CHILDREN IN CHINA

CHILDREN IN CHINA ———

Orna Naftali

polity

First published in 2016 by Polity Press

Polity Press
65 Bridge Street
Cambridge CB2 1UR, UK

Polity Press
350 Main Street
Malden, MA 02148, USA

ISBN-13: 978-0-7456-8054-5
ISBN-13: 978-0-7456-8055-2 (pb)

A catalogue record for this book is available from the British Library.

Library of Congress Cataloging-in-Publication Data

Naftali, Orna, author.
  Children in China / Orna Naftali.
    pages   cm
  Includes bibliographical references and index.
  ISBN 978-0-7456-8054-5 (hardback) – ISBN 978-0-7456-8055-2
(pbk.)   1. Children–China–Social conditions.   I. Title.
  HQ792.C5N337 2016
  305.230951–dc23
      2015023559

Typeset in 11.5 on 15 pt Adobe Jenson Pro
by Toppan Best-set Premedia Limited
Printed and bound in Great Britain by CPI Group (UK) Ltd, Croydon

For further information on Polity, visit our website: www.politybooks.com

Contents

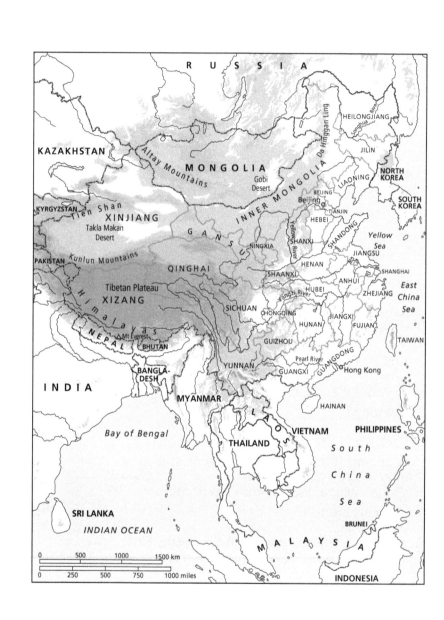

RUSSIA

KAZAKHSTAN

MONGOLIA

Altay Mountains

Gobi
Desert

HEILONGJIANG

JILIN

NORTH
KOREA

KYRGYZSTAN

Tien Shan

XINJIANG

Takla Makan
Desert

INNER MONGOLIA

Da Hinggan Ling

LIAONING

SOUTH
KOREA

BEIJING

Beijing

TIANJIN

HEBEI

SHANXI

SHANDONG

Yellow
Sea

JIANGSU

PAKISTAN

Kunlun Mountains

GANSU

NINGXIA

Yellow River

HENAN

QINGHAI

SHAANXI

SHANGHAI

Tibetan Plateau

XIZANG

Himalayas

NEPAL

Mt Everest

BHUTAN

BANGLA-
DESH

SICHUAN

Yangzi River

HUBEI

ANHUI

ZHEJIANG

East
China
Sea

CHONGQING

HUNAN

JIANGXI

FUJIAN

GUIZHOU

TAIWAN

INDIA

YUNNAN

Pearl River

GUANGDONG

GUANGXI

Hong Kong

MYANMAR

HAINAN

Bay of Bengal

LAOS

VIETNAM

PHILIPPINES

THAILAND

South

China

SRI LANKA

INDIAN OCEAN

Sea

BRUNEI

MALAYSIA

INDONESIA

0   500   1000   1500 km
0   250   500   750   1000 miles

Chronology

1894–1895	First Sino-Japanese War
1911	Fall of the Qing dynasty
1912	Republic of China established under Sun Yat-sen
1927	Split between Nationalists (KMT) and Communists (CCP); civil war begins
1934–1935	CCP under Mao Zedong evades KMT in Long March
December 1937	Nanjing Massacre
1937–1945	Second Sino-Japanese War
1945–1949	Civil war between KMT and CCP resumes
October 1949	KMT retreats to Taiwan; Mao founds People's Republic of China (PRC)
1950–1953	Korean War
1953–1957	First Five-Year Plan; PRC adopts Soviet-style economic planning
1954	First constitution of the PRC and first meeting of the National People's Congress
1956–1957	Hundred Flowers Movement, a brief period of open political debate
1957	Anti-Rightist Movement
1958–1960	Great Leap Forward, an effort to transform China through rapid industrialization and collectivization

March 1959	Tibetan Uprising in Lhasa; Dalai Lama flees to India
1959–1961	Three Hard Years, widespread famine with tens of millions of deaths
1960	Sino-Soviet split
1962	Sino-Indian War
October 1964	First PRC atomic bomb detonation
1966–1976	Great Proletarian Cultural Revolution; Mao reasserts power
February 1972	President Richard Nixon visits China; "Shanghai Communiqué" pledges to normalize US–China relations
September 1976	Death of Mao Zedong
October 1976	Ultra-Leftist Gang of Four arrested and sentenced
December 1978	Deng Xiaoping assumes power; launches Four Modernizations and economic reforms
1978	One-Child family planning policy introduced
1979	United States and China establish formal diplomatic ties; Deng Xiaoping visits Washington
1979	PRC invades Vietnam
1982	Census reports PRC population at more than one billion
December 1984	Margaret Thatcher co-signs Sino-British Joint Declaration agreeing to return Hong Kong to China in 1997
1986	Compulsory Education Law of the People's Republic of China introduced
1989	Tiananmen Square protests culminate in June 4 military crackdown
1991	Law of the People's Republic of China on Protection of Minors introduced

1992	Deng Xiaoping's Southern Inspection Tour re-energizes economic reforms
1993–2002	Jiang Zemin is president of PRC, continues economic growth agenda
1994	"Outline on the Implementation of Patriotic Education" published
1999	"Education for Quality" reform plan introduced nationwide
November 2001	WTO accepts China as member
2002–2012	Hu Jintao, General-Secretary CCP (and President of PRC from 2003)
2002–2003	SARS outbreak concentrated in PRC and Hong Kong
2006	PRC supplants US as largest CO_2 emitter
August 2008	Summer Olympic Games in Beijing
2010	Shanghai World Exposition
2012	Xi Jinping appointed General-Secretary of the CCP (and President of PRC from 2013)

Acknowledgements

My research and writing of this book would not have been possible without the generous support of many individuals. Primarily, I want to express my heartfelt thanks to the editors at Polity Press. Emma Longstaff first approached me with the idea for the book, and I am extremely grateful for the faith she has placed in me, as well as for her enthusiasm and helpful guidance throughout the early phases of the project. My deep appreciation also goes to Jonathan Skerrett at Polity for suggesting many concrete improvements, and to two anonymous reviewers who provided encouraging feedback and thoughtful comments on the draft manuscript.

Many people, colleagues, and friends, have given me ideas and opportunities to explore the themes that appear in the book through personal conversations, seminars, and symposia. At various stages, I benefited greatly from conversations and discussions with Vanessa Fong, Andrew Kipnis, Terry Woronov, Esther C.L. Goh, Sabine Frühstück, and Dafna Zur. Special thanks go to my research collaborator in China, Yang Junhong, whose enduring friendship, help, and advice have been a source of encouragement throughout the years.

I would like to acknowledge the sustained support of my colleagues at the Hebrew University of Jerusalem, Yuri Pines, Gideon Shelach, Michal Biran, Lihi Yariv-Laor, Jooyeon Rhee, and Nissim Otmazgin. I am also deeply indebted to my students, Shachar Kessler and Hagar Iron, both of whom provided enthusiastic and unstinting help as my research assistants on this project.

Most of all, I want to thank my father, Gideon, who has always been an inspiration, as well as my husband, Dean, and my daughters, Eleanor and Tamara, for putting up with the long hours of writing. Without their love, patience, and understanding, I would not have completed this book, and I dedicate this book to them.

Introduction

The period of life prior to adulthood is always a time of dramatic change. It is during childhood that social and gender roles are learned and personal identity is formed. But the perception of these changes in different historical and cultural contexts and the way these perceptions are felt in the lives of children of different social backgrounds is far from uniform. This book explores how recent processes of social and economic change are re-shaping the experience of childhood and the subjectivities of children in the People's of Republic of China, a country that has undergone a period of exceptionally rapid transformations, reversals, and innovations over the past decades.

Due to rapid economic development and demographic transitions, especially since the implementation of the One-Child Policy in the late 1970s, the size of China's child population has declined in recent decades and particularly over the past ten years or so. Yet China still has the largest population of children in the world. According to data from the country's Sixth National Census conducted in 2010, people under the age of 18 make up 21 percent of the nation's population and number 279 million (National Bureau of Statistics of China 2013). The massive size of the country and of its child population render any attempt to generalize about the nature of Chinese childhood or the experiences of individual children difficult.

Recognizing this limitation, this book nonetheless seeks to identify some of the major transformations that have occurred in the lives of children and in the meanings of childhood in post-1978 China. These transformations include the rising importance of global, scientific models of childrearing and education, and the growing attention to children's personal rights and psychological needs – developments that in turn contribute to Chinese children's increasing empowerment and individualization at home and at school.

These developments are similar in many respects to those that took place in liberal, capitalist societies from the beginning of the eighteenth century onwards (see Ariès 1962; Zelizer 1985; Stephens 1995; James et al. 1998; Heywood 2001; Archard 2004; Walkerdine 2005). What makes the Chinese case unique is not just the distinct political and socioeconomic conditions under which these processes have occurred, but also the exceptional pace and scale of the changes. As this book will show, a modern notion of children as autonomous individuals separate from the family and the kinship group had already begun to form in China during the republican and socialist periods. This idea became much more salient, however, following the introduction of market reforms, the One-Child Policy, and the Open Door Policy in the late 1970s. Due to the country's rapid demographic shift to an aging society, contemporary Chinese children have in a relatively short period been provided with an increased "scarcity value" and have been viewed as more deserving of precious attention. The emergence of a globalized consumer culture in post-socialist China, particularly since the 1990s, has further contributed to children's empowerment and individualization. New products, media, and services geared specifically towards the needs and interests of the young have reached the market, and children have won a new role as independent consumers and as key agents of cultural interpretation and social change.

These developments do not necessarily imply that contemporary Chinese children are "freer" or "happier" compared to their predecessors. The introduction of market reforms and the country's increasing integration within the global market economy may have provided many children, especially those in urban areas, with better life conditions, but these processes have also contributed to a growing commercialization and standardization of Chinese childhood. As elsewhere in the post-industrial world, the lives of many children in China are also becoming more regimented to suit the demands of a neoliberal market economy while children's subjectivities are increasingly embedded in the normalizing regimes of modern psychological science.

Further, like adults, contemporary Chinese children do not escape structural constraints (see Bluebond-Langner and Korbin 2007: 242). Their ability to exercise their personal agency in the spheres of education, consumption, and family relations is crucially shaped by their socioeconomic backgrounds, as well as by their gender and ethnic identities. One of the central arguments I wish to make in this book is that the recent transformation in the nature of Chinese childhood and the increasing empowerment and individualization of Chinese children have been most evident among the ranks of urban, middle-class families of Han descent. Among these relatively affluent city families, a majority of children are now singletons whose lack of siblings has given them more power vis-à-vis their teachers, parents, and grandparents. Furthermore, urban caregivers who belong to – or wish to become members of – China's newly formed middle classes also tend to encourage their only-son or only-daughter to assert their individuality while viewing children's empowerment as a sign of their own "civility" and "progressivity".

In contrast, with the decline of social security and the widening gap between rich and poor in China, many rural families have to scramble to ensure their basic economic survival. Unlike urban boys and girls of middle-class backgrounds, China's migrant children living with their parents in the city, and rural children or ethnic minority children residing in the country's poorer areas, have also been much less able to assert their personal interests and desires at home or at school. These children must struggle for the attainment of a full course of basic education and a physically and emotionally sound environment in which to develop.

Recent transformations in the nature of Chinese childhood are marked by additional contradictions and dilemmas. Even in the country's urban, more affluent areas, children's growing independence and consumer power have given rise to much apprehension among adults who fear that these developments might lead to moral chaos, social instability, or the loss of a distinctive cultural and national identity among China's young. As government institutions, teachers, and caregivers attempt to grapple with these perceived threats, they draw on – and negotiate with – divergent cultural models of childrearing and education.

These models are informed not only by global, neoliberal prescriptions for producing "high-quality", individualized citizens and workers for the new market economy, but also by a deep sense of nostalgia for the collectivist, egalitarian ethos of the Maoist period. Contemporary educators and caregivers further draw on the indigenous precepts of filial piety. Though this long-held ethos has undergone considerable mutations and modifications in the modern and contemporary period, it nonetheless continues to offer people in China a meaningful framework for raising a child who would become not only a successful laborer and consumer but also – and no less importantly – a moral, caring person.

THE STUDY OF CHILDHOOD AS A SOCIAL CONSTRUCTION

Unlike biological immaturity, "childhood" is neither a natural nor a universal feature of human groups but a specific structural and cultural component of societies (James and Prout 1997 [1990]: 8). Now a common theoretical premise for researchers working in the field of childhood studies, the idea of childhood as a social construction is in fact a relatively recent theoretical development. Until the late 1970s, the anthropological study of childhood largely concentrated on how childrearing practices accounted for a particular "cultural personality"; on how socialization practices allowed a person to learn the ways of a given society or social group; or on linguistic and cognitive development in children (Hardman 1973; Bluebond-Langner and Korbin 2007). This body of work has supplied rich evidence for the variety of childrearing practices across different cultures. It has nonetheless overlooked the fact that childhood is a social category that is historically constructed and has also failed to consider that children may themselves contribute to the production of their own social lives (James and Prout 1997 [1990]; Schwartzman 2001; James 2007).

Recognizing these weaknesses and informed by developments in history, sociology, gender studies, and cultural studies, scholars have in recent decades begun to formulate a new conceptual framework for the study of childhood worldwide. This new framework posits that every society must recognize children as distinguishable from adults since such a recognition plays a crucial role in assuring physical care and socialization for vulnerable, immature human beings (Stephens 1995; Corsaro 1997: 53). However, different societies may at different times hold unique notions concerning the duration of childhood. Societies may also differ in the perceived features that distinguish "children" from "adults," and in the significance these features acquire in particular social and political contexts (Caputo 1995; Archard 2004: 31).

The study of childhood as a social construction therefore aims to analyze how different discursive practices produce different childhoods, "each and all of which are 'real' within their own regime of truth" (James and Prout 1997 [1990]: 27). When asking which set of attributes are accorded to children in a given time and place, scholars recognize that in all societies, notions of childhood are shaped in relation to structural variables, such as rates of fertility and life expectancy, organization of family life and kinship patterns, and different ideologies of care and philosophies of need and dependency. They further consider how children's assigned attributes are intertwined with issues of gender, ethnicity, and class (Scheper-Hughes 1992; Jenks 1996).

Building on these theoretical insights, this book regards Chinese childhood not as a singular, uniform social construct, but rather as composed of distinct multiple categories that are products of ideational, demographic, and socioeconomics processes. These in turn shape the lives of boys and girls, Han and ethnic minority, and rural, urban, and migrant children in potentially different ways. Moreover, the category of childhood in China and elsewhere has important political, ideological, and social uses. Within the home, childhood plays a central role in the organization of production and consumption and in the transmission not only of genes, but also of ideas, identities, and property. Outside the home, childhood constitutes the primary site of pedagogy and cultural learning (Scheper-Hughes and Sargent 1998). State protection of children and the extension of this protection to the home can appear as a sign of humanity, benevolence and enlightenment of the modern nation-state. In fact, it also marks the extension of state surveillance and control to the private sphere and to the individual "souls" of children and their caregivers (Rose 1989: 122). This book therefore examines childhood in China as a primary nexus of mediation between the state and the family, between public norms and private life, and between "consumption and production, objective need and subjective desire," distinctions on which the post-socialist party-state and the new market economy now depend (see Stephens 1995: 6; Scheper-Hughes and Sargent 1998: 1).

To understand fully the roles Chinese children play within the moral and political economy of the nation-state, we must also recognize that these roles are intimately linked to global forces and structures. Particularly since the 1970s, globalization processes, defined as the acceleration and intensification of social, cultural, political, and economic links across frontiers, have led to "a heightened entanglement of the global and the local" (Inda and Rosaldo 2002: 9). In recent decades, childhood scholars have begun to ask how this local–global entanglement shapes the experiences of childhood in different national and cultural contexts. Does the extensive borrowing of pedagogical theories and childrearing practices across national borders means that we can speak of "a globalization and standardization of childhood"? Or is it more useful to examine how global models interact with indige-nous notions of education and care to open "a third space," character-ized by "heterogenization and mutual imbrication" (Bhabha 1994: 218; Inda and Rosaldo 2002: 22)? Alternatively, should we discard the dichotomy of the "global–local" altogether? After all, the argument that the global entails homogenization whereas the local preserves hetero-geneity and difference includes an implicit, false assumption that the differences in local childcare notions and practices are in some sense natural, or at least that their origin remains beyond question. Such a view can easily devolve into a kind of "primordialism that fixes and romanticizes social relations and identities" (Hardt and Negri 2001: 44; see also Appadurai 1990; Featherstone 1990). The dichotomy of the global and the local in the field of childhood studies is further complicated by the fact that a relationship of coexistence as well as creative interaction between the transnational and the indigenous may actually match the everyday experiences and desires of many local populations (Hannerz 2002 [1989]: 42).

These broader theoretical concerns have also informed the burgeon-ing field of childhood studies in China, a country that, over the past three-and-a-half decades, has undergone a major transformation in almost all areas of life. Economic reforms initiated by the Chinese Communist Party (CCP) in 1978 have entailed de-collectivization in agriculture and relaxation of state controls in urban productive sectors. These changes in turn have given rise to entrepreneurial experimenta-tion and a renewed emphasis on profit and prosperity. Since the late

1970s, the country has also witnessed an increased openness to the outside world. China's reintegration within the global economy has brought not only capital investments, renewed trade links and technology exchanges, but also increased flows of people, ideas, and cultural products across its borders.

Beginning in the 1990s, China's economy has experienced sustained growth and rising per capita income. The combined forces of market reforms, the ensuing relaxation of internal migration restrictions by the Chinese government, and the sweeping trend of globalization have also led to an unprecedented growth of economically driven rural-to-urban migration. Compared with the results of the 2000 population census, in 2010, the proportion of urban residents in the country rose by 13.46 percent while the size of the rural population – which in the early 1980s was estimated at 80 percent of the total population – shrank to 50.32 percent (National Bureau of Statistics of China 2011).

These developments have reduced the poverty level in China and have brought prosperity to many Chinese citizens. However, they have also been accompanied by acute problems, such as a growing regional and class inequality, the explosive growth of a migrant labor underclass, wide-scale environmental destruction, ethnic unrest, and a loss of security and jobs for many state sector urban employees. Partly to alleviate these uncertainties and conflicts, the Chinese government has, since the 1990s, initiated sweeping legal reforms which have expanded the scope and exercise of the rights of citizens. Over the past decade or so, the CCP leadership has also asserted its intent to build a sustainable "harmonious society" (hexie shehui) by focusing on the needs and interests of regular citizens rather than on rapid economic growth alone. Indeed, in the reform era (1978–present) the party-state has gradually withdrawn from many areas of social and economic life. In pursuit of what the CCP has termed a "socialist market economy with Chinese characteristics," mechanisms of state control, such as the household registration and work-unit systems have weakened; power has been decentralized in favor of more regional autonomy; and a majority of the rural population is now practicing "village democracy."

Nonetheless, these developments have not precipitated large-scale political reform; China is still governed by a one-party system, and organized opposition to the party remains banned. Further, while reform-era leaders have gradually moved to disengage the government from control over land, labor, and markets, they have also devised new ways of insinuating the state into the private lives of Chinese citizens. The launch of the One-Child Policy in the late 1970s, which aimed to turn China into a powerful and modern country and to "raise the quality (*suzhi*)" of the nation, signifies perhaps more than anything else the intent of the post-socialist party-state to continue to play a prominent role in the lives of individuals and families in China.

CHILDREN IN CONTEMPORARY CHINA: KEY THEMES AND THEORETICAL CONSIDERATIONS

In recent decades, scholars have begun to explore the implications of these broader transformations for the nature of Chinese childhood, and the political deployment of children by the nation-state in the age of market reforms, economic globalization, and the One-Child Policy. Some have argued that Chinese state policies towards children and their education reflect the ascendancy of global, neoliberal paradigms of care which aim to foster children as self-governing, individualistic flexible laborers and consumers (see, e.g., Greenhalgh and Winckler 2005; Greenhalgh 2011).

Others posit that contemporary Chinese childrearing and pedagogical paradigms may reflect the construction of an increasingly influential "ethic of autonomy" (Zhang 2008; Yan 2011). But they also cohere with alternative models of childcare and education, which may be informed by Confucian, authoritarian, and/or (neo)socialist goals and techniques (see, in particular, Anagnost 1997; Fong 2004b, 2007a;

Kipnis 2006, 2008, 2011b; Woronov 2007b, 2009a; Hansen 2015; Kuan 2015).

Building on these important insights, this book explores the interaction between current discussions about children's care and education, and the shifting nature of power, morality, and governance in post-socialist China. It recognizes that contemporary ideas about raising and educating the young in China draw much of their inspiration and legitimation from global models that in recent decades have been dominated by a neoliberal ideology. Children everywhere are being prepared for participation in a rapidly changing adult world by fostering their ability for self-governance, their autonomy, and their creativity to ensure that society has a sufficiently flexible body of "human capital" (Stephens 1995: 20).

Contemporary public thinking and child-related policies in China are crucially informed by this ideology. However, Chinese understandings of global neoliberal models also reflect historical and cultural-specific notions of social order and disorder, citizenship and personhood. As these notions are themselves undergoing change in the post-socialist era, a new concept of children as autonomous, entrepreneurial individuals is increasingly evident in educational publications, government policies, and media articulations. However, this concept co-exists with a nationalistic ethos that subsumes individual children to state projects of "national rejuvenation". It is also partially deflected by a nostalgic harkening back to the socialist, more frugal morality of the Maoist period, and by long-held folk beliefs concerning the proper way to care for and educate the young.

In exploring the tensions and contradictions that characterize contemporary Chinese thinking about children and childhood, the book further considers how idealized visions of the child and the person are applied to children of both genders, and how Chinese caregivers from diverse social backgrounds respond to new official and media discourses of childhood. Do parents and grandparents of different locales and age cohorts perceive the upbringing of children in a similar way? If not, how can we account for the differences and how do these differences affect the experiences of boys and girls of different backgrounds? No less importantly, how do children themselves perceive their lives and negotiate "worlds that they create for themselves (such as peer groups), worlds others create for them (e.g., schools), and worlds in concert with others, such as families, marketplaces, and neighborhoods" (Bluebond-Langner and Korbin 2007: 245)?

To address these questions, I draw on empirical data presented by a growing number of studies published since the 1980s in the fields of sociology and anthropology, education, social history, cultural studies, and social work, while seeking to identify and analyze some of the emergent themes and theoretical currents within the burgeoning body of work on contemporary Chinese childhood. The discussion further relies on the results of my own ethnographic work conducted among Chinese children, schools, and families since the mid-2000s, and on the analysis of Chinese-language primary sources, including government, media, and academic publications which have appeared in the PRC in the past several decades.

Some caveats are in order. Due to practical limitations, this volume focuses on childhoods in the Chinese mainland, where the social, political, and economic conditions of the socialist revolution have shaped the lives of caregivers and children in distinct ways and where notions of childhood in many respects differ from those found in Hong Kong, Taiwan, or Chinese diaspora communities. That said, the book does on occasion refer to scholarship on children in Taiwan or Hong Kong, when such work can provide a useful conceptual framework for a discussion of mainland notions and practices. The book also reflects the Han-centered nature of most contemporary scholarship on Chinese childhood but does consider the unique experiences of ethnic minority children residing in the countryside, especially regarding schooling and education.

The insistence that children be regarded as social actors in their own right, and that they be given voice in studies of and about them has become a staple in recent sociological and anthropological literature worldwide (see, e.g., Stephens 1995; James and Prout 1997 [1990]; James et al. 1998; Scheper-Hughes and Sargent 1998; Schwartzman 2001). Some of the contemporary scholarship on Chinese childhood has also started to reflect this crucial recognition and to incorporate children's views rather than focusing on adult notions and practices. Continuing this important shift, the discussion in this book attempts to document children's experiences in their own words and from their own perspectives wherever these are available, to reveal what James (2007: 264) describes as the "the hidden hurts and humiliations that many children experience and which adults often dismiss as unimportant or regard simply as playground rough-and-tumble."

STRUCTURE OF THE BOOK

To recognize the meaning and magnitude of the changes that have occurred in post-1978 Chinese ideas and practices of childhood, it is crucial that we view these changes within their historical context. Chapters therefore focus on the momentous changes that have occurred in the experiences and conceptualizations of Chinese childhood since the late 1970s, but they also seek to highlight differences and continuities with earlier trends in the lives of children and in notions of childhood.

The book begins with a brief historical overview of the conditions that have led to the emergence of new concepts of new patterns of childrearing and education in twentieth-century China. Chapter 1 presents some of the main tenets of the pre-modern Chinese concepts of childhood, including the prominence of the Confucian ethos of filial piety, of ancestor worship, and of patrilineage; and the notion of hierarchy, which determined an authoritarian nature of the parent/child relationship and depressed the status of girls in imperial China. The main part of the chapter will then address the crucial changes that have occurred in these ideas from the turn of the twentieth century until the late 1970s.

The discussion will show that modernization processes and the socio-political transformations of the last century created by the republican and socialist revolutions of 1911 and 1949 respectively, have changed the perception of children, leading to the rise of a decidedly "modern" yet unmistakably "Chinese" concept of childhood. Beginning in the early decades of the twentieth century, Chinese reformers and political leaders have sought to eradicate time-honored notions of childrearing and education in favor of modern, scientific ideas about children and their capabilities introduced mainly from Europe, the United States, and Japan. These endeavors, which received their impetus from the national crisis China experienced during this period, have contributed to the emergence of new ideas concerning the temporal boundaries of childhood; the perceived qualities of children; and the social and political roles of the young within the family and society.

The implementation of child-related policies and initiatives after the socialist revolution of 1949 led to a considerable improvement in children's welfare and to a relative elevation in the social and familial status of both boys and girls. Through the expansion of schooling and the employment of mass propaganda campaigns, the Maoist regime sought to destroy the old kinship hierarchy and to transform children from loyal family members into dutiful citizens of the new socialist state. These attempts undermined the principles of age and gender hierarchy that had determined children's subordinate status within the family. In the process, they also produced children as increasingly atomized individuals. However, long-held ideas about the proper way of raising the young and former practices of childrearing and education did not disappear in post-1949 China. Public discussions about children and their upbringing continued to draw on the "tradition/modernity" dyad, while reflecting broader debates about questions of personhood, state and society, and national and cultural identities.

As chapter 2 shows, these debates preoccupy Chinese government officials, educators, and caregivers to this day. Recent decades have witnessed the introduction of global, neoliberal notions of childrearing and education to China, manifested in school reform plans and in a new and increasingly popular genre of psychological advice literature. Striving to improve the lives of individual children and raise the "quality" (*suzhi*) of the nation, official, media, and academic discourses in China have promoted an idealized notion of childhood as a time of innocence and play rather than political activity or manual labor. They have also sought to encourage Chinese children to exercise independent thinking and free choice. Chapter 2 considers the circumstances that have led to the introduction of these new notions, their modes of circulation among urban and rural populations, and their effects on family and school life in China. The chapter argues that the growing importance of global, neoliberal models of childrearing and education has contributed to children's increasing empowerment and individualization, particularly among the ranks of urban, middle-class populations in China. However, this process has also produced new conflicts and dilemmas, as adults and children attempt to negotiate new ideals of the child and the person with pragmatic concerns and pre-existing beliefs and practices regarding the proper way of governing the young.

A key factor that has contributed to children's increasing empowerment in contemporary China is the demographic shift caused by the One-Child Policy. Chapter 3 examines the components of this crucial policy and considers its implications for the lives of Chinese girls and boys of different social backgrounds. The present generation of Chinese singletons has often been described as willful "little emperors," who are insufferably spoiled, showered with attention, toys, and treats by anxiously overindulgent parents and grandparents. As chapter 3 shows however, this is far too simplistic a picture. The Chinese government's population policy has undoubtedly contributed to the production of a new generation of individualized singletons in some parts of the country but has also introduced new concerns and anxieties to the lives of caregivers, and new constraints and pressures into the lives of children.

Some children, notably those residing in the city – where a majority of couples have until recently been allowed only one child – are spoiled by parents and two sets of grandparents. But they are also made to bear the weight of their caregivers' hopes and expectations. Many of these children experience heavy psychological pressure to perform well at school so that they can build a successful career and support their parents in old age. Meanwhile, the One-Child Policy has also influenced Chinese girls in complex, non-uniform ways. Following the decision of the Chinese government to allow rural families to have a second child if the first is a girl, many families have resorted to the use of sex selection methods during pregnancy or have avoided registration of their second female child with the authorities. In some parts of the country, unwanted girls have been given up for adoption, while others have suffered neglect and maltreatment. In this respect, the One-Child Policy has contributed to growing gender discrimination and to a severe gender imbalance. At the same time, there are also indications that the demographic shifts brought on by the policy have resulted in a relative empowerment of increasing numbers of girls, particularly those born and raised in urban, single-child families.

These contradictions notwithstanding, the One-Child Policy and its accompanying demographic shifts have contributed to a significant transformation of the family institution in contemporary China, including the nuclearization of the household and the rediscovery of the emotional "value" of children. Together with the launching of market reforms and the country's increasing integration within the global economy, these developments have also led to the emergence of Chinese children as independent consumers and to a dramatic growth in familial consumption of children's products and services. Chapter 4 considers the implications of these new trends for children's identities, social practices, and for adult–child relations in different parts of the country.

The discussion demonstrates that Chinese children of the early twenty-first century have grown richer and less frugal, and are exercising their influence over a greater volume of family spending. Children, particularly singletons in urban areas, now have more say in purchases of food, entertainment, and large commodities, including numerous items that affect their health, education, and training. As elsewhere in the post-industrial world, many have also become avid consumers of television, computer games, and the Internet, and exhibit a preference for global media products.

Their choices have given rise to much public concern in China. Like parents everywhere, Chinese caregivers worry about excessive snack consumption, television viewing, Internet surfing, and computer gaming, which they regard as harmful to children's health and education. The Chinese mass media has also published alarmist reports on the magnitude and extravagance of children's consumption practices, expressing anxiety about children's (perceived) materialism and its implications for their moral integrity and for the wellbeing of Chinese society as a whole. Joining these concerns, government officials worry about the possible effects of extensive foreign media consumption on Chinese children's cultural and national identities as well as their loyalty to the nation-state. These fears translate into an ambiguous attitude toward children's consumption on the part of the state, the school, and caregivers.

With the decline of fertility rates and the rise in personal incomes since the 1980s, even the Chinese countryside has had its share of "spoiled," empowered children, particularly in prosperous villages and small towns. At the same time, however, the country is also experiencing rising economic inequality, particularly between east and west and urban and rural areas. The discussion in chapter 5 explores the effects of economic restructuring and the growing rural–urban gap on the lives of children in the countryside. It examines the main problems rural children have faced in the areas of education, familial relations, and social wellbeing while paying attention to the unique difficulties experienced by rural girls, by ethnic minority children who are over-represented within the poor rural population, and by rural children with disabilities or those whose family members have been diagnosed with HIV/AIDS.

The combined forces of market economic reforms, the relaxation of migration restrictions, and the widening gap between rural and urban areas have led to an unprecedented growth of economically driven rural-to-urban migration in China. Though population movement can counteract inequality, it has also had some negative implications for the lives of children. The structural limitations of China's household registration system have forced many parents to leave their children in the countryside in the care of grandparents or other people. The discussion in chapter 5 considers how parental migration affects these children's schooling as well as their relations with peers and family members. Whether parental migration really has a negative impact on rural children's education remains a contentious issue. However, a majority of scholars agree that rural "left-behind children" suffer from a lack of parental supervision and emotional support, and often experience alienation toward the absent parents. Further, many of these left-behind children are at a particularly high risk of becoming victims of child trafficking.

While a majority of migrant workers who move from rural areas to Chinese cities for work choose to leave their children behind in their hometown villages, increasing numbers are electing to bring their children with them, or to raise their city-born children in urban areas. Much of the research literature on migration in China has focused on first-generation adult migrants, especially their labor rights and the workplace discrimination they face. However, as more people participate in the migration process and as migrants expand the duration of their stays in cities, children increasingly become part of the migration stream. Chapter 6 discusses the unique difficulties that migrant children face in the cities, while exploring the effects of migration on children's perceptions, expectations, and social identities; their relationships with their families and their peers; as well as their education attainments.

Owing to restrictions from both the household registration (*hukou*) system and the educational system tailored for urban residents, an immediate difficulty facing Chinese migrant families concerns the education of their children. These difficulties include exclusion from public schools, higher tuition fees for migrant children, and mental maladjustment for many. The migration experience has also exposed many children to the negative social stigmas of permanent urban residents who frequently consider migrant children to be of lower "quality" (*suzhi*) compared to those of urban descent. Under these conditions, Chinese migrant children find it much more difficult to express their individual wishes or to pursue their personal interests at home and at school.

The concluding chapter of the book summarizes the key features of contemporary Chinese childhood, while pointing out some of the main contradictions that characterize the lives of children across the country. The discussion presents questions for further consideration and identifies issues that have so far received little attention in the literature on Chinese childhood. As the conclusion argues, recent developments in notions of childcare and education play a crucial role in the formation of new class identities and in the changing relationship between society, the individual, and the state, and in this sense constitute a key mechanism of social and cultural change in China. The study of children and childhood is therefore vital to our understanding of the social, economic, and political processes that have taken place in the country since the late 1970s. It can reveal much about how Chinese society now perceives its past and how it is attempting to shape its future in the coming decades.

Chinese Childhood in the Modern Era

Twentieth-century China witnessed a series of political upheavals, national and civil wars, and major social and economic transformations triggered by no less than two revolutions in 40 years: the republican revolution of 1911 and the socialist revolution of 1949. These conflicts caused far-reaching changes to the structure of the Chinese family and led to the development of new thinking about the temporal boundaries of childhood; the needs and capabilities of children; and the roles youngsters should play within the family and society.

This chapter provides an overview of the major changes that have occurred within official and popular thinking about childhood in modern China, and considers the effects of these new ideas on the living conditions of individual children from the early decades of the twentieth century to the late 1970s. The aim of this chapter is not to provide an exhaustive account of children's experiences throughout the period but to highlight some of the key moments in the development of a modern concept of childhood in twentieth-century China. In so doing, the chapter seeks to situate the discussion of childhood in post-1978 China within an appropriate historical context, and to identify the main factors that have contributed – and which continue to contribute – to the shaping and re-shaping of Chinese childhood today.

The chapter is divided into three sections. The first offers a brief introduction to the dominant notions of childhood in late imperial

Chinese society. The other two sections consist of a more detailed examination of the social and political conditions under which a modern conceptualization of the child emerged during the twentieth century. As the first section will show, orthodox views of the child in imperial China were primarily shaped by the cult of ancestor worship, by the Confucian ethos of filial piety, and by the centrality of patrilineage. Beginning in the early decades of the twentieth century, however, sustained attempts at social reform and successive political revolutions led to a major transformation in public notions of childhood and to a considerable elevation in the status of children, particularly girls, in modern China.

The second and third sections consider the distinct historical conditions that have prompted these changes, beginning in the republican revolution of 1911 and leading up to the end of the Maoist era (1949–76). The second section shows that since the early decades of the twentieth century, the development of a modern Chinese notion of childhood was inextricably linked to issues of public interest and national duty. In their quest for the formation of a powerful nation-state that could stand up to its imperial aggressors, early twentieth-century Chinese political leaders, reformers, and educators were preoccupied with the question of how best to transform children's upbringing and education in order to develop a modern Chinese citizenry. The treatment of children thereby came to acquire heavy symbolic significance as "an ideological showroom" in which ideal images of citizens, communities, and even the nation were put on stage (Thøgersen 2002: 5). As the third section will indicate, modernization processes and the establishment of the People's Republic of China in 1949 resulted in the increasing empowerment and individualization of Chinese children. However, these processes were also accompanied by an unprecedented encroachment of the Chinese state upon the domestic and the familial realm. They have also led to an extensive politicization of children's lives.

FILIAL CHILDREN AND THE CRISIS OF
CHILDHOOD

In his landmark study of European social history, *Centuries of Child-hood*, Philippe Ariès made the provocative claim that "the idea of child-hood did not exist" before modern times (1962: 128). It is a claim that has since come under substantial criticism. However, Ariès was advancing the crucial notion that our contemporary conception of childhood as a separate stage of life, and of children as subjects requiring unique forms of treatment, is not a universal phenomenon but a product of specific historical and social circumstances. Certainly in China, a notion of childhood as a stage of life distinguishable from adulthood had existed in some form prior to the modern era (Kinney 1995a; Wicks and Avril 2002; Hsiung 2005). In fact, despite variations in historical periods, geographical locations, ethnic origins, gender, and social status, Chinese ideas of the child from the Han period (206 BC–220 AD) to the late Qing Dynasty (1644–1911) carried a number of discernible features.

First, there was a widespread popular, ritualistic, and philosophical perception of childhood as a time of crisis, when vulnerable children struggled against recurring physical and spiritual threats both in the outside world and within themselves (Furth 1995: 176; Stafford 1995: 18). It was not until the age of seven *sui* (or six years by Western reckoning), that a child was considered to have passed the most dangerous period of its life. It was also at this stage that children were thought to have reached "the age of reason," acquire an awareness of their social gender, and develop a sense of shame and embarrassment. Consequently, children before the age of seven generally did not receive much disciplining, nor did they have legal responsibility for any wrongdoing (Dardess 1991: 73; Bai 2005b: 17).

A second, related view stipulated that children came into the world with inherently good, yet incomplete moral faculties (Bai 2005b: 12).

Both Confucian and Neo-Confucian perspectives stressed the child's unformed state and its need for lengthy instruction as part of a larger argument that education is the foundation of a humane society (Kinney 2004: 3). Early Confucian teaching viewed external phenomena, environmental influences, and learning activities as the most crucial factors in a child's growth, stressing the need to employ rituals that would gradually transform the child into a mature person (*chengren*), or in other words, "a social being" (Bai 2005b: 12). A person's maturation, perceived mainly in terms of self-cultivation and moral growth, was regarded as a holistic progression of "realizing one's authentic human nature" – a process which began in early childhood and did not end even with old age (Tu 1976: 113). The belief in the human potential for transformation through proper external stimuli was further illustrated in the Chinese doctrine of "fetal education" (*taijiao*) in which the mother's moral and physical practices were thought to affect her child's future health and personality. The stress on environmental influences continued during the lactation period, giving imperial-era Chinese mothers a heavy responsibility for their infants' health and vitality (Kinney 2004: 16–29; see also Furth 1987, 1995).

Third, imperial Chinese thinking placed little value on the childhood stage in and of itself. Pre-modern Chinese advice books, medical texts, family instructions, primers, and the like reflected the predominant notion, couched in Confucian precepts, that education should instill adult standards in children as early as possible, making few concessions to so-called "childish" mentalities (Dardess 1991: 79). Moreover, the requirements of the classical language and the Civil Service examination system induced children to learn philosophical and historical texts that had little to do with the world around them (Saari 1990: 45). When Confucian writers wrote about and for children between the ages of seven and fourteen, they concentrated on the "proper rules" for children's behavior, expounded in the Confucian classics (Dardess 1991: 75; Kinney 1995b: 12). These tended to uphold children who acted with adult seriousness and wisdom as exemplary models while discouraging aimless play and unrestrained activity even in the very young (Kinney 1995b: 12; Bai 2005b: 9). Children, especially those of the gentry class, were told not to be "frivolous, noisy, critical, vulgar, and lighthearted" (Saari 1990: 45), whereas qualities such as juvenile precocity, self-restraint, sober moral judgment, and studiousness were strongly encouraged (Dardess 1991: 75; Kinney 1995b: 12).

This was mainly true for elite boys, however. Male children from wealthy families were expected to study for the imperial examinations in order to acquire a position in the imperial bureaucracy. Accordingly, they were more restrained by Confucian regulations and formalities compared to peasant children who frequently worked alongside their parents in the fields and were allowed more free play (Bai 2005a: 15). Family instructions for girls often put more emphasis on the qualities required of a good wife and mother, including softness and tenderness, humility, and obedience. Yet here, too, one finds the same warning against "frivolous" behavior and "vigorous physical and outdoor activities" contained in family instructions addressed to boys (Hsiung 2005: 186–90).

Age reverence was a fourth leading factor that shaped the experiences of Chinese children in pre-modern times. A common feature of late imperial didactic works aimed at children of both sexes was a child's deep obligation toward his or her parents. Confucian thought had always emphasized the reciprocity involved in the "five relationships" of society (ruler/minister, father/son, husband/wife, elder brother/younger brother, friend/friend). However, late imperial ritual texts, philosophical references, family instructions, and legal documents ascribed to children a "subordinate, humble, and inferior status" to that of their elders, ancestors, and others in a hierarchically superior position (Hsiung 2005: 21). In Confucian orthodox thinking, a child's subordinate status vis-à-vis its elders was most pronounced in youth, yet was not necessarily tied to young age, a fact illustrated, for instance, in the popular saying: "As long as his parents are alive, a son is always a boy" (*"fu yi bei, zi yi bei"*). Indeed, until the death of one's parents, or whenever speaking or acting in the presence of the elders in the house, any offspring at any age always assumed the position of a "child" (*zi*) (Furth 1995: 178; Stafford 1995: 28; Hsiung 2005: 21). Unlike many pre-modern European societies, in Chinese families of the imperial era, children also did not gain substantial familial authority or family headship even when they married. Rather, they remained subordinate to their parents (or in the case of married women, parents-in-law), particularly their father, until either death or disability caused the latter to relinquish his familial power (Whyte 2003: 6).

This hierarchy of age and status compelled the child to observe his or her own place in the kinship group through, among other factors, the cult of ancestor worship and the norms of filial piety (*xiao*), a central virtue in Confucian thinking that made Chinese children feel overwhelmingly indebted to parents for their very existence. Part of this debt was for the biological gift of life itself, but part was for the care that the child received during his or her early years, a debt created by the perseverance of the parents in the face of the trouble and anxiety caused by the child (Hsu 1967 [1949]; Wolf 1970; Saari 1990).

Over the centuries, a series of writings on the topic of filial piety conveyed the message that a worthy child is one who gladly exerts extra efforts to meet the needs of, and provide pleasure to, parents. Ideally, a child should place the welfare of parents (or in the case of girls, parents-in-law) ahead of the welfare of himself (or herself) and his or her offspring – and persist in such behavior even if the parents are unpleasant or even abusive (Whyte 2003: 7).

The prescriptions of filial gratitude dictated much of the course of a child's future. Upon reaching adulthood, sons were expected to express their devotion to parents by passing the Civil Service examinations, winning prestige for the whole family. Most important of all, a son had to make sure that the family line would be continued. Dying without a male heir was one of the worst offenses against the concept of filial piety. Since women became part of their husband's family through marriage, filial conduct for a woman meant faithfully serving her in-laws, in particular her mother-in-law, and giving birth to a son. By fulfilling these duties, she also gained prestige for her own family. Within this ideological, social, and ritual framework, the birth of a child was regarded "not so much as the birth of an individual with its own individual right to existence but as one link in a network or continuum of lives connecting ancestors with descendants" (Kinney 1995b: 7). Children functioned as status symbols in a complex power game in which each adult player had different stakes and each child a different value (Bray 1997: 336). They were certainly desired, but were also "disposable." In theory, they could even be sold or killed (for instance, if rations were insufficient to feed everyone), as they were replaceable and one's parents were not (Wolf 1985: 205; Bray 1997: 336).

The notion that children belong to parents was filtered through gender (Furth 1995: 177). The enduring importance of ancestral worship (whose origins some scholars trace back as far as China's Neolithic period) emphasized the role of the male child as "a living representative within a line of descent emerging from the past and extending into the future" (Kinney 1995b: 1–2). The dominance of the patrilineage meant that female offspring were perceived as contributors to their husbands' lineage rather than that of their natal families. Traditional notions of hierarchy further depressed the status of girls and contributed to the sense that sacrificing a (female) child is acceptable if the sacrifice works for the greater good of the family (Kinney 1995b: 11; Waltner 1995: 208–11).

According to some estimates, as many as 10 or even 20 percent of newborn female infants, varying in different regions and classes, were killed in late imperial China. Girls aged between one and five also died more frequently than their brothers (Maynes and Waltner 2001:

20n10). For instance, a missionary (and naturalist) observer in the late nineteenth century interviewed 40 women aged over 50 who reported having borne 183 sons and 175 daughters, of whom 126 sons but only 53 daughters survived to age ten. By their account, these women had destroyed 78 of their daughters. The preference for a male child apparently had little effect on the survival of the first female child, however, as she was useful in helping to care for younger siblings and for performing tasks associated with the female role in the household. A female child with one or more older sisters, however, seems to have been especially unwelcome in comparison with a second or third male birth (Coale and Banister 1994: 472).

These aspects of childhood as a time of physical vulnerability, moral incompetence, and pronounced subordination to elders and seniors dominated Chinese concepts of the child throughout much of the imperial era. However, these views were sometimes challenged. Alongside the widespread, Confucian perspective that put an emphasis on children's inferior social status and downplayed the significance of childhood as a life stage, a Daoist view extolled the spontaneity and "innate innocence" of the young (Hsiung 2005: 23–4). This positive view of childhood became particularly dominant in the sixteenth and seventeenth centuries when central Neo-Confucian thinkers like Wang Yangming (1472–1529) equated the child's mind with "spiritual perfection," and regarded it as superior to the adult mind, which, "was often confused and corrupted by too much learning" (Dardess 1991: 79; Kinney 1995b: 5).

Despite this range of attitudes, scholars agree that the treatment of children in late imperial China was fundamentally invested in the past, in the sense that childrearing methods consistently upheld "traditional" beliefs and aspirations, and above all, emphasized the obligation to please and honor ancestors (Kinney 1995b: 1). In the late nineteenth century, and particularly the first few decades of the twentieth century, however, Chinese evaluations of both "tradition" and of childhood underwent a dramatic change. Public discourses began to celebrate childhood as the most valuable period of life, and the young were accorded an indispensable role in constructing a modern nation-state. What prompted this significant shift was nothing less than a large-scale national and social upheaval that led to a complete reappraisal of imperial culture and resulted in two political revolutions.

CHINESE CHILDHOOD UNDER REVOLUTION AND REFORM (1912–1949)

At the turn of the twentieth century, China was struggling with a number of major social crises. Its population had climbed to more than 300 million, but the country lacked sufficient industry or trade to absorb the available labor. Mounting poverty in the towns and the scarcity of land in the countryside led to widespread discontent and a breakdown in law and order, which a weak and corrupt bureaucratic and military system was unable to quell. Localized revolts erupted in various parts of the Qing Empire, culminating in the disastrous Taiping Rebellion (1851–64), which cost the lives of close to 30 million people. At the same time, the Chinese Empire was coming under increasing pressure from without.

After its defeat by the British in the first Opium War (1839–42), China was forced to sign the "unequal treaties" which enabled a number of foreign powers, including not only Britain but also Russia, Germany, France, Belgium, the United States, and Japan, to form special zones of influence to facilitate the exploitation of China's resources. In the last decade of the nineteenth century, another humiliating military defeat – this time to the Japanese – prompted last-minute attempts to reform and modernize China's political, educational, and military systems while maintaining the core values of Chinese culture. When these attempts failed, the Qing Dynasty collapsed in 1911, ending millennia of imperial rule. In place of empire, a democratic republic was established in 1912, but in 1917, the country fractured into a number of warlord territories. A further, crucial blow to China's sovereignty came when the Treaty of Versailles awarded to Japan the territories in Shandong that had formerly been controlled by Germany. On May 4, 1919, university and middle school students in Beijing protested against the treaty. The protest rapidly spread to other cities, crossing class boundaries and leading to the formation of a widespread movement for reform.

The New Culture Movement, also known as the May Fourth Movement (roughly dating from 1919–23) was led by young urban intellectuals who attacked all elements of "traditional" Chinese culture. Its proponents charged Confucian culture for being "unnatural and retrogressive," leading "first to stagnation and then to extinction." The basic unit in pre-modern Chinese society, they argued, was "the old instead of the young; and its emphasis [was] placed in the past rather than the future" (Farquhar 1999: 61). Convinced that Confucian values and family morality were the main sources of China's backwardness, May Fourth intellectuals promoted an alternative vision that emphasized rational scientific thought, democratic political and social organizations, and the valorization of the young and the new (Schwarcz 1986).

In their quest to turn China into a rich, powerful nation that could stand up to its foreign aggressors, many radicals of the period looked outside for new models of thinking about childrearing and education. In the early decades of the twentieth century, Chinese students returning home with degrees from Japan, Europe, and the United States imported a succession of foreign pedagogical models into the country's new education system (Pepper 1996: 519). It was the "West" though, with its strong conceptualization of "the self, an ethic of rebellion, and a paradigm of critical thought" (Schwarcz 1986: 117), that most attracted the attention of these early educational reformers.

Influenced by thinkers such as American philosopher John Dewey (1859–1952) and his ideas of Progressive Education, leading Chinese reformers like the author Lu Xun (1881–1936), leader and scholar Hu Shi (1891–1962), and founder of the CCP Chen Duxiu (1879–1942) believed that the development of individuality was a crucial condition to China's modernization. Through the norms of filial piety, they argued, the family and the state in China had "collaborated to keep the individual bound and gagged emotionally, intellectually and spiritually" (Schwarcz 1986: 109; see also Glosser 2003).

In his famous 1918 story, "Diary of a Madman," published in the New Culture movement's radical magazine, *New Youth* (*Xin qingnian*), the Chinese author Lu Xun equated Confucian virtue with cannibalism and pleaded with readers to "save the children" from being "devoured by their families." A year later, he again set out to attack the old order of priorities in an essay titled "How are we to be fathers today?," in which he used the authority of evolutionary biology to further condemn the Chinese family system as being perversely "against nature" (cited in Schwarcz 1986: 109, 111; see also Saari 1990: 44). He posited that parents must increase their "sense of duty toward their sons and daughters" and do their utmost to "quench concern with their own rights, in order to pave the way for a moral order in which the young set the standards" (cited in Pease 1995: 284).

Lu Xun and other liberal intellectuals of this period further held that a child's perspective provided fresh insights into social and political issues. To May Fourth intellectuals, the figure of the child functioned as a "symbol of 'naturalness', the perfect image of the Chinese citizen as yet untainted by the artificial strictures of Confucianism" (Farquhar 1999: 36). In the Darwinian discourse of struggling races, nations, and groups, which gained wide popularity among intellectuals of the time, children as a group and childhood as a segment of the life cycle were further valued and given important function (Saari 1990: 67). It was also during this period that the new academic disciplines of child psychology and educational psychology began to be established in China, and scientific and practical knowledge about the nature of child development circulated to the reading public.

In the cities, especially in Shanghai, children's literature emerged as part of the commercial publishing world and as a central element in the process of modern education. The notion of children as separate from the adult population, evident in these developments, implied recognition of the child as a proper subject of adult observation, description, instruction, and discipline (Farquhar 1999: 124; Jones 2002: 700, 713). Childhood began to be viewed as a distinct and critical phase that held the potential for a renewed vision of human capability (Pease 1995: 287), and the proper rearing and development of the young was deemed a necessary condition for nation building and modernization.

This latter notion received further reinforcement beginning in the mid-1920s, when China witnessed a new, anti-imperialist wave of militant nationalism. Fueled by the May 30, 1925 incident, in which British-led police in Shanghai fired on and killed Chinese demonstrators, a widespread conservative reaction undercut the assumption that China could only be saved by the "New Culture" formerly advocated by May Fourth intellectuals (Keenan 1977: 225). What China needed now, argued social and political activists, was a strengthening of the nation through the fostering of a strong sense of solidarity, community, and duty to the state. In this context, liberal, "child-centered" pedagogies were gradually displaced by an emphasis on patriotic political education and military training for children, copied from China's principal aggressor at this time, Japan (Bastid 1987: 12; see also Culp 2006; Plum 2012).

Like many of their European and American contemporaries, Chinese intellectuals of the 1930s and 1940s came to regard children and youths more as "national assets," whose proper education and regulation was crucial to the survival of the nation-state, than as autonomous individuals who should be allowed to develop freely. This instrumental view of the child became particularly potent in China as the reform attempts of early Chinese radicals were a response to imperialist invasion and were deeply and consciously embedded in a nationalist agenda. With the issue of national survival in mind, modern Chinese educators may have advocated freedom and autonomy of the child from authoritarian, patriarchal forces, but often rationalized this agenda with the need to achieve collective progress. Above all, they hoped that modern education would liberate Chinese children and youths who would then be able to "sweep away national humiliation, poverty, and technological backwardness," and thereby "salvage the nation" (Thøgersen 2002: 240; see also Anagnost 1997; Farquhar 1999).

These considerable expectations met with some pragmatic results in the realms of children's welfare and education. During the 1920s and the 1930s, literacy (which then stood at merely 10–15 percent of the total population) was advocated as a key to modernization, first for national cohesion and then for rural reconstruction, even among women and girls. Republican-era educational reforms therefore included the development of a modern school curriculum, citizenship education, and girls' education (Ross 2005: 9). In 1935, the Nationalist government initiated a drive for the universalization of basic education. Between 1935 and 1940, the plan called for all children to receive at least one year of school, between 1940 and 1944 two years of school, and after 1944, all children were to receive at least four years of primary schooling. This limited goal was ultimately beyond the financial resources of rural Chinese communities. While more children went to school during the republican era, the impact on long-term literacy was forestalled both by the short time children spent in school and the war with Japan (cited in Ross 2005: 10; see also Thøgersen 2002).

For its part, the Chinese Communist Party (CCP) also struggled to reach and gain the support of rural residents through educational and literacy programs implemented in Communist liberated areas. Both the Nationalist party and the CCP had hoped to build a large youth contingency, which would become a revolutionary vanguard reaching out to workers and merchants, and even to peasants (Saari 1990: 69; Gold 1991: 598). The CCP, in particular, concentrated much of its efforts on children and youth. Like other Marxist-Leninist parties of the day, the leaders of the CCP saw children as less tainted by the old, bourgeois society and therefore more ready to follow the new, socialist ideology. Successfully cultivating young people as revolutionary successors, it was thought, could help prevent the old society from reproducing itself and guarantee a large body of citizens who could be mobilized for the socialist cause (Gold 1991: 596; see also Kinney 1995b). After the Communists' victory in 1949, Chinese youngsters therefore came to play an ever more crucial role in the social and political transformations of the modern era, while the CCP sought to foster children as productive citizens and revolutionary fighters who would be loyal to the socialist nation-state rather than to their families and extended kinship group.

PUBLIC CHILDHOODS AND HEROIC CHILDREN IN THE MAOIST PERIOD (1949–1976)

Soon after the establishment of the People's Republic in 1949, the new CCP government signaled its intent to overhaul the institution of the patriarchal family by promulgating a new Marriage Law. The law called for the abolition of the "arbitrary and compulsory feudal marriage system" which ignored the interests of women as well as of children. It banned arranged marriages, polygyny, concubinage, and minor marriage (defined as marriage between men under the age 20 and women under 18). While reasserting the duty of adult children to support and assist their parents, the law also emphasized the duties of parents toward their offspring, particularly children's right to survival and to adequate treatment.

In subsequent decades, the Chinese government would make systematic efforts to improve children's welfare. Government policies worked to eradicate the custom of infanticide and to establish maternity and health- and childcare facilities across the country (Croll 1980). By the 1960s, these endeavors had led to high fertility rates, low infant mortality rates, and to a decline in excessive female mortality. In the early to mid-1970s, infant mortality was reduced to somewhere between 50 and 100 infant deaths per 1,000 live births from a level close to 300 per 1,000 in 1929–31. Due to the general improvement in the country's healthcare system, most Maoist-era mothers were likely to have at least one surviving son, and no longer had to resort to sex selection (Banister 1984: 718; Coale and Banister 1994: 472).

The Maoist state further sought to limit the patriarchal power associated with three-generation households through a sustained attack on the structure of patrilineage. After 1949, lineage property was confiscated in the name of land redistribution and collectivization, and the political and economic functions of lineages were replaced by the collectives and by party cadres (Potter and Potter 1990: 255; Yan 2003: 213). The destruction of the economic basis of lineage power was accompanied by an attack on ancestor worship. Striking directly at the cultural and religious core of the extended family, the ban on ancestor worship reduced the past prerogatives of the elderly by removing state sanction for these beliefs and rituals and making it harder for parents to invoke the threat of supernatural punishment against children who failed to respect them (Davis-Friedmann 1991; Davis and Harrell 1993). Together with the New Marriage Law of 1950, these state measures contributed to considerable shift of power from the old to the young in post-1949 China (Yang 1959; Diamant 2000; Yan 2003).

Government campaigns to promote gender equality also helped to raise the social and familial status of girls. During the Mao years, state pronouncements emphasized the obligation and opportunity of all women to contribute to society, expressed in the slogan "Women hold up half the sky" and in Mao Zedong's pronouncement, "Times have changed. Whatever men comrades can do, women comrades can do" (cited in Hershatter 2004: 1013). The CCP's stated ideology of gender equality had practical implications for female education. Back in 1949, 80 percent of the entire Chinese population and 90 percent of women were illiterate; the general enrollment rate of primary schools was below 20 percent, and the junior secondary school enrollment rate stood at a mere 6 percent. The figures for girls were even lower (Kessen 1975: 2; see also China.org.cn 2009).

The first two decades of socialist rule saw a massive expansion in China's school population. From the 1950s until the 1970s, modern schooling and mass education extended into all Chinese communities, including in rural and remote areas. In the early 1970s, some 127 million students reportedly attended primary school, ten times more than before 1949, and a very high proportion of the relevant age group (Kessen 1975: 2; see also China.org.cn 2009). By 1959, illiteracy rates among youths and adults (aged 12–40) fell from 80 percent to 43 percent; and by 1979, this figure had dropped to 30 percent. Though data from the period suggests that boys were still given priority in education, the gender gap did start to narrow in the mid-1960s, when the male illiteracy rate had also fallen. This convergence was probably due to the cumulative result of earlier government literacy programs that targeted girls and women (World Bank 1997: 49).

Structural problems of gender inequality and entrenched views regarding the supposedly "limited" capacities of women remained throughout the Maoist period (see, e.g., Evans 1997) but the Chinese state also sought to present girls with new models for emulation. Propaganda campaigns encouraged girls to become "women students," "women workers," or "women scientists," all of whom could participate fully in socialist construction (Wang Zheng 2001; Chen 2003). Many Chinese women recall these campaigns as enabling the transgression of gender boundaries and regard them as a positive legacy of their childhood under Mao (Hershatter 2004: 1013; see also Honig and Hershatter 1988; Evans 1999).

The new status accorded to Maoist-era children of both genders was equally evident in the official parlance of the period. Discourses and images produced by the socialist state tended to characterize the young as having "more culture" than the old and assigned children and youth the role of enlightening the older generation on various matters, especially pertaining to politics (Kessen 1975: 47). Represented as fighters for the country and for the revolution, even young children received the status of responsible actors in society's struggles. Stories, films, and propaganda posters of the period often depicted the brave deeds of "child martyrs" who were involved in violent or even murderous activities, fighting against Japanese aggressors or Nationalist forces (Donald 1999: 80–5, 95; see also Xu 2011; Naftali 2014b, 2014c). In times of national emergency, for instance during the Korean War or when relations between China and the Soviet Union deteriorated to an armed conflict, children as young as seven or eight were further encouraged to take part in digging tunnels as air raid shelters in order to defend the country (Xinran 2003: 174).

One of the main avenues through which children could prove their political commitment was by joining the Young Pioneers (also referred to in the literature as "Little Red Pioneers"). Modeled on a similar institution in the Soviet Union, this organization was founded by the CCP in 1949, and served as the first Communist Party affiliation for Chinese children aged seven to thirteen. Qualified teenagers could later apply for membership in the Communist Youth League. Similar in many ways to organizations such as the Boy and Girl Scouts, the Young Pioneers of the Maoist era was nonetheless a politically elite organization. Membership, which began in the third grade, was first restricted to the most enthusiastic and most academically diligent children. Later, successive groups of well-behaved children were also invited to join, so that by the end of the fourth grade, it was considered shameful not to wear the Young Pioneer "Red Scarf." Weekly activities included hobby clubs, voluntary labor for the school, or song-and-dance performances. To train the children to be socially conscious, the Young Pioneers also organized children to help needy people, do housework at old people's homes, or to plant trees for the nation (Chan 1985: 15; see also Unger 1982).

Young Pioneer members were encouraged to develop a sense of discipline and self-control. Activities were usually played out in tightly organized units, and structured criticism sessions took place on a regular basis. Children elected the leaders at the company and platoon levels on their own and those who served in leadership positions were encouraged to display initiative and to organize various activities (Ye and Ma 2005: 38). In a sense then, membership in the Young Pioneers granted even young children responsibility and autonomy. At the same time, child activists were also expected to serve as a model of good behavior and correct political ideology and to maintain the "rectitude and seriousness of adults" (Chan 1985: 25).

The politicization of childhood in the Maoist period was accompanied by an attack on the so-called "absurd and barbaric notion" that children constituted "the private property (sichan) of their parents." As one article in the CCP mouthpiece, the People's Daily, explained, parents had to realize that "from the time a child lets out its first cry coming into this world, he/she has already become a future citizen (gongmin) of the socialist state" (Xiao 1955: 3). This idea was also a crucial element in the cult of Mao which reached its zenith during the Cultural Revolution (1966–76). In campaigns of this chaotic period, gratitude to parents – the mainstay of the Confucian notion of filial piety – was to be replaced with gratitude to the Party and to Chairman Mao who had "given life" to a new Chinese society (Yang 1994: 259). Children and youth received encouragement to "draw the line" (huaqing jiexian) between themselves and their "counter-revolutionary" family members (Zang 2000: 65; see also Xinran 2003; Ye and Ma 2005; Lupher 1995). As Chinese historian Ye Weili recollects:

> It was not uncommon for children to struggle against their parents. During the big Xinhua parade, for instance, a man was humiliated by his children, with his estranged wife watching and cheering. The older child was only about ten and the young no more than eight. I had been fond of them because of their doll-like faces. Now they followed their father and spat at him. Violence didn't have to be physical. Psychological torture could be even crueler, especially if it was done by your own children (cited in Ye and Ma 2005: 80).

In some cases, children were even induced to spy on their parents and report them to their radical peers, occasionally with fatal consequences. To be sure, not all children and youth acted against their parents in this way (Rosen 1982). In conversations with young Chinese women in the early 1980s, Margery Wolf (1985: 208) found, for instance, that even those who were participants in the violent actions of the revolutionary Red Guards did not necessarily relate their activism to their relationship with their parents. In fact, she suggests, "far more young people simply dropped out of school and sat out the Cultural Revolution at home." However, it is safe to assume that growing up at a time when "exposing one's parents became a politically fashionable thing to do" (Ye and Ma 2005: 59) did cause injury to the parent–child relationship and certainly affected the life conditions of many children in urban areas. Parents who were persecuted as "rightists," "bad elements," or "counter-revolutionaries" often did all they could to send their children away to live in other cities or in the countryside in order to protect them from persecution. The less fortunate were held in detention centers, while their underage children were placed in special homes or left to care for themselves for extended periods (Zang 2000: 65–7; Xinran 2003).

State attempts to appropriate children from the care of the family were in evidence well before the Cultural Revolution, however. To allow large numbers of women to enter the workforce, the Chinese government had constructed nurseries, as well as kindergartens, primary, and middle schools with boarding facilities from the mid-1950s onward. Reports and studies nonetheless suggest that the clear majority of children under the age of seven were still cared for by parents, friends, relatives, or, in many cases, grandparents (Kessen 1975; Wolf 1985). This was partly due to resistance on the part of Chinese parents to collective childcare institutions which were often viewed as a threat to the family unit (Honig and Hershatter 1988). Contradictory official messages may have also played a role. Despite sustained efforts to convince Chinese women that devoting "too much time to their families" was "bourgeois and selfish" (Jacka 1992: 126), official propaganda posters and women and youth journals published from the 1950s to the 1970s continued to depict women as possessing "natural responsibilities to the domestic sphere," including the responsibility for childcare (Evans 2008: 84; see also Naftali 2014b).

Practical reasons further contributed to the continued importance of the extended family in children's care and education. While the expectation was that both parents would work full time, places in nurseries and kindergartens were often in short supply. Since grandmothers retired in their early fifties, just at the time when their sons and daughters had children of their own, many of the older women ended up taking over the care of the younger children (Wolf 1985; Jacka 1992; Evans 2008). Maoist-era women may have been told that "it was only a matter of time before the state and, to a limited extent, their husbands would be in a position to reduce their 'double burden'" (Evans 2008: 103), yet there is ample evidence that women continued to care for children within the home up until the very end of the Maoist period. In this sense, the intermittent attempts of the Maoist state to collectivize children's care were only partially successful.

CONCLUSION

China's socialist revolution transformed children's lives and subjectivities in dramatic ways. However, the significance of post-1949 reforms lies not so much in their new contents, but in the systematic and rapid attempt of the socialist state to extend processes already under way among the urban educated elite to other segments of Chinese society, namely the urban working classes and the peasants (Yang 1959; Yan 2003). As this chapter has shown, PRC state reforms and propaganda campaigns resulted in a weakening of family obligations, a re-shaping of relations within the domestic sphere, and an elevation in the status of children of both genders within society as a whole. The relative empowerment of Chinese children, who for centuries had been regarded as morally and cognitively "incomplete," constituted a clear, direct challenge to long-held Confucian notions of childhood and personhood.

Through the expansion of schooling and the employment of mass propaganda campaigns, the Maoist regime sought to destroy the old kinship hierarchy and to transform children from loyal family members into dutiful citizens of the new socialist state. These attempts contributed to a weakening of the horizontal kinship bonds that had been the mainstay of Chinese society. They also undermined the principles of age and gender hierarchy that had determined children's subordinate status within the family. In the process, however, they produced children as increasingly atomized individuals (Yang 1994: 187). Liberated from the strict control of elders and seniors, Maoist-era children gained "new social spaces for individual development" (Yan 2003: 231). At the same time, they were also brought into an ever more direct and close relationship with the power of the modern socialist state. Moreover, children's willingness to rebel against parents, teachers, and other authority figures during tumultuous periods such as the Cultural Revolution was in effect conditioned upon the approval of the ultimate authority figure: Mao himself (Lupher 1995: 335).

Mao's death in 1976 brought the collectivist period and the Cultural Revolution to its official end. The ascendance of a new CCP leadership bent on modernizing China's stagnating economy signaled a renewed and strengthened emphasis on academic excellence in children's education. Under the leadership of Deng Xiaoping, the post-Maoist state reintroduced the nationally unified college entrance examination and increased its investment in elite schools, mostly in urban areas. The introduction of market reforms and the Chinese government's Open Door Policy resulted in increasing openness to global, neoliberal agendas in the realms of childrearing and education, as well as to the emergence of a new consumer market targeting youngsters and their caregivers. As will be shown in the following chapters, these developments have led to an intensification of the process of children's empowerment which had begun 70 years earlier. They have also contributed to a greater individualization of the child at home and at school. At the same time, some important elements of Confucian, early modern, as well as socialist repertoires of childrearing and education would continue to shape the lives of children and the conceptualizations of childhood in twenty-first-century China.

2 | Raising Children in Contemporary China: Discourse and Practice ————

In 1978, the Chinese government launched a series of extensive reforms with the aim of rapidly modernizing the country's economy and renewing and expanding its cultural and diplomatic ties with the world. Three-and-a-half decades later, these reforms have led to considerable economic growth as well as to a far-reaching social and cultural transformation that has also affected the raising and educating of children. This chapter outlines the main contours of – and the political, economic, and sociocultural factors contributing to – China's recent transformation in ideas and practices of childrearing and education. The discussion identifies the main institutions and agents involved in the production and dissemination of new ideas about children and their care, and notes how caregivers and children of different social backgrounds interpret and experience these new ideas in their daily lives. While recognizing the increasing influence of neoliberal notions and prescriptions in the realms of childcare and education, the chapter argues that these notions are crucially shaped by competing ideologies and divergent practices on the ground, resulting in the development of multiple models of what it means to be a child and a person in twenty-first-century China.

Since the late 1970s, government policies and legal codes, academic publications, and childrearing literature in China have promoted more "modern" and "scientific" ways of treating the young. The declared aim has been to improve the lot of individual children but also to raise the "quality" (*suzhi*) of the entire nation. At the same time, the past few decades have also seen the rise of an idealized notion of childhood as a time of innocence and play rather than political activism or physical toil. Largely suppressed during the Mao era, this view – which first emerged in China in the early decades of the twentieth century – has re-emerged and become more popular in recent decades, particularly among the ranks of a younger generation of urban, middle-class parents born after 1978.

These new currents share many similarities with ideas currently circulating elsewhere in the world. They draw much of their inspiration from a global, neoliberal discourse which seeks to educate children everywhere as innovative and independent-minded future laborers and consumers. As these notions spread to schools and homes in China, they contribute to a standardization of Chinese childhood along the lines of global models of thinking. They further result in children's growing empowerment and individualization both at home and at school.

These developments are nonetheless characterized by tensions and contradictions that stem from inherent conflicts between new, global visions of childhood and personhood, and alternative notions about the proper way of governing children – ideas that draw on the cultural repertoires of the socialist-collectivist period and on long-held notions of moral and filial conduct. As the discussion will illustrate, both of these earlier repertoires continue to hold sway among government officials, educators, and caregivers in China, even as the country undergoes considerable social and economic transformations.

Social class and the gender of the child also play an important role in the reception of new notions of childrearing and education. Some Chinese parents, particularly those of urban, well-educated backgrounds who wish to associate themselves with a "modern," "middle-class" civility, tend to be more receptive to the neoliberal logic of childrearing, with its emphasis on fostering a child's freedom, autonomy, and individuality. Others, particularly those with lower levels of education, believe that such tendencies should be encouraged in boys, less so in girls. Yet others, including grandparents who continue to play a prominent role in caring for young children in China, remain ambivalent about the implications of introducing a more liberal, individualizing code of conduct into family life. They therefore continue to teach children the value of obedience to elders and seniors, and to exercise relatively harsh disciplinary methods with their child.

For their part, however, even young schoolchildren in China are becoming more aware of – and more vocal about – their individual rights than ever before. But they too are conflicted about whether they should assert their personal interests or respect the wishes of their seniors as dictated by the notion of filiality. To negotiate these inherent conflicts, children and caregivers of different social backgrounds employ myriad creative strategies, resulting in hybrid, complex paradigms of childrearing, education, and morality.

SCIENTIFIC CHILDREARING AND "EDUCATION FOR QUALITY"

In the late 1970s, the leadership of the CCP turned from an emphasis on socialism and revolution to "science" and "modernity." In line with this official, gradual retreat from collectivist, egalitarian agendas to one of economic growth based on market reform, Chinese society also witnessed the rise of individualism; the growing importance of the private sphere; and an increasing attentiveness to the exploration of selfhood (Yan 2010: 1–2; Kleinman et al. 2011: 28). Particularly since the 1990s, this shift has been illustrated by the exponential growth of hotlines, radio call-in programs and advice literature, ranging from self-help titles to professional books on psychology and psychoanalysis, including translations of European and American authors (Erwin 2000; Farquhar 2001).

This intensified popular interest in emotions, personality, and self-development has spilled over into the educational and familial domains (Kleinman et al. 2011: 29). Chinese caregivers, particularly in urban areas, are now swamped with psychological advice through lectures, books, websites, newspapers, and magazines, as well as through talk shows on CCTV stations which devote episodes to parenting issues with the help of psychology professionals (Kuan 2011: 79–80; see also Naftali 2010b, 2014a). In line with these developments, writers and media producers for young audiences in China have started to pay attention to the "unique features" of childhood as defined by the principles of developmental psychology. Accordingly, children's literary and media works in the post-1978 era tend to portray young characters engaging in a world of play and fantasy rather than violent political struggle, as was the case in the latter part of the Maoist period (Naftali 2014c: 4–5).

The growing influence of this modern, psychological discourse of childhood in academic works and popular media products has received further impetus from the Chinese government's campaign to improve the "quality of the population" (*renkou suzhi*). Following the launch of market reforms and the One-Child Policy in the late 1970s, a broad array of state programs and scientific research plans have called on the Chinese public "to reproduce less in order to nurture better." Targeting caregivers, the campaign includes the publication of books on child health and psychology as well as the launch of state-sponsored adult-education programs that disseminate "correct" childrearing knowledge. Local and national competitions and the bestowal of honors to households for achievements in childcare and education further attest to the government's current interest in raising the quality of the nation through the promotion of more "modern," "objective" models of caring for and educating children (Anagnost 1995, 2004; Greenhalgh and Winckler 2005; Kipnis 2006, 2011a, 2011b; Woronov 2009a).

Much of the official and academic discourse that now proliferates in China emphasizes the intensification of parental investment as part of what is termed quality "family education" (*jiating jiaoyu*) (Anagnost 2008: 59). In this context, even ordinary parents receive a prominent role in the major political project of modernizing China by "modernizing" the subjectivity of their school-age children (Kuan 2015: 209). Just as national development is now predicated on rational management and capital investment, the government's program of raising children's quality stipulates that parents should educate their children using methods proven by scientific experts rather than those absorbed in the home through the example of family elders. Caregivers are further called on to orient their children's developmental goals to the global market and to invest in capital equipment such as computers and educational services which foster children's various competencies (Woronov 2007a: 32; see also Greenhalgh and Winckler 2005). Though Chinese guidebooks commonly address "parents," there is a general assumption that mothers in particular should take primary responsibility, or are already primarily responsible for the crucial task of raising the "quality" child (Honig and Hershatter 1988; Milwertz 1997; Anagnost 2008; Kuan 2011, 2015).

Alongside this new emphasis on scientific parenting and in particular scientific motherhood, the Chinese government has also launched an extensive reform plan to advance "education for quality" (*suzhi jiaoyu*) in the nation's schools. Introduced in 1999, this ambitious program summarizes a series of educational experiments implemented at the local and provincial levels since the 1980s. It includes an overhaul of the curriculum, teaching, and assessment methods of state schools, with the goal of fostering a "well-rounded" child – a child who is developed intellectually (*zhiyu*), morally (*deyu*), physically (*tiyu*), and aesthetically (*meiyu*) – and who would acquire the occupational skills necessary to compete in a global labor market (Woronov 2008: 407; 2009a: 572; see also Kipnis 2006).

In practice, the breadth of the plan is matched by a singular lack of specificity: precisely how these changes are to be created is never clearly defined. However, the launch of the "education for quality" reforms has opened a new discursive space in which parents, teachers, administrators, and officials in China contest and challenge the meaning of "quality" – and how to raise it in children (Woronov 2008: 406; see also Kipnis 2006).

The plan and the proliferating discourse which surrounds it is partly informed by Confucian traditions of self-cultivation, but also by a Marxist emphasis on physical, intellectual, and moral training of children (Kipnis 2006: 307). Its main source of inspiration, however, is Western, neoliberal educational theories. The North American notion of "competence education," which emphasizes training students in specific competencies rather than in exam success, is particularly popular among contemporary Chinese academic writers (Kipnis 2006: 300; see also Naftali 2008). That said, in many popular volumes and even some academic works published in China in the 2000s, the "West" frequently functions as a self-referential construct whose features are determined more by local standards than by actual realities. In parallel, the imaginary construct of "Chinese culture" is often seen in these publications as the source of inadequate educational and childrearing skills and as an obstacle preventing Chinese children from achieving "Western-style" economic success (Woronov 2007a: 47–8).

The notion of "quality" (*suzhi*) is central not only in the Chinese government's population policy documents and in educational discourses relating to modernity and civility, but also in the anxieties and aspirations of caregivers, and in particular the urban middle classes. In the everyday parlance of both parents and children, the term "high quality" (*gao suzhi*) currently represents a kind of "ideal personhood associated with urban modernity" (Fong 2007a: 86), while "backward peasant thinking (*nongmin yishi*)" is condemned as a hindrance to the country's further development and modernization (Anagnost 2004: 196; Woronov 2009a: 571; Lin 2011: 318–19). As Ann Anagnost further notes, "[t]he discourse of *suzhi* appears most elaborated in relation to two figures: the body of the rural migrant, which exemplifies *suzhi* in its apparent absence, and the body of the urban, middle-class only child, which is fetishized as a site for the accumulation of the very dimensions of *suzhi* wanting in its 'other'" (2004: 190).

Such views are evident among not only caregivers, but also officials and educators. A recent ethnographic study conducted in a Beijing suburban school finds, for instance, that some schoolteachers regarded students with a rural background negatively in relation to all attributes, including manner, attitude, mental ability, aptitude, and physical appearance. They described rural children as "brutal," "impolite," "retarded," "self-abased," "dirty," and "dark," while attributing these negative features to "a lack of family education or discipline as a consequence of the low educational level of their parents," which "have caused the children to lack good habits, broad horizons, self-esteem, and high academic achievement" (cited in Lin 2011: 319).

In another ethnographic study by anthropologist Andrew Kipnis, a Beijing education official similarly explained that a student's "quality (*suzhi*) is a product of social environment, school environment, teachers, family, and level of individual effort." Whereas rural children may work hard and attain high grades, noted the official, their "overall quality" is necessarily lower compared "to a child who lives every day in such an information-saturated environment [as Beijing]" (cited in Kipnis 2001: 22).

As illustrated by such statements, the ubiquitous discourse on "quality" often assumes that the way to improve or modernize the rural populace lies in either education or mobility (Lin 2011: 315). In practice, however, children of rural migrant workers who have moved to the cities in search of work continue to be regarded by local urban officials, teachers, and parents as essentially inferior to their urban counterparts, thereby belying the promise of social mobility under the new market reforms (Froissart 2003; Woronov 2009b; Lan 2014).

Discrepancies between theory and practice within the discourse of "scientific," "quality" childrearing are further illustrated in regards to the perceived roles of grandparents in children's care and education. Most contemporary media and government publications in China direct their messages at young parents who are expected to fulfill a primary role in tending to the child's physical, cognitive, and emotional needs. When grandparents are mentioned, their caretaking style is often attacked and usually considered "backward" (Binah-Pollak 2014: 33). In reality, however, many grandparents continue to play an important and sometimes primary role in caring for young children.

Because the labor supply far exceeds demand, Chinese urban women are unable to use part-time jobs as a way of balancing work and childcare. Even in the country's rural areas, where agricultural work is considered more compatible with childcare, women have to combine multiple work activities. Moreover, many rural couples who migrate to the cities are often forced to leave their children behind. Given these difficulties, parents in both urban and rural areas frequently rely on help from grandparents (Ye et al. 2010; Chen et al. 2011: 576; Goh 2011; Binah-Pollak 2014). The expectation that parents play a primary role in tending to the child's needs and disregard grandparents' "unscientific" childrearing knowledge is therefore at a clear disconnect from the practical realities of family life in China and may alienate those grandparents who are in fact the child's primary caregivers.

Finally, the ambiguity surrounding the current drive to promote "scientific childrearing" and "education for quality" also stems from the contradictions that characterize the current prescriptions for raising a "quality" child. The next two sections will discuss these contradictions at length, by focusing on two central themes that are now at the center of much debate in China: the importance of study versus play in childhood; and the importance of autonomy versus discipline in children.

CHILDREN'S STUDY AND PLAY

A growing number of field studies conducted in China since the 1990s suggest that the lives of children, particularly those residing in urban areas, have undergone increased regimentation. Many parents try to ensure that children's spare time will be spent studying or engaging in various skill-enhancement activities designed to raise the child's "quality." As a result, Chinese children have few opportunities for play and relaxation (Fong 2004b; Greenhalgh and Winckler 2005; Woronov 2007a, 2011; Anagnost 2008; Cockain 2011; Kuan 2015).

In Shanghai of the mid-2000s, for instance, primary school children of middle-class backgrounds typically had to wake up at 6:30 a.m., stay at school until 4:30 p.m., and return home with a large amount of homework and test preparation assignments. By the time they had reached fourth grade, many children failed to finish their schoolwork before nine or ten in the evening, sometimes even waking up early in the morning to complete their unfinished tasks. Shanghai children of middle-class backgrounds also had to attend a plethora of after-school activities during weekdays as well as at weekends. These activities were chosen by parents with the intention of making their son or daughter attain a higher "quality," and when they began to interfere with academic test-based success, they were often discarded (Naftali 2010b: 599; see also Cockain 2011).

Alongside – or indeed in response to – the production of these highly disciplined childhoods, which in many respects resemble similar patterns of "concerted cultivation" in urban, middle-class families in East Asia and beyond (see, e.g., Field 1995; Abelmann 2003; Lareau 2003), the past two decades have also witnessed the emergence of an alternative strain of thinking. Drawing on the principles of developmental psychology, some academic writers and advice book authors in China have begun to insist that if children are to develop fully and healthily, they must be allowed to experience a "proper" childhood, ideally defined as a time of leisure and play rather than ceaseless study (Naftali 2010b: 590–1; see also Binah-Pollak 2014). This notion is portrayed as a crucial step in solving what is thought to be one of the most pressing problems facing Chinese children today: emotional difficulties caused by excessive pressure at school and high expectations at home.

Particularly since the late 1990s, Chinese state-run media have paid much attention to the so-called national malaise of too much homework, frequent testing, and heavy parental demands, all of which are said to be detrimental to the mental health of the nation's children. Media reports in China often cite statistical surveys, which show that the country's children, and in particular singletons residing in urban areas, suffer from a range of acute mental problems, including Internet addiction, psychosomatic skin diseases, and suicidal tendencies. As one such report suggests, these problems stem from the fact that Chinese children "spend longer hours at school than their parents spend at work," "have little time to play," and consequently "are experiencing *joyless childhoods*" (*People's Daily* 2007, emphasis added).

The Chinese government appears to be listening to the experts. Since the late 1990s, it has introduced various measures to alleviate school pressure and protect the "mental health of schoolchildren" in accordance with the "development characteristics…of [their] growth" (Communist Party of China 2000: 231–2). China's 1999 "education for quality" plan calls, among other things, for a limit on the number of school hours and examinations, the abolition of school-based extracurricular study and cramming sessions, as well as a reduction in the amount of work assigned to young students (Communist Party of China, 2000; see also Woronov 2008: 413). The implementation of these measures has nonetheless met with some difficulty and even outright resistance on the part of caregivers in both rural and urban areas.

In his 2001 study of rural schools in Shandong Province, Kipnis discovered, for instance, that even after the implementation of the "education for quality" reforms, students in some rural primary schools spent four hours each Saturday doing extra work on their mathematics and Chinese. Rural county officials and teachers candidly related that many caregivers in the countryside are concerned that "they don't have the educational background to help their children study at home" and therefore do not approve of shortening the school day since they are "afraid that their children will fall behind" (cited in Kipnis 2001: 15).

Concerns about maintaining children's competitive edge are also evident among middle-class, urban caregivers, who in response to the reduction in schoolwork have sometimes assigned children extra homework to keep them on their toes (Woronov 2008: 408). Fieldwork I conducted in Shanghai primary schools and homes of the mid-2000s reveals that teachers in the city continued to assign large amounts of homework due to pressures from both below and above (Naftali 2010b: 599). As noted by informants, the difficulty in reducing children's workloads largely lies in China's current selection and evaluation system. To gain acceptance to a good university, a student has to do well on the National College Entrance Examination (the *gaokao*). However, in order to achieve that coveted goal, he or she first has to attend a good middle school, and admission depends on the results of the middle school entrance examination (the *zhongkao*). In the minds of many parents and children, doing well on the *gaokao* determines not only one's chances of entering a top university but also of securing a good position later in life. In reality, that is not always true, but parents of different socioeconomic backgrounds nonetheless continue to cherish this dream for their child, pressuring him or her to study hard in the hope of raising talented, successful offspring (see also Fong 2004b; Croll 2006; Woronov 2007a, 2008, 2011).

Some children have started to publicly object to these continued pressures. In 2004, for instance, a large number of participants in Shanghai's Fifth Conference of Young Pioneers submitted public petitions demanding that parents and school officials "start listening to the experts," "let up the pressure," and allow children "*to have a childhood*" (cited in China Daily 2004, emphasis added). In an insightful ethnographic study, researcher Alex Cockain asked China youth about their experiences in senior middle school, and found that despite recognizing the importance of academic success, many informants expressed frustration at the way in which their academic scores were used to classify them. His young interviewees complained:

> The most important thing is your test scores. Both teachers and parents only focus on this.

> All teachers and parents think that scores are the most important thing. They think that is the most important standard to evaluate a person.

> It is necessary for all people to be classified and ranked. Students are no different, but the importance of the exam places a lot of pressure on young people. If they fail the *gaokao*, parents and teachers will view them as bad boys even if they might be good in many other respects.

> If you are good at study, everything is fine [said in exasperation] and there is no problem. If your grades are good, then you are good. If your grades are bad, then you are bad. You are bad. You are bad, and there is nothing you can do to change this (cited in Cockain 2011: 110).

By voicing these objections to the researcher, Chinese students showed that they could deconstruct the rigid binaries used to classify them (Cockain 2011). Others employ poetic forms to express their frustration. In 2011, Yueyue, a girl in fifth grade in the city of Nanjing, wrote a poem entitled "Mom, I'm under such pressure." Posted on the Chinese Internet, where it created much interest, the poem was written after a fight Yueyue had with her mother who insisted that she finish a math worksheet before the final exam. The daughter protested with a rhyme poem written in three minutes:

> Mom, I'm under such pressure [...]
> I want to explore each blade of grass and every flower [...]
> Mom, I promise I will not fail you when I grow up.
> Please don't cut me from nature. Please give me a break

The poem was also published in the state-run newspaper, the *China Daily* (2011), which further reported that the fifth-grader saw the fight with her mom as "a fight for the right." Yueyue's mother told the newspaper she was touched by the poem, "I thus knew my child was not happy, because she was restrained from what she likes and forced into what she hates."

Like this Nanjing mother, some of the middle-class parents I interviewed in Shanghai sympathized with their schoolchildren's plight but many also reported feeling trapped. One well-educated Shanghai mother told me that both she and her husband placed their child's "unfettered development" over his academic success but she admitted that, like many of his peers, her seven-year-old son participated in various enrichment classes. Between regular school assignments, studying for exams, taking lessons in art and conversational English, and competing in Chinese chess tournaments during the weekends, the boy had little time left for rest or spontaneous play (cited in Naftali 2010b: 601).

As noted, the situation appears to be worse for older children, and Chinese adolescents commonly describe themselves as "over-worked and under-rested" (Cockain 2012: 81–2). Preparing for the *gaokao* is a rite of passage so normalized that it is considered the central experience of the Chinese teenager. Moreover, there is also a strong moral hierarchy among students; they assess and rank each other based on fewest hours of sleep because they are studying so hard (Woronov 2011: 92). Many urban, middle-class parents say that they would like to do "what the experts recommend – to be more humane and to attend to a child's psychological needs" (cited in Kuan 2015: 210). However, they also see these recommendations as a threat to developing their child's ability to succeed in the market economy he or she would have to face one day. In China's highly competitive academic and labor environment, parents feel that they cannot afford to reduce the pressure on their children.

There are some indications, however, that caregivers' attitudes toward children's study and play may be undergoing a change, particularly among younger cohorts of parents. According to some reports, urban, educated parents born after the introduction of the One-Child Policy in the late 1970s are often more determined to allow their own son or daughter a more carefree childhood. Parents of this generation – most of whom are only-children – may be more willing to decrease children's pressure not only because they regard this attitude as more "modern" and "scientific" but also because they themselves grew up with the pressure of being better and smarter than their peers (Guan 2009).

The desire to allow children to experience a less stressful childhood is also evident among a slightly older cohort of Chinese parents who had been young children during the Cultural Revolution (1966–76). Some remember this chaotic decade with a surprising degree of nostalgia, as a time of carefree play on a permanent holiday from school. This image of a "happy childhood" during the collectivistic period often crops up in their misgivings about the regimented childhood experience of their son or daughter today (Anagnost 2008: 64). In contrast, however, urban parents who had experienced the Cultural Revolution as adolescents often did not have a chance to complete a full course of basic education, let alone the opportunity to attend university. Deprived of a proper education in their own childhood, they want their own children to do better, even if that means missing childhood fun and games (Milwertz 1997; Chee 2000; Davis and Sensenbrenner 2000; Fong 2004b; Anagnost 2008). These findings highlight the importance of generational factors in shaping the attitudes of many contemporary Chinese parents toward issues of study and play, as well as childrearing more generally.

Finally, the expectation that children devote a majority of their time to schoolwork may also stem from the view that a child's academic success serves as a form of future guarantee that the parents would receive sufficient care – emotionally, financially, and/or physically –

when they reach old age (Milwertz 1997; Fong 2004b; Whyte 2004). This pragmatic expectation in turn draws on the long-held ethos of filial piety (*xiao*) and the notion of reciprocal family relations.

With rising incomes and the emergence of private insurance and commercialized elderly care, some middle-class urban parents are becoming less interested in the value of children as future providers of old-age security (Kuan 2015: 181). However, as indicated by a number of studies conducted in mainland China, as well as in the more advanced economies of Hong Kong and Taiwan, many Chinese parents, even those of relatively affluent means, continue to believe that they have a "moral duty" to train their child to succeed in school. Children, in turn, must ensure that their parents' efforts and sacrifices had meaning and strive to repay their mothers and fathers for their care and investment by working as hard as they can in order to obtain good grades and eventually a successful career (see Chao 1994; Stafford 1995; Wu 1996; Fong 2004a, 2007b; Kipnis 2008). Accordingly, Chinese parents expect their sons or daughters to invest the best of their childhood years in study rather than play.

AUTONOMY, DISCIPLINE, AND OBEDIENCE

Children's autonomy is another hotly contested issue in contemporary China. Whereas Maoist-era discourse stressed children's autonomy as political actors, it also promoted the value of self-abnegation and individual sacrifice for the collective good. In contrast, China's contemporary "education for quality" program extols the importance of allowing children to protect their individual interests and express themselves freely. Since the 1990s, educational authorities have been revising the curriculum to promote new visions of students as responsible subjects rather than passive receptacles of knowledge, while school administrators in both urban and rural areas have been experimenting with "democratic" student elections to promote the ability of children and youth to take initiative and exercise "self-governance" (Naftali 2008; Hansen 2015).

In order to foster innovative, independent-minded learners and eventually workers, parents and teachers are now advised to allow children to develop creative thinking and to refrain from the use of harsh disciplinary methods which curtail children's autonomy (Drulhe 2002; Greenhalgh and Winckler 2005; Woronov 2009a; Kuan 2012; Binah-Pollak 2014; Naftali 2014a). Creating a direct link between the importance of fostering children's ability to make their own choices and decisions and their future happiness and success, some psychology professionals in China recommend that caregivers respect the wishes of their child in order to foster his or her sense of individual identity and separateness. Others emphasize that in contrast to previous generations, contemporary children are increasingly exposed to alternative, diverse sources of knowledge and are therefore better able to form their own judgments and have "the necessary cognitive and emotional capabilities to enjoy and even demand rights" at a relatively early age. Chinese parents should recognize that "even young children have a voice of their own" and that this voice "deserves to be heard and respected" (cited in Naftali 2009: 87).

Contemporary parenting guidebooks further associate the fostering of children's freedom and autonomy with the goal of improving the nation's "quality" by comparing local educational practices to those thought to exist in other countries, particularly the United States. This genre of guidebooks has now become highly popular. A noted example is the 2000 best-selling volume *Suzhi jiaoyu zai Meiguo* [*Education for Quality in the US*]. Authored by educational consultant Huang Quanyu, the book criticizes Chinese education for its emphasis on respect for authority and praises American pedagogies for emphasizing the ability of children to recognize and express their own needs and desires. American attitudes, suggests the author, are able to contribute to the production of "confident," "entrepreneurial" subjects who possess an increased ability to creatively express themselves (cited in Woronov 2007a: 40–3). In another volume of the same genre, Chinese educator Shen Ning similarly contrasts what he describes as outdated Chinese concepts concerning the "limited rational capacities of children" with "American notions of childhood," which argue that even young children possess the ability to make judgments in matters concerning them. Parents should bear this ability in mind, argues the author, not only because it is more "scientifically correct," but also because China's shift to a market economy requires workers to exhibit qualities such as "independence, individuality, and self-awareness" (cited in Hu 2000: 154).

This new emphasis on children's individuality and autonomy has received further impetus from the introduction of a new law designed to protect the rights of minors. As noted in chapter 1, earlier republican- and Maoist-era discourses already attempted to reconstitute children in the role of responsible agents who can partake in revolutionary struggles. However, it is only in the late twentieth century, particularly from the early 1990s onward, that we see a significant expansion of a public discourse surrounding children's individual rights, together with the introduction of a law devoted to the interests of the young in China (Naftali 2009: 82).

Addressing such basic issues as a child's right to survival and education, as well as the endemic problem of child labor, China's Law on the Protection of Minors (in effect since 1992 and amended in 2006) details specific new rights to which minors – defined as persons under the age of 18 – are now entitled. These include the right to protection from acts that "humiliate the personal dignity of the child," such as physical abuse and – for the first time in PRC legislation – a child's right to privacy (*geren yinsi*) (China.org.cn 2015).

Following the adoption of this benchmark law, parts of which clearly evoke the rhetoric of international documents such as the 1989 UN Convention on the Rights of the Child, Chinese legislation in the areas of family and criminal law has started to reflect the idea that children constitute autonomous persons who should be consulted in matters concerning them. When parental custody is disputed in divorce cases and in adoption proceedings, Chinese courts are instructed to hear the opinions of children aged ten and older, and to consider their voices as decisive factors in their eventual judgment. A child who has become involved in judicial proceedings is also now allowed to express his or her "personal views" (cited in Naftali 2009: 84).

The issue of children's rights, including the right to protection from violence, is now taught in Chinese primary schools. Interviews conducted with parents in Shanghai suggest that some children have successfully internalized these lessons. Citing the new law, they demand that parents "stop hitting them" and use persuasion instead of physical force. Some parents attempt to heed their children's requests. Others, however, continue to use corporal punishment though they now acknowledge that "it is wrong to do so" (Naftali 2014a: 78).

Different cultural expectations about childrearing practices can, of course, affect perceptions of what constitutes "corporal punishment" and "child abuse" in different parts of the world (Korbin 1991). In recent decades, opposition to the use of corporal punishment of children has nonetheless grown due to greater worldwide awareness of children's rights and the way childhood experiences affect later life. In China, however, "child abuse" is still a relatively new concept not commonly used in social contexts (Qiao and Xie 2015: 1–2; see also Naftali 2014a: 6–12; 69–74). Moreover, field research conducted in the last 20 years or so confirms that physical punishment remains a prevalent practice in many Chinese homes (see Qiao and Chan 2005; Qiao and Xie 2015).

In-depth interviews with 20 parents and quantitative surveys conducted among more than 1,000 Beijing adults between 2004 and 2012 revealed, for instance, that child beatings and other types of corporal punishment are still considered by many adults to be legitimate and effective methods for parents to educate and discipline their children (Qiao and Xie 2015: 1). Based on the explanations offered by interviewed parents who hailed from different socioeconomic backgrounds, parental child beating mainly resulted from the child's poor study habits, disobedience, defiant responses, and moral misconduct. Respondents were hesitant to consider the beating of one's own child (by biological parents) as a case of "child physical abuse," a category that in their view, only included parents beating their children "malevolently and frequently, so as to cause serious physical injuries" (Qiao and Xie 2015: 3–4, 7).

Ethnographic work by Schoenhals (1993), Kuan (2011), and Goh (2011) similarly shows that urban Chinese caregivers of various socioeconomic backgrounds commonly employ physical punishment with their children. The practice is equally prevalent among rural migrant workers in the city (Xiong 2015: 181), and is especially common among caregivers – and even teachers – in the Chinese countryside. A qualitative study conducted in a northern rural Chinese county reports, for instance, that physical punishment was ubiquitous and even "valued" by virtually all adult participants, including teachers and caregivers (see Katz et al. 2011: 99). An ethnographic study of two rural middle schools in southwest China similarly found that girls and boys alike were "kicked by female teachers' high heels or slapped on the face when they misbehaved in class" (Wu 2012b: 667). Though village teachers in this area were familiar with the precepts of "education for quality," which ban the use of harsh discipline, in practice teachers continued to hold physical discipline as imperative in order "not to let the students get an upper hand" (Wu 2012b: 666). The school vice-headmaster further rationalized the persistence of such harsh practices by explaining to the researcher: "Unlike the urban children, our mountain kids are wild little monsters and have no self-motivation in learning. If we practice child-centered teaching and don't use discipline, we are doing our students a disservice" (p. 664).

This ambiguity is also evident in PRC legislation. Some Chinese laws prohibit the abuse of children, including not only the PRC Law on the Protection of Minors (Article 10), but also the Constitution of the PRC (Article 49), the Marriage Law of the PRC (Article 3), and the Criminal Law of the PRC (Article 260). However, none of these laws specifically defines what constitutes child abuse. Moreover, there is no executive department or departmental public body in charge of child abuse in the Chinese government at any level, nor is there a special unit dedicated to dealing with child abuse investigations or protection by the police, hospitals, or schools (Qiao and Xie 2015: 2). The government's indecisive stance regarding the issue of physical punishment echoes and further reinforces mainstream public attitudes that sanction these childrearing practices.

Nonetheless, there are some indications that the use of physical punishment is becoming at least a subject for debate. In 2011, a book entitled *Suoyi, Beida xiongmei* (*That's Why They Go to Beijing University*) generated a great deal of public discussion in China. The book, which followed the success of Amy Chua's 2011 volume, *Battle Hymn of the Tiger Mom*, describes how the author and businessperson, Xiao Baiyou (whom the Chinese media quickly dubbed "Wolf Dad"), beat his children into China's top school, Beijing University. Xiao relates that even in preschool, his children would spend "days reciting Chinese classics ranging from poetry to philosophy. If they failed to meet his standards, they would be beaten with a feather duster on the legs or the palm of the hand" (cited in Xinhua News Agency 2011; see also Lim 2011). The book became a bestseller in China, yet Xiao's methods were heavily debated. Some urban parents were quoted in the press as saying that they "fully understand why Xiao administers physical punishment to his children." Other city caregivers, as well as education experts, argued however that "too many beatings...can lead to psychological problems for children" and that the root of the problem was a way of thinking that ignores "children's personal choices and feelings" (cited in Xinhua News Agency 2011).

As this example illustrates, China's official media has in recent years tried to instill greater awareness of the adverse effects of corporal punishment by drawing on the logic and rhetoric of developmental psychology and on the idea of children as autonomous individuals. The efficacy of such rhetoric remains uncertain, however. Qiao and Xie (2015) argue, for instance, that Chinese parents generally "do not consider the problem of child abuse from the perspectives of individual child rights or the negative consequences for the physical and mental development of the child" (p. 5). Nonetheless, they concede that younger respondents and those with higher levels of education are less likely to show tolerance of parental child beating, findings that are congruent with studies conducted in other cultural contexts (p. 9).

My own work among Shanghai caregivers with high levels of education, especially those who consume psychological childrearing guides, lends support to this finding. It shows that though urban, well-educated informants of means continue to employ physical punishment, they are nonetheless becoming more ambivalent about the use of harsh disciplinary methods with children and tend to express this ambivalence by employing the idioms of a child's "developmental needs" and his or her moral "rights" (Naftali 2014a). Others feel that abstaining from corporal punishment is crucial to raising an independent-minded, creative child, who can compete in the global, market economy. Yet others are willing to adopt more liberal disciplinary strategies because they associate these with modern "civility" and are eager to distance themselves from "the masses of China's rural backward hinterland" (Naftali 2009: 98). As one Shanghai mother explained, "people in China previously went by the old saying: '*gunbang chu xiao zi* [a stick produces filial sons]', and hit children because they thought it was the only way to teach them right from wrong." Nowadays, however, "most parents, especially those who are civilized/cultured (*you wenhua*) and well-educated, don't agree with this idea anymore" (cited in Naftali 2014a: 78).

Caregivers may nonetheless feel uneasy about the experts' recommendation that they respect children's autonomy and individuality in all spheres of life. To some, allowing children "to be themselves" implies emotional distance and lack of human warmth among family members. These parents are concerned that their relations with their own children would "resemble cold, heartless, capitalist social relations the way they do in the US" (cited in Woronov 2007a: 47; see also Naftali 2014a: 123). Some urban parents may criticize the "Chinese tradition of paternal authority" as constraining children's freedom and independence, but they are also concerned that the next generation of urban, single children will be overindulged, self-centered, and difficult to control (Anagnost 1997: 216, 218; see also Naftali 2014a). Even when parents are ready to embrace lenient disciplinary methods, they may run into conflict with the older generation. Many grandparents who, as noted earlier, play an important role in caring for the young, often continue to believe in the merits of strict physical and moral guidance rather than in encouraging children's freedom and autonomy (see Goh 2011, 2013; Binah-Pollak 2014).

The gender of the child may also affect parental attitudes toward his or her autonomy. A 2007 study conducted by Vanessa Fong reveals, for instance, that urban parents are especially likely to tell daughters to be obedient, saying that disobedient women were likely to be seen as unpleasant by their husbands, parents-in-law, and employers. Another study, conducted in the mid-2000s, similarly records the gender-specific expectations of urban parents of various social backgrounds. A girl's mother from a relatively high socioeconomic background explained to the researcher the difference between boys and girls:

> As I observe, boys have a sort of inner potential. Whenever it comes to difficulties, boys are always stronger than girls. […] With a boy, parents

only need to set broad boundaries for him and let him play heartily. You do not need to worry about him, for naughty boys will turn out to be intelligent. Boys who are not naughty will not accomplish much (cited in Liu 2006: 497).

In contrast, this mother and other parents who took part in the study described daughters as being ideally "gentle and soft." Although some parents indicated it is good for a girl to be "lively," they immediately added that "it is bad for her to be too unrestrained." Indeed, some of the girls had caused their parents to complain that they "were too active and not at all like a girl" (Liu 2006: 495).

Although they were seen as "naturally" less obedient than girls, boys in Fong's (2007b) study were also encouraged to be submissive because parents believed that defiance could hinder their success in the educational system and in their future careers (Fong 2007b: 91). As noted by Fong (2004b, 2007b) and others (e.g., Fung 1999; Xiao 2001), while many parents expect their children to bring their families and society the benefits of modernization, they also want their son or daughter to internalize the longstanding Chinese value of obedience to parents, teachers, elders, employers, and the state. The contradiction between these goals creates confusion and sometimes friction between parents and children, but it can also result in creative engagements and necessary modifications of the filial ethos.

NEGOTIATING THE FILIAL ETHOS

The notion that respect for one's elders has been – and should remain – an important feature of family relations in China continues to be influential among many caregivers as well as schoolteachers. In interviews I conducted in Shanghai primary schools in the mid-2000s, educators stated that parents "have sacrificed themselves to raise their children, so children should be grateful and repay their parents by showing deference." These beliefs found expression not only in teachers' comments but also in school activities. Educators in Shanghai schools took pains to teach children not only their new rights under the law but also how to show their parents gratitude and appreciation by doing chores around the house or through symbolic gestures such as washing parents' feet after a long workday (cited in Naftali 2009: 100). Well-educated, middle-class caregivers I met in Shanghai viewed such initiatives positively, though none reported that they actually expected their school-aged child to implement these recommendations at home. Contemporary Chinese children "are so busy with schoolwork that they barely have time for anything else," they explained, "we wouldn't want to burden children with making them take care of us" (cited in Naftali 2014a: 124).

These remarks indicate parents' growing ambiguity toward some of the traditional tenets of filial piety. On the one hand, parents and grandparents are keen to teach contemporary children the value of *"zhang you you xu"* ("respect and observe the hierarchy of order from old to young"). On the other hand, contemporary parents are less ready to take concrete disciplinary action when children's behavior challenges the authority of elders. As a result, young children in China learn that expressed principles of this traditional precept do not always coincide with the reality of everyday practices (Goh 2011). They enjoy an elevated position at home with enhanced leeway regarding their expression of agency and, as will be discussed in more detail in chapter 4, are increasingly able to negotiate some elements of their lives, such as television viewing or food choices (Cockain 2012; Naftali 2014a).

That said, some studies do indicate that children's increased autonomy at home is mediated by their awareness of traditional discourses that stipulate certain filial obligations to the larger familial structure (Fong 2007b; Goh 2011; Cockain 2012; Naftali 2014a). Chinese families have certainly become much more flexibly structured as a result of the rising importance of the individual, increased divorce rates, a higher degree of mobility both within China and outside, as well as the One-Child Policy (Fong 2004b; Cockain 2011). However, the family continues to play an important role in shaping children's attitudes and practices, and the ethos of filial piety has not lost its importance, though it has undergone some notable changes (Whyte 2003).

In a study of intergenerational relations among urban families in Xiamen, Esther Goh found that some parents employ a "consultative" parenting style and try to "explain things nicely to their child" rather than assert physical power in order to control him or her (2011: 79–80). Their children, who are frequently the center of attention for the adults in the family, respond by attempting to exercise their agency and independence vis-à-vis their parents and grandparents (Goh 2011: 79). However, children also continue to receive messages about the importance of respecting and tending to the needs of their elders, and these messages are deeply internalized even by relatively young children. For example, when asked "whether he would take care of his parents and grandparents when they grow old," seven-year-old Wei Wei readily told the researcher: "I will give them money, buy food for them, cook for them, take care of them and help them with chores." When asked why he would want to care for them, the boy further explained:

> They treated me so nice since [I was young], so I will look after them. *Jing lao ai you* (respect the elder and love the young), don't we say "*jing lao ai you*"? I will buy a three-story house, my father would stay on the top floor, my grandparents on the second floor and I stay on the ground floor (cited in Goh 2011: 81).

As the researcher observes, what is noteworthy is that the remark "*Jing lao ai you*" was repeated twice in the boy's response. The boy's tone of voice, she observes, "was as if to 'respect the elder and love the young' was an accepted fact of life." He even seemed puzzled about why the researcher would ask him this question (Goh 2011: 81).

The idea that children should show gratitude to parents who suffer so that their children would have a better life continues to be reinforced in contemporary China by the assertion that parental illness is caused by their anxiety about the child's academic performance. Anthropologist Vanessa Fong, who studied urban families in China of the late 1990s, notes that when parents came down with various ailments, from arthritis and fatigue to diabetes, heart disease, and high blood pressure, they, their children, and their relatives often attributed these illnesses at least partly to the physical, emotional, and economic sacrifices parents made for their children. Parents in turn were comforted by the idea "that they were suffering so that their children would have a better life" (2004b: 143). This notion, observes Fong, induces guilt and a heightened sense of filial obligation in children. Indeed, teenagers told Fong "they would never put their parents in nursing homes. They dreamed of supporting their parents in luxury" and pointed to "the cultural model of filial piety as one of their greatest motivations for pursuing academic studies and socioeconomic success." Like the seven-year-old boy quoted above, these urban teenagers often expressed their love in material terms and told the researcher "detailed fantasies about expensive gifts they would someday buy their parents" (Fong 2004b: 144).

In practice, of course, children do not always follow the precepts of filial piety, even if they uphold them. Some are becoming ever more defiant of their parents because they are well aware of their increased power as singletons. Fong describes a heated argument she had witnessed between an eighth grader and his parents, which reflects this new position. During the incident, the boy was angry with his parents, who did not allow him to go out with his friends, and refused to finish his private English lesson. When his father hit him and threatened that he will continue beating the boy as long as he refused to study, the boy replied defiantly, "Beat me now and I'll beat you when you're old!" (cited in Fong 2004b: 153).

Additional studies likewise suggest that even though the cultural model of filial piety holds sway in contemporary China, the principle of mutual care now replaces the historically hierarchical intergenerational relationship and reciprocal exchanges that had previously underlined the filial ethos. This development in turn reflects a contemporary renegotiated and reinterpreted "intergenerational contract" in which both generations make investments (Chen et al. 2011; Goh 2011; Naftali 2014a). Though the filial ethos has not disappeared in contemporary China, the introduction of global, neoliberal paradigms of childrearing, coupled with the effects of the One-Child Policy (discussed in further detail in the next chapter), have led to an important transformation in the nature of the child–adult relationship, and to an extensive empowerment and individualization of Chinese children.

CONCLUSION

China's economic reforms and opening-up to the world in the past three-and-a-half decades have hastened the country's modernization and integration within the global market economy in ways that most Chinese people consider highly desirable (Fong 2007b). However, these processes have also created significant conflicts regarding the proper way of raising and educating children. The new discourse that the government and academic establishment have promoted since the early 1980s advocates childrearing in a "scientific," "modern" manner in order to "raise the quality" of the population. It requires parents to give increased attention to the child on the emotional and educational levels, signifying a retreat of the extended family as well as the socialist system in favor of the nuclear family and the private sphere (Drulhe 2002).

Reflecting a modern, neoliberal relationship to the child as a "self-cultivating," "self-regulating" subject, this new discourse rejects the patriarchal system of authority. It reinforces children's individualization and promotes the idea that they are autonomous human beings who should be given the personal freedom to express their inner worlds. This discourse therefore plays a central role in the formation and dissemination of an individualistic ethos among China's young and arguably among adult caregivers as well (Zhang 2008; Yan 2009, 2011; Hansen 2015).

As we saw, some caregivers, especially those born after 1978, who belong to – or aspire to belong to – the new urban middle classes, accept that China's increasing links to the global economy mean that they must adopt new family strategies and new ways of using childrearing "to link their families with global sources of value" (Woronov 2007a: 40). Others, however, resist the new individualizing paradigms or attempt to negotiate them with the ethos of filial piety, with its emphasis on respect and obedience for elders and seniors. Government plans such as the 1999 "education for quality" program further reveal the extent of public ambiguity in China regarding the proper way of governing children. Caught between the promotion of collectivism and individualism, obedience and independence, forceful control and self-governance, contemporary childrearing and educational agendas above all reflect the moral and ideological problem of "how to link the next generation with the nation's past, yet prepare them for the future?" (Woronov 2009a: 570).

As this chapter has shown, there is no simple answer. Contemporary Chinese discourses and practices of childrearing and education are therefore best described not as "authoritarian" or "democratic" or as "Confucian" or "neoliberal" but as a hybrid, which combines different cultural repertoires to meet the challenges of the new market economy while also attempting to maintain a sense of safety, family intimacy, and stable national identity. Such negotiations are evident in other non-Western, developing countries, and in this sense may not be unique to China.

A central factor that nonetheless distinguishes the experiences of childhood in contemporary China from other parts of the world (as well as from previous historical periods in the country) is the introduction of the One-Child Policy in the late 1970s. The next chapter will focus on the implications of this unprecedented population policy for the life conditions and changing subjectivities of Chinese boys and girls in both urban and rural areas.

3 | Children and the Effects of the One-Child Policy

In the late 1970s, China's government introduced an unparalleled birth control program. The aim was to reduce the country's population growth and allow for rapid modernization and economic development. The implementation of the "One-Child Policy," as it has come to be known outside China, led to huge demographic shifts and a major restructuring of the Chinese family. It has also contributed to a transformation in the experiences of childhood and the subjectivities of children.

This transformation has nonetheless been far from uniform among boys and girls residing in the country's rural and urban areas. The present generation of Chinese singletons, many of whom live in the cities, has often been described as willful "little emperors": insufferably spoiled, showered with attention, toys, and treats by anxiously overindulgent parents and grandparents who focus their energies and resources on catering to the whims of a single child. As the present chapter will show, however, this is an overly simplified picture.

The One-Child Policy has undoubtedly contributed to the emergence of a new generation of urban children who enjoy greater parental investment and greater power within families of diminishing size. As the fertility rate declines and personal income rises, even the countryside has had its share of spoiled children. However, the policy has also led to the rise of new concerns and anxieties among caregivers and has imposed new constraints and pressures on the lives of children.

Girls have been particularly affected. The demographic shifts brought on by the One-Child Policy have resulted in a relative empowerment of many girls, especially those born and raised in single-child families in urban areas. With no competition for family resources, these single urban daughters have come to enjoy better treatment and greater educational opportunities. They can be said to have benefited from the policy. In other parts of the country, however, the effects on the lives of Chinese girls have been less benign. Due to intense rural resistance, the Chinese government has, since the mid-1980s, been forced to alter its original program by allowing rural families to have two children if the first is a girl. Following this change and due to strong male preference coupled with social and economic pressures, many families have resorted to the use of sex selection methods during pregnancy or have avoided registration of their female child with the authorities. In some parts of the country, unwanted girls have been given up for adoption, while others have suffered neglect and maltreatment. In this respect, the One-Child Policy, which initially had been gender-neutral, has contributed to growing gender discrimination and to a severe gender imbalance in China.

In the past decade or so, the Chinese government has been trying to address these and other issues caused by the policy, while further attenuating some of its regulations. There are also growing indications that the program may undergo additional modification or even be scrapped altogether in the coming years. Nonetheless, the launch of the policy three-and-a-half decades ago has already played a major part in the transformation of the material conditions of Chinese childhood, the structure of urban and rural households, and the nature of intergenerational relations within the family. As this chapter will argue, these transformations have provided Chinese children with an increased "scarcity value" (Zelizer 1985: 211), and in turn have contributed to an acceleration and intensification of children's empowerment and individualization within the family and society.

THE ONE-CHILD POLICY: BACKGROUND, GOALS, AND DEMOGRAPHIC EFFECTS

The roots of China's current population policy can be traced to the Maoist period (1949–76). After the socialist revolution, the population grew rapidly, increasing by 80 percent between 1950 and 1980 as a result of improved social and economic conditions that greatly reduced mortality. In the mid-1950s, when the PRC government encouraged a pro-natalist approach, China's total fertility rate exceeded six children per woman. In the 1960s and 1970s, however, the Maoist government shifted its approach and started to encourage a curb on birth rates. A family planning campaign that was launched in 1971 encouraged later marriages, longer intervals between births, and fewer children. As a result, China's fertility rate had fallen to 2.7 by the late 1970s. However, the large numbers of children born during the "baby boom" years caused concern among Chinese leaders.

By 1978, China's population was thought to be closing in on the one-billion mark, and Mao Zedong's successors, who were intent on ending the revolutionary turmoil and economic stagnation of the Maoist period, believed that drastic containment of population growth was a necessary prerequisite. Faced with a population that was enormous, and overwhelmingly rural, poor, and young – and thus poised to reproduce itself on an even larger scale – the Chinese government led by Deng Xiaoping introduced a one-child birth planning policy to reduce the country's population growth and allow for rapid modernization (White 2006; Feng et al. 2014).

The "One-Child Policy" or the "Family Planning Policy" (*jihua shengyu*), which is the official term in Chinese, was initially distinguished by the stringency of the one-child rule, the economic sanctions taken against those not adhering to these rules, and the degree of state intervention in family affairs which it represented. To achieve the goal of one child per family, an unprecedented bureaucratic control system was developed, led by the State Family Planning Committee, with parallel committees organized at administrative levels down to the local commune/village level. The system featured numerous rules and regulations, mechanisms for control and surveillance (including monitoring of menstrual cycles and pregnancies), provision of family planning services, and fines and other punishments for children born outside the official plan. To compensate for the sacrifice made by young couples, parents who pledged to have just one child were awarded the one-child certificate, which entitled their only child to special benefits, such as improved healthcare and education (Greenhalgh 2003; Scharping 2003; Croll 2006).

However, after a five-year experiment, often conducted with considerable harshness and heartbreak, the Chinese government embarked on a series of modifications that permitted the birth of a second child in a range of circumstances. In 1984, the government modified the one-child regulations so that families in rural areas could have a second birth if the first-born was a daughter, while the policy was most stringently implemented in the municipalities of Beijing, Shanghai, Tianjin and the largest cities (Croll 2006: 170). In 2002, the first Population and Family Planning Law put in place a national legal framework which aimed to replace localized rules and regulations and extended the number of categories permitted to have a second or even a third child. The number and range of exceptions to the rule mean that it has not been appropriate to speak of a national One-Child Policy for some time.

As of the late 2000s, Chinese fertility policy imposed a one-child limit on urban couples; a 1.5-child policy limit in most rural areas, where close to half of China's population currently resides; and a two- or three-child policy limit for provinces in remote areas. The policy has also granted exclusions to various groups, including Chinese ethnic minorities and those employed in dangerous occupations (Ebenstein 2011: 787). In recent decades, even in the largest cities, the local government has further modified its one child per couple policy to allow more parents to have two children, for instance if two parents are single children themselves (Croll 2006). At the end of 2013, China's central government expanded this modification and announced that the policy will allow couples all over the country to have two children even if one of the parents is an only child (Xinhua News Agency 2013).

These modifications notwithstanding, the population policy has contributed to a rapid decline in fertility and family size, constituting one of the most dramatic demographic shifts worldwide. The Chinese government estimates that since the launch of the policy in the late 1970s, it has resulted in a reduction of some 400 million people in China. The fertility rate fell from 2.29 children per woman in 1980 to between 1.5 and 1.6 in 2013, below the replacement rate of about 2.1. The fertility rates in China's biggest cities are among the lowest in the world at well below 1.0. While in much of the Chinese countryside it is still common for children to have at least one sibling, in the largest cities, more than 90 percent of the young are single children (Croll 2006: 171; Xinhua News Agency 2013; Feng et al. 2014: 17).

In part thanks to the government's enormous educational and propaganda efforts over the past three-and-a-half decades, the trade-off between population size and economic development has been regarded as common sense among a majority of urban residents, who have largely – if grudgingly – accepted the policy as a necessary condition for national development (Milwertz 1997). The relative success of the policy in the cities can also be explained by the fact that, in general, urban couples tend to experience less family pressure to have more than one child as a substantial proportion of grandparents were themselves the parents of singletons (Ikels 1996; Fong 2004b). Most urban couples also have not found the One-Child Policy a threat to their immediate prosperity or to financial security in old age (Davis and Harrell 1993: 4). Though they may perceive the policy as an oppressive intervention of state power (Davis and Harrell 1993: 4), a large majority of urban couples, especially administrators, intellectuals, and those with higher levels of education, appear to have accepted the official government rhetoric. They believe that the policy is a radical but necessary solution to China's problems of population growth, "backwardness," and lack of development (Croll 1985; Kane 1985; Gates 1993; Anagnost 1995; Milwertz 1997). Many urban parents also see having only one child as a sign of "modernity," as well as a "patriotic duty" (Woronov 2008: 405; see also Anagnost 1995).

Yet merely reducing the size of the population has not been enough. The state's efforts to restrict population numbers have been closely linked to another initiative, that of guaranteeing the "quality" (*suzhi*) of the next generation (Greenhalgh and Winckler 2005: 234–5; Woronov 2008: 405; see also Kipnis 2006). As noted in chapter 2, the attempt to ensure this process is embodied in the slogan "superior birth, childrearing and education" (*yousheng, youyu, youjiao*), which embraces a broad and eclectic array of scientific research programs, state policies, and social activities promoting top-quality healthcare and education for the young (Greenhalgh and Winckler 2005: 234–5; see also Bakken 1999).

For the birth-planning establishment in China, promoting the raising of the "quality child" has justified the push for low quantity and legitimized the government's claim to be a scientific modernizer capable of transforming China's people into a well-off populace equipped to compete in the global marketplace of the future. At its most basic and popular conceptualization, the government's argument is that the quality of the population can rise only when the quantity goes down; when the quantity is sufficiently low, the quality of individual Chinese can then coalesce into sufficient aggregate quality to bring wealth, power, and respect to the nation as a whole (Woronov 2008: 405). The state's concern with ensuring children's "quality" both taps into and further provokes parents' anxieties about whether their one (or, in the villages, two) offspring would not only survive but also grow into healthy, well-educated, competitive young adults, able to succeed and provide for them in old age (Greenhalgh and Winckler 2005: 235).

Parents' concern about their future welfare is not unjustified considering that China's population policy has led to a decrease in the size of the labor force. The country now has about 940 million workers, a figure that is estimated to decrease by about 29 million over the current decade. Meanwhile, the country's growing population of over-sixties, which currently accounts for 14.3 percent of the population, is forecast to exceed one third of the population in 2050 (Xinhua News Agency 2013). As a result, China now faces the risk of a population crisis consisting of a quickly aging society with too few young people to support their parents and grandparents.

Some Chinese demographers, including those who advise the government, believe the policy should have been relaxed long ago, if not scrapped altogether (The Economist 2013). As the next section will show, increasing debates in China about the costs of the policy have also centered on its problematic gendered effects, illustrated in the growing imbalance in the number of male and female births and in the ill-treatment of unwanted girls, especially in rural areas.

"MISSING" AND "UNREPORTED" GIRLS UNDER THE ONE-CHILD POLICY

One of the gravest unintended consequences of the One-Child Policy has been a distorted gender ratio. According to government statistics, China's sex ratio at birth has drastically increased from 108.5 to 113.8, and to 119.9 boys for every 100 girls in 1982, 1990, and 2000, respectively. In some areas of Hainan and Guangdong Provinces, the ratio has risen as high as 130 boys to every 100 girls (China Daily 2004; Li et al. 2011: 1535–6). At the end of 2013, China's overall sex ratio at birth was 117.6 boys to every 100 girls. This is an improvement compared with the 2000 figure, yet still indicates a serious deviation from the biologically stable range of 103–107 boys to 100 girls (Xinhua News Agency 2014d).

These figures reflect the fact that over the past two decades or so, roughly 9 million females are "missing" from naturally occurring birth patterns (Ebenstein 2011: 784). Scattered historical statistics indicate that China has had a traditionally male-biased sex ratio. However, the sex ratio at birth was relatively stable and was only marginally higher than western countries from the founding of the PRC in 1949 to the beginning of the One-Child Policy in the late 1970s. One exception was the 1956–8 birth cohort – those born just before the great famine resulting from the disastrous Great Leap Forward campaign of 1958–61 (Banister 2004). Since the launch of the current population policy, however, China's sex ratio has become severely distorted. Data from previous censuses further reflect that the high overall sex ratio at birth is due to extremely large fractions of sons following daughters, and very low fertility for those who already have sons (Ebenstein 2011: 785).

Scholars largely agree that the increase in China's sex ratios since the late 1970s is a result of the decline in fertility caused by the One-Child Policy, combined with the strong tendency for son preference. Studies in other nations reveal that son preference generated for cultural and economic reasons plays a key role in affecting sex ratios at birth. In Taiwan, India, and the Republic of Korea, for example, where no family planning is implemented, distorted sex ratios at birth have also been registered in the past several decades, though not as high as in the PRC (Goodkind 2011). In China, the limitations mandated by the One-Child Policy coupled with sex selection via infanticide and the increasing availability of gender-selection technology account for the dramatic increase in the gender gap since the 1980s (Zhu et al. 2009; Li et al. 2011: 1536). In particular, the introduction of ultrasound technology appears to have greatly facilitated the availability of sex-selective practices (Ebenstein 2011: 787).

The gender imbalance is true mostly for Han-dominated regions; in rural ethnic minority areas, the sex ratios tend to be much lower, a fact which could be attributed not only to the relatively relaxed policy among these groups but also to the fact that some ethnic minorities have weaker son preference than Han Chinese (Goodkind 2011: 309). Goodkind (2011) further suggests that parental propensities to use sex selection among Han Chinese are prevalent both in the countryside and in urban areas. Most studies nonetheless maintain that the highest sex ratios exist in provinces that allow rural inhabitants a second child if the first is a girl.

In rural Chinese society, the patrilineal family system continues to bestow on male descendants economic, sociocultural, and religious benefits and obligations, which create preference for sons and unfavorable social status for daughters. Male children in the countryside still enjoy a dominant status in inheriting property, in living arrangements, in continuity of families, and in family power structure. Moreover, the social security system in rural China is weak. The family remains the dominant provider of old-age support, and the traditional gender division makes women economically dependent on men. Married-out daughters provide mainly auxiliary help such as emotional support and assistance with daily activities for their parents, while sons provide the basic economic support. Since the reduced number of children mandated by the population policy entails a lower probability of having a son, people in rural areas turn to sex-selective abortion to ensure at least one male offspring (see Banister 1987; Greenhalgh 2003; Zhu et al. 2009; Jiang et al. 2011).

Parental gender bias is illustrated not only by pre-natal sex selection of unborn children but also in maltreatment of infant girls. A pioneering study conducted by Zhu and her colleagues in a county in Shanxi Province, which reported a higher death rate of female children, revealed that more boys were delivered in hospitals while girls were mostly born at home. Boys were fed with better and more nutritious foods than girls and were sent to hospital more quickly when they got ill. Many girls were cared for at home and had to rely on their own resistance to illnesses. The researchers concluded that son preference is the fundamental factor in the birth culture that exists in these rural communities (cited in China Daily 2004).

At the same time, some scholars maintain that the documented distortion in China's sex ratio is a product not only of sex-selective abortions or of maltreatment of girls, but also of widespread under-reporting of female births (Greenhalgh 2003; Ebenstein 2011; Good-kind 2011). Unfortunately, the absence of reliable statistics makes it impossible to calculate either how many unreported births have taken place since the launching of the policy or how many of those unreported infants have remained outside the register to become unreported persons. According to some official statistics, between 1979, when the One-Child Policy was introduced, and 1999, as many as 82 million unreported births took place. High as this number seems, it is probably far below the real figure. Some Chinese demographers believe that because of underreporting and other forms of statistical doctoring, the number of births counted in official surveys was understated by as much as 20 to 25 percent in the late 1980s and 30 to 35 percent in the 1990s (cited in Greenhalgh 2003: 207). There are also indications that about 19 percent of children at ages 0–4 were unreported in the 2000 census, more than double that of the 1990 census (Goodkind 2011: 302, 311).

The vast majority of unreported infants, virtually all second or higher-order offspring, are girls. Unregistered female infants are at greater risk of abandonment, a fate that may result in death, institutionalization in a state-run orphanage, or, for the fortunate ones, adoption (Greenhalgh 2003: 207; Jiang et al. 2011: 622). Some reports suggest that as many as 160,000 Chinese infants are abandoned annually, the vast majority of them female (White 2005: 198). The number of orphans in social welfare institutes in China has soared since the early 1980s and orphanages have been populated mostly with girls at rates as high as 75 to 95 percent – a figure which is comparable to that of late imperial and republican times (Apter 2014: 6; see also Yoxall 2007). This statistic likely underestimates the size of the problem, as many abandoned girls may never enter state institutions such as those managed by the civil affairs bureaucracy. Instead, birth parents often try to identify likely prospects for adopting the child, such as couples who have a son but no daughter (White 2005: 198). China opened its doors to international adoption in 1990 and the Chinese government reported a total of 60,000 adopted births sent to foreign countries between 1992 and 2006 (Ebenstein 2011: 797; Yoxall 2007). In 2005, for instance, the United States naturalized nearly 8,000 Chinese adopted children. More than 95 percent of these children were female (Ebenstein 2011: 797).

Discussions with Chinese population specialists suggest that a majority of unreported female infants are probably raised by their birth parents. Some manage to acquire registration for their children at a later stage, while others are raised as "black children (hei haizi)," implying that they are not included in the household register (Greenhalgh 2003: 207). Parents have a good reason to conceal an out-of-quota child. To encourage full reporting when the 1990 census was conducted, parents were assured that they would not be punished if they revealed an unregistered child. However, those who did were indeed punished in some localities by birth planning authorities (Goodkind 2011). Moreover, the fine for out-of-quota births has risen to two or three times annual wages beginning in the 1990s, double what it had been earlier (Scharping 2003).

Parents of means can nonetheless buy themselves out of trouble. In a highly publicized 2014 court ruling, famous film director Zhang Yimou was ordered to pay a fine of 7.48 million yuan (US$1.22 million) for having no fewer than three children (Xinhua News Agency 2014d). Other couples make hefty "donations" to obtain school places for undocumented children. However, disadvantaged couples often cannot afford the birth fines and many families are either unable to pay or go into debt to do so (Branigan 2013). Parents of unregistered children are subject not only to steep fines, but also to a loss of state-sector jobs, expulsion from the Communist Party, and many other punitive measures (Greenhalgh 2003: 206–7).

As a result, an unknown proportion of unreported infants fail to obtain official registration and the social, economic, and psychological costs of being a "black child" are very steep. As illegitimate persons who are ineligible for inclusion in the household register, unreported children – most of whom are girls – are denied a wide range of benefits, including access to state-sponsored healthcare and education. A 20-year-old unregistered girl related, "I have never been to school. I can't buy a train ticket. I can't even buy certain cold medicines, which require an identity card. I don't have medical insurance. It's impossible to get a job" (cited in Branigan 2013).

The Chinese government has been slow to acknowledge the link between its population control policy and China's distorted gender balance. Although surveys conducted in the 1980s and 1990s suggest that the sex ratio at birth was becoming ever more skewed, it was only in the early 2000s that the imbalance was openly recognized as a problem and drew a concerted policy response. The delay may have occurred because China's leadership feared that recognizing and confronting the problem would imply criticism of the birth planning policies. However, a convergence of factors, including mounting statistical evidence, eventually led to public recognition of gender distortions as a social problem (Murphy 2014a: 782). In March 2004, China's former president, Hu Jintao, called for a lowering of the sex ratio to normal levels by 2010, a call reiterated by many officials, including the Vice Minister of the National Population and Family Planning Commission. In addition, an experimental "Care for Girls" program was enacted in a pilot county in each of 24 provinces in order to enforce the anti-sex-selection edicts that had already been on the books for many years. In 2006, the Care for Girls program was formally extended across all counties (Ebenstein 2011: 784; Goodkind 2011: 306; Jiang et al. 2011: 624; Murphy 2014a: 789).

The program includes the use of sanctions, economic incentives, and educational tools such as lectures to parents and grandparents on gender equality, and courses that aim to teach rural women modern production skills that will enable them to contribute to the family income (Murphy 2014a: 789). Economic incentives include giving small loans to families with only daughters to help them develop an income-generating household economy as well as offering assistance in education, living conditions, and livelihood (China Daily 2004; Murphy 2014a).

The Care for Girls program does suffer from several problems, however. Benefits such as school sponsorship and scholarships are only offered to rural girls without brothers. As a result, the female population that actually faces the greatest competition for parental investment in their education is excluded (Murphy 2014a: 795). Further, while the program offers access to life insurance, healthcare and old-age security for parents of only girls, some of these benefits are not necessarily viewed or represented as "support" or "reward" by rural people. Instead, they are often understood as a form of "compensation" given to sonless families in recognition of their difficulties in achieving economic self-reliance (Murphy 2014a: 797–8).

These and other problems limit the effectiveness of the program in advancing girls' rights or inducing a real change in rural caregivers' notions concerning the inherent value of girls (Murphy 2014a: 801). As the next section will show, however, in China's urban areas, where until recently a majority of parents were allowed only one child, a discernible shift in caregivers' attitudes toward girls has been more evident.

THE ONE-CHILD POLICY AND GIRLS' EMPOWERMENT

Although the One-Child Policy has contributed to the rise in discriminatory practices against girls in some parts of the country, studies suggest that urban daughters have benefited from the demographic pattern produced by the policy. As noted in a pioneering (2002) study by anthropologist Vanessa Fong, under the One-Child Policy, urban singleton daughters enjoy unprecedented parental support because they do not have to compete with brothers for parental investment. Low fertility in the later decades of the Maoist era has also enabled the mothers of these contemporary only girls to find paid work and gain the ability to demonstrate their filiality by providing their own parents with financial support. By comparing the experiences of daughters born in the 1980s with the experiences of their mothers and grandmothers, Fong further shows how singleton daughters have a unique degree of power to deal with gender norms in ways that benefit them.

Other studies note that the One-Child Policy has had the unintended consequence of introducing greater gender equality to the education of urban boys and girls. Using data from a 1998–9 survey of more than a 1,000 eighth graders in the city of Wuhan, Tsui and Rich (2002) explored the differences between single-girl and single-boy families with regard to parental expectation and investment in children's schooling, children's own educational aspirations, and mathematics performance. The researchers found that, contrary to the intra-family discrimination against girls common among families of pre-one-child generations (and still common among rural families with more than one child), there were no gender differences related to education between single-girl and single-boy families. The study documented equally high educational aspirations and similar mathematical performance for male- and female-only children. It also found that parents of female-only children spent more on education than the parents of male-only children, presumably in order to give daughters a competitive advantage in the job market and to counter employment discrimination against women in China.

Additional studies suggest that in some areas in the country, the status of rural girls in two-child families has also improved over the years. A longitudinal study on changing fertility preferences and behaviors among rural Hubei families from 1993 to 2004 found, for instance, that, confronted with the population policy and the rapidly changing social and economic environment, some rural families have shifted from "active resistance against" to "conscious decision for" the one-child limit. The widening rural–urban divide, together with the state's new emphasis on enhancing the quality of the population, has brought new pressures and strains to rural parents. They now recognize education as the best way to guarantee a more successful future for their children and yet the high cost of education severely constrains rural parents' ability to afford the best teaching. Because of the mounting burden and pressure of raising "high-quality" children and of living up to the new standards of good parenthood, more young rural parents choose to raise just one child. In turn, smaller family size, coupled with new economic opportunities and social mobility for rural young, has increased the value of daughters in some rural families and heightened their filial roles (Zhang 2007).

A more recent ethnographic study conducted by Hansen (2015) in a rural high school in Zhejiang Province likewise finds that, although the wish to have a boy remains strong among many rural parents in the region, people also emphasize "the social and emotional advantages of having at least one daughter." They regard daughters "as more affectionate, well behaved […], concerned about their parents, and better than boys at adapting to the schools' demands for diligence, obedience, and patience" (p. 38).

Admittedly, such notions also indicate that patterns of differences in parental expectations based on gender remain even under the One-Child Policy. In interviews with parents in urban north China, some stated, for instance, that boys must be "masculine" and girls must be "feminine," while further maintaining that appearance matters for a girl but not for a boy. Caregivers of higher socioeconomic backgrounds were somewhat distinguished by their indication that they would like their only-daughters to develop some so-called "manly characteristics," such as "strong will, toughness, boldness, ambitiousness, competitiveness," and "independence." However, their statements ultimately confirmed the long-held association of "being strong and weak to males and females respectively" (Liu 2006: 500).

Gender-specific expectations are evident even among school educators who may be concerned about the distinct effects of the One-Child Policy on boys' masculinity. A Shanghai female teacher in her mid-thirties complained in a personal interview, that nowadays

> Many [boys] are quite fragile (*cuiruo*) because most of them are only-children and everyone in their families spoils them. Not only that, but it is mainly mothers who take care of children. Men don't participate so much in raising children … so boys are becoming more and more like girls. When they come across all sorts of problems at school, they have no idea what to do and will often start crying. That's not good at all (cited in Naftali 2014a: 49).

Comments of this sort suggest that it would be over-optimistic to believe that only-child status and the equally high academic aspirations many urban parents hold for boys and girls have removed all the deep-rooted factors against gender equality in Chinese society. Nonetheless, there are some indications that a change may be underway among a younger generation of urban parents who are themselves only-children, and who are now starting to have children of their own. A large-scale longitudinal study conducted between 1999 and 2013 by Kim and Fong (2014) finds that child gender preferences are becoming neutral, especially among young urban men in China. The study suggests that this may be the result of more gender equity in educational opportunities and earning power. The One-Child Policy may have influenced the child gender preferences of the generation born under it by encouraging their parents to accept their child's gender (Kim and Fong 2014: 23).

The positive effects of only-child status on the education and well-being of city girls as well as boys indicate that the One-Child Policy has had the unintended consequence of producing a child-centered culture in contemporary urban China. As discussed in the next section, it has also introduced new strains to the lives of urban children and to their relationships with their various adult caregivers.

CHINA'S URBAN SINGLETONS: PAMPERED "LITTLE EMPERORS" OR OVER-WORKED LEARNERS?

With singletons now making up a majority of the children enrolled in city nurseries and schools, the impact of the population policy on the lives of urban children and families has been dramatic. Since the 1980s, popular and media discourse in China has portrayed urban singletons as a generation of "little emperors" (*xiao huangdi*) who are "insufferably spoiled, self-centered, and difficult to control" (Jing 2000: 2; Anagnost 1997: 216). Chinese media discourse frequently emphasizes how the singletons born under the policy are timid and unable to care for themselves. Many PRC scholars and journalists have also claimed that singletons tend to be "moody," "bad tempered," "neurotic," and "psycho-logically disturbed" (cited in Fong 2007b: 87).

Scholarly work on the social and psychological features of the first generation of singletons in China has nonetheless produced widely differing, even contradictory, theories. For example, Jiao, Ji, and Jing (1986) collected peer evaluations of schoolchildren in the Beijing municipality, and found that the only-children in the sample were evaluated as being low in independent thinking, self-control, cooperation, peer prestige, and persistence, and high in frustration proneness and egocentrism. Additional studies (see, e.g., Liu et al. 2005) suggest that urban only-children in China, in particular boys, tend to suffer more from depression and anxiety, and experience higher interpersonal dependency than urban non-only-children.

In contrast, other studies conclude that the personalities of only-children, as judged by their peers, parents, teachers, and themselves, were no different from those of their peers with siblings (see, e.g., Falbo & Poston 1993; Sun and Zhao 2006). Moreover, Falbo and Poston's 1993 study, which included surveys of thousands of only-children in several provinces, found that singletons had very similar personality characteristics and physical growth as classmates with siblings. There was one difference, however: the only-children generally had higher academic skills than their peers, both in terms of their school grades and their performance on standardized tests of academic skills, findings that mirror the results of the meta-analyses of studies of only-children in North America and Western Europe (see also Falbo 2012: 45).

In light of this mixed picture, some sociologists and anthropologists have suggested that the widespread concern in China about the rising generation of "spoiled singletons" may reflect public anxieties about the perceived dangers of modernity rather than children's actual traits (Bakken 1993). Anthropologist Vanessa Fong has also made the persuasive argument that parental complaints about pampered children may be linked to the fact that many caregivers in China of the 1990s and 2000s have been brought up in larger families with lower parental investment. For these parents and for grandparents, only-children can seem maladjusted and pampered, a complaint heard in many societies in the developed world where declining fertility rates are an integral part of the modern economy (Fong 2004b).

Unlike their parents, who had grown up during the Cultural Revolution (1966–76) and spent many hours doing house chores or taking care of younger siblings, China's contemporary singletons are socialized in a system where education serves as the primary determinant of socioeconomic status (Fong 2004b: 163). Parental anxiety over an only-child's academic success may, in some instances, translate to excessive doting. One mother included in Fong's study recounted how during her son's high-school years, she used to put toothpaste on his toothbrush every morning "to save him a few precious seconds as he prepared to go to school" (p. 164). Taking the cue from their parents, the urban singletons Fong spoke to felt entitled to freedom from the most time-consuming household duties. They admitted they were "lazy" when it came to doing chores, but insisted that it was only because they "had more important priorities," or as one student explained, "What if I fail to get into college because of the time I waste taking out the garbage?" (p. 166). As noted by the researcher, singletons' sense of entitlement may seem unremarkable in post-industrialized, developed economies, where the household duties of minors have been light for generations, and where children have become consumers of education rather than producers of labor (Fong 2004b: 162). However, these attitudes and practices starkly diverge from those of Chinese children in the countryside or those who have migrated with their parents to the city, a majority of whom continue to take part in both housework and income-generating chores (Ming 2014: 65).

Parents of urban singletons, particularly those who were educated before 1978, view their children's attitudes as problematic. Though they themselves granted their own children freedom from housework, they do not feel their children are *entitled* to this freedom, and are therefore distressed when their singleton son or daughter refuses to do housework even when he or she is not studying (Fong 2004b: 164).

As noted in chapter 2, contemporary urban parents may encourage singletons' autonomy but they also want their children to express virtues of respect and obedience to elders and seniors. As one Shanghai mother complained in a personal interview: in the past, "children used to respect their parents and teachers....[and even] had to wait until the adults sat at the table before they could touch their chopsticks. Now, people treat children as if they were adults!" Other caregivers and educators I met with in Shanghai made similar objections, reflecting the notion that the boundaries between the social categories of "child" and "adult" were becoming increasingly blurred in contemporary China.

The origins of this process may be traceable to the Maoist era and in particular to the time of the Cultural Revolution (1966–76), when schoolchildren and youths took part in violent struggles against their teachers and in public denunciations of "counter-revolutionary" parents. However, many informants saw the introduction of the One-Child Policy as the more decisive turning point. The policy, they argued, has produced a generation of "self-centered" children, who expected adults to serve them rather than the other way around (cited in Naftali 2009: 100).

The reduction in the number of children in urban families has meant that the single child has become the focus of attention for two parents and four grandparents, so that the so-called 4:2:1 families have become increasingly child-centered. Since there is usually one child in each family to satisfy the emotional needs of the host of caregivers, each puts a greater weight on the interactions with that child (Goh 2011). In some instances, caregivers even compete for a singleton's favor, a reversal of the circumstances in which previous generations of Chinese children had been brought up. As further indicated in Goh's (2011) study of only-children in three generational families, the positions of parents and grandparents within the urban family have declined compared with the status of only-children. It is now the only-children who enjoy an elevated position at home with enhanced agency in inter-actions with the multiple caregivers who revolve around them.

Yet it may be premature to conclude that urban only-children differ from their peers with siblings in terms of their general attitudes toward the family. Fuligni and Zhang (2004), who surveyed urban and rural middle school students in Shandong Province, were surprised to dis-cover similar notions of family support and respect among the two groups of students. The researchers postulate that only-children in China experience many countervailing pressures during their develop-ment of attitudes toward family obligations. Some pressures, such as the pursuit of success in a market-driven economy, push them away from traditional attitudes of filial piety, while other pressures, such as a close parent–child bond, may push them toward meeting the long-held notion which obligates children to display respect and support toward elders.

The diminishing size of the Chinese family has nonetheless contrib-uted to a re-shaping of the filial ethos already noted in chapter 2. Far from reducing the need for a child in old age, changes brought about by wage reform, mandatory retirement, the reduction in pensions and state subsidies for healthcare, and the growing geographical mobility of children, appear to have reinforced the importance of family support for the elderly among Chinese urban families (Ikels 1993; Whyte 2003; Fong 2004b). Only-children are now expected to be the primary providers of support and care for their retired parents, grandparents, and parents-in-law, and only a very lucrative position will allow them to provide for so many dependents.

The Chinese government continues to promote this model of filial piety because it has allowed the state to devote its resources to promot-ing economic growth instead of social security (Fong 2004b: 127–8). The heavy emotional and economic investment in singletons is driven by parents' fear that their sole offspring might eventually abandon them, financially and/or emotionally. By "drowning" their only child "with love" (*ni ai*), urban parents arguably seek to strengthen the child's attachment to the immediate family and thereby ensure that their son or daughter would take care of them in old age (Greenhalgh and Winckler 2005: 243; see also Ikels 1996; Milwertz 1997; Davis and Sensenbrenner 2000).

Regardless of parents' motivations, their increased investment in their only offspring has had a positive effect on children's education, as singletons consistently have a higher chance of school attendance than children with an older sibling for those beyond compulsory education (Yang 2007; see also Tsui and Rich 2002). At the same time, however, urban singletons have also been experiencing acute pressure in the academic realm. Many caregivers see education as the main achievable route to upward social mobility, and the pressure for educational performance is further exacerbated by the One-Child Policy because the educational aspirations of the entire family are placed on the one child (Fong 2004b; see also Kipnis 2006; Woronov 2008; Naftali 2010a, 2010b; Goh 2011).

In many singleton households, the completion of schoolwork or participation in various after-school activities often comes at the expense not only of household chores but also of play and social activities (Fong 2007b; Naftali 2009, 2010b; Goh 2011: 119; Goh and Kuczynski 2014). As one Shanghai mother explained, "the only form of entertainment kids have nowadays is playing the piano, and even that is forced on them: some parents think that if their child can't play the piano, he is not as good as the neighbors' child. I've even heard of children who cut their hands so that they wouldn't have to play anymore!" (cited in Naftali 2010b: 600).

Though the 4:2:1 ratio of caregivers to child ensures that urban singletons are often well cared for, it also means that they have little time to be alone or with other children without adult supervision. Chinese singletons seldom venture outside unsupervised by an adult and many remain relatively isolated. They are under constant surveillance and often experience frustrations at being so closely watched by parents and grandparents without a chance to play with their peers (Drulhe 2002; Goh 2011). Only-children sense the clash between their desire to exercise autonomy and their parents' and grandparents' concern about bad influences and safety quite acutely. Some take out their frustrations on their caregivers. For instance, Wei Wei, a seven-year-old boy in Xiamen, related to researcher Esther Goh (2011: 119) that he believed he was "old enough and tough enough" to walk the ten-minute trip to and from school on his own. However, his desire was frustrated by his paternal grandmother, who always accompanied him, and the boy expressed his frustration in the form of temper tantrums in the presence of his grandmother. Other children express ambivalence about being the only child. Tian Tian, a 10-year-old girl who lived in Xiamen with two parents and two grandparents under the same roof, explained the dilemma:

> To be an only-child is good and bad at the same time. Good because I am treated like the precious one and always the one to get all the rewards. Bad because if anything went missing they would accuse me. So I sometimes wish to grow up quickly. But other times I don't want to grow up. [...] *Hen mao dun* (very conflicting) (cited in Goh 2011: 118).

As indicated by this statement, the One-Child Policy has led to an unprecedented empowerment of singletons of both genders and to a concentration of adult attention on the individual child. Paradoxically, however, many urban only-children have also become subject to an intensified surveillance and discipline (Anagnost 1997: 214). The close monitoring of singletons' movements and the strict regimentation of their free time in order to ensure their "quality" upbringing and successful education no doubt signals caregivers' love and deep concern for their only-child's wellbeing. However, particularly for those from well-off backgrounds, it has also resulted in the shutting of urban children in a "gilded cage," where they feel they are deprived of personal "breathing space" (see Goh 2011: 119).

CONCLUSION

Three-and-a-half decades after its introduction, China's One-Child Policy has largely succeeded in its stated goals. It has also produced a number of acute social problems and some unintended consequences for the lives and subjectivities of contemporary children. The reduction in fertility brought on by the policy may have accelerated modernization and economic growth, but the policy has also contributed to deepening discrimination against girls in some parts of the country and to the severely imbalanced sex structure of China's population. The cumulative demographic effects of the phenomenon of "missing girls" on future population growth should not be underestimated. The shortage of marriageable females has already caused a squeeze on males in the marriage market. The imbalance is predicted to further decrease the number of births in the coming decades and will certainly affect the aging of China's population. The imbalanced gender structure has given rise to other social problems, including an increase in births out of wedlock, increasing prostitution, and abduction of, and trafficking in, girls and women (Jiang et al. 2011: 622–3).

These issues have contributed to the growing criticism of the policy in Chinese academic circles and in recent years among the wider public as well. The 2013 decision to relax the policy by allowing couples to have two children if one of the parents is a singleton serves as a clear indication that China's leaders recognize the severity of these issues. Recent media statements by government sources and population experts further suggest that China could be on the verge of introducing a two-child policy for all couples in the near future (see Philips 2015; Wang 2015).

To date, however, the policy still stands, and many suspect that the fines for excessive births – known in China as "social compensation fees in recognition of the extra cost to society" – give birth planning officials a strong incentive to resist further reforms (Branigan 2013). Even with the recent relaxation in the policy, it is unlikely that China's birth rate will show a dramatic rise, since in recent decades, the desire for larger families has been considerably blunted by the rising costs of healthcare, education, and housing. Thus, even where two children are permitted, parents in China rarely exceed that number.

While the One-Child Policy may be on its way out, the process will be gradual, and the social and psychological effects of previous measures on a generation of children born under this policy would continue to be felt in decades to come. As this chapter has shown, the policy has led to a nuclearization of the household and to a rediscovery of the emotional "value" of children. In this sense, it has played an important role in the intensification and acceleration of Chinese children's empowerment and individualization in the age of market reforms.

Indeed, one of the most visible manifestations of the growing power of the young in post-socialist China has been the emergence of children as independent consumers and the dramatic growth in consumption of specialized children's products and services by caregivers. The next chapter will consider this recent trend, while noting its intersection with another important development: the rise of new classes of affluent customers and families, particularly in the country's urban areas. Children's consumption plays a central role in the making of these new social classes in China.

<table>
<tr><td>4</td><td>Childhood and Consumption in the New Market Economy</td><td>—————</td></tr>
</table>

4 Childhood and Consumption in the New Market Economy

Since the 1990s, China has undergone a revolution in consumption. Millions of people have gained access to new modes of communication and novel forms of leisure through commercialized outlets. With the increase in consumer choice and the raising of material standards of living, particularly in urban areas, Chinese citizens have also gained new spaces in which to explore and construct their personal and social identities outside the purview of the party-state (Davis 2000: 2–3; see also Yu 2014).

Children constitute key agents in this important new development. China's market reforms and increasing integration within the global market economy have introduced new products and services geared specifically towards the young, contributing to the growing commercialization and standardization of Chinese childhood. Meanwhile, the diminishing size of the family under the One-Child Policy and the rise of new classes of urban, affluent customers have contributed to the emergence of children as independent consumers with unprecedented power and influence over family spending habits.

As avid participants in a new type of global media culture, Chinese children have also come to serve as cultural brokers; their consumption choices facilitate the flow of global products, values, and ideas into the country, and shape contemporary lifestyles and values in important ways. Just as China's education reforms and One-Child Policy have led to a devolution of adult power in favor of children, so the consumer revolution plays a central role in children's increased individualization and greater agency in the post-socialist era.

The present chapter discusses these developments by examining the consumption habits of children and their families in various areas, including food, educational services and products; toys and leisure activities; and media products. It further considers the relationship between children's consumption habits, and government and public concerns about young people's morality and their cultural and national identities. As the discussion will demonstrate, these concerns are not entirely founded. Above all, they reflect the deep tensions in China between an increasingly influential individualistic ethos, which celebrates material pleasures and the fulfillment of personal desires, and a more frugal moral code on which a large share of Chinese educators, parents, and grandparents were raised during the collectivist period.

The Chinese government has also sent mixed messages about children's consumer choices. On the one hand, it has vigorously promoted children's participation in the construction of a consumer society, which serves to fuel the nation's economic growth and global prestige. On the other hand, official rhetoric and school teachings continue to celebrate socialist-era values of thrift and diligence, and encourage the "patriotic" consumption of "local" rather than "foreign" media products.

At the center of these cultural and political debates, children in China attempt to reconcile these conflicting notions. As the discussion will show, Chinese youngsters may have become consumers in their own right and fervent actors in an electronically mediated popular culture market, which includes Japanese cartoons and animation, Korean pop songs as well as American films, television shows, and computer games. However, contemporary Chinese children also retain and reiterate a sense of local and national identity, while exhibiting a critical view of money, spending, and the role of material products in the construction of the self.

CONSUMPTION FOR CHILDREN AND THE RISE
OF THE CHILD CONSUMER IN CHINA

Over the last two-and-a-half decades, children have become the single most important new category of consumers in China, and raising them has become subject to increased commodification (Yu 2014: 131). Together with their parents, children and youth were among the first consumer groups targeted by both foreign and domestic marketing and manufacturing companies (Croll 2006: 169). Due to the deepening rural–urban divide, this trend has been most visible in the cities, where a majority of children are also singletons and where incomes are much higher than in the countryside.

According to a recent report by the National Bureau of Statistics of China (2014), the annual per capita disposable income of rural households is 8,896 yuan (US$1,456). In urban households, income is three times higher, reaching 26,955 yuan (US$4,411) in 2013. A large share of this income is now spent on products and services for children. Already in the mid-1990s, the average couple in urban China was spending as much as 40–50 percent of their combined income on their child. Family resources were directed to children's food and dietary supplements, toys, travel, computers and other electronic equipment, and educational products and services (Guan 2003a). A study by Credit Suisse conducted in 2013 found that Chinese couples typically spend over 22,500 yuan ($3,600) a year to raise a child to the age of 18. That is more than three-quarters of the average annual disposable income per person of urban households. A 2015 government report further showed that in the first five years of a child's life, city parents spend twice as much as rural ones (The Economist 2015).

Chinese children have played an important role in shaping their parents' spending habits, influencing around two-thirds (68 percent) of family purchases, surpassing the approximately 40 percent level of

US children (McNeal and Yeh 1996). In 1995, children in Chinese cities received an aggregated yearly income of US$5 billion in the form of weekly allowances and birthday and holiday gifts from their parents and grandparents (Jing 2000: 5–6; see also Milwertz 1997). Less than a decade later, in the mid-2000s, children's income had doubled. They were being given regular larger allowances, and their spending had almost tripled. Children's independent store visits also increased 32 percent and the number of stores at which they shopped independently grew by 81 percent (McNeal and Yeh 2003).

As these figures illustrate, urban Chinese children of the early twenty-first century have grown richer and less frugal, and are exercising their influence over a greater volume of family spending (McNeal and Yeh 2003). They are making more decisions on what their family ought to eat at mealtimes (Gillette 2000; Guo 2000; Watson 2000), and on entertainment and large commodity purchases, including numerous items that affect their health, education, and training (Greenhalgh and Winckler 2005: 244). Behind the economic reality of increased consumption on and by children are sweeping changes that are remapping Chinese society.

The privatization of education, health, and leisure services and products, on the one hand, and the rising income of many families, particularly in urban areas, on the other, has caused a consumer revolution in China (Davis 2000). The government itself has encouraged this change through such measures as public endorsements of private enterprise and the promotion of the household as a locus for consumption (Hershatter 2004: 313; see also Wang Jing 2001; Yan 2003). Particularly since the 1990s, the state has reduced or eliminated socialist-era welfare provisions, and devolved responsibilities for employment and welfare onto individuals.

Meanwhile, and as discussed in chapter 2, social reproduction and the fostering of children as future laborers and consumers is increasingly seen as the responsibility of caregivers and families (Woronov

2007a: 30). Parents' and grandparents' growing spending on children is driven not merely by government discourse, but also by historical and psychological factors. The parental generation's entry into the new consumer system in post-1978 China was marked by their experiences of socialism under Mao. Many parents and grandparents of this generation had experienced Spartan times and childhoods had been blighted by either the shortages of the Great Leap Forward in the late 1950s or the disruptions of the Cultural Revolution in the mid-1960s, both of which affected children's health, education, and quality of family life at the time. Often dubbed the "lost generation," and in part to compensate for their own years of hardship, many Chinese parents who grew up during the Cultural Revolution are particularly determined to give their offspring every possible advantage.

In the era of market reforms, caregivers who grew up during the collectivist period eagerly examine each new product or service as a means not only of giving their children "better childhoods" than their own, but also of allowing them to fully develop their individual talents. In the words of one contemporary Chinese mother: "no sacrifice is too great to give my child all the things that I didn't have in order to ensure her happiness" (cited in Croll 2006: 172; see also Davis 2000; Zhao 2006; Anagnost 2008).

This frenzied consumption by parents and grandparents further reflects a shift in the conceptualization of Chinese children's "value" in both a material and a psychological sense. As noted in chapter 3, the introduction of the One-Child Policy in the late 1970s has made urban children in China – both boys and girls – into "precious commodities" of the sort Viviana Zelizer described in her 1985 seminal work on children's changing status in modern, capitalist societies. Since the launch of the Chinese government's population policy, urban parents and grandparents have invested ever more heavily in children in an effort to ensure their educational and career success in an increasingly competitive environment (Milwertz 1997; Jing 2000; Davis and

Sensenbrenner 2000; Fong 2004b; Rosen 2004; Goh 2011). Arguably, the new opportunities for consumption, particularly in the city, have also helped to mitigate popular opposition to the population policy in urban areas (Croll 2006: 172). China's strict birth quotas may have denied young couples the freedom to define family size, but the flood of affordable consumer goods has enabled urban mothers and fathers to spend money on educational products, toys, and leisure activities that they believe would cultivate their child's individuality and strengthen his or her emotional attachment to the immediate family (Davis 2000: 8). Expenditure on educational commodities, including books, supplies, and proper "life experience" for children, is seen by some Chinese parents as an essential aspect of building children's "quality" (*suzhi*) (Woronov 2009a: 584). This view has been further motivated by government and media discourse on the future of the Chinese nation and its ability to transcend its perceived inferior status, whether in terms of the "quality of its population (*renkou suzhi*)" or its living standards (Anagnost 1997: 197; Woronov 2007a: 32).

Among the new urban middle classes or those who aspire to become middle class in China, increased spending on children may additionally function as a household strategy to guarantee the future of the family and to ensure that parents can maintain their class position in a society undergoing rapid social and economic change. For wealthy urban families, spending lavishly on children carries potent symbolic value. Highly priced products and services act as markers of a family's economic capacity and success, and by extension, for parents' openness and adjustment to change. They announce Chinese "parents' arrival as full subjects of late modernity" (Zhao and Murdock 1996: 212). Buying the best children's products and services can therefore be seen as a form of "conspicuous consumption" and a prime mechanism in the formation of a new middle-class sensibility in China, a means to distinguish themselves from the country's "uneducated masses" (see Donald and Zheng 2008).

Such ambitions are not unique to Chinese caregivers of course: similar changes in patterns of family relations and consumption on children are evident in many of East Asia's metropolitan areas, and indeed may be part of a transnational transformation of childhood in the changing conditions of early twenty-first-century capitalism (see Anagnost 1997: 196). The rise of PRC children as independent consumers and their growing ability to shape family consumption patterns is also related to another global development of late modernity: the emergence of the idea that even the very young have a capacity – and indeed should be encouraged – to make independent decisions.

As discussed in chapter 2, this idea has in recent years gained increasing influence in China, especially among well-educated urban caregivers who see children as autonomous persons with personal rights, including the right to consume (see Naftali 2009, 2014a). A Shanghai office worker in the mid-2000s, who was married to a successful entrepreneur, noted that, for instance, until recently, she and her husband had made all the decisions for their 11-year-old son. Now that he was older, they made a point of "discussing all sort of things with him" and respected "his wishes" even when these contradicted their will. Believing that parents "should trust their child's judgment and not try to control everything he does," the couple had consulted their son and asked for his opinion before they purchased their current apartment, in order to "make sure he liked the place as much as they did" (cited in Naftali 2014a: 51).

For this middle-class Shanghai couple as well as for many other urban, affluent caregivers in China, allowing children to make consumer decisions signals the parents' association with a more "modern," liberal childrearing style, which empowers children and takes heed of their individual choices. However, in the area of educational consumption, Chinese mothers and fathers frequently face a dilemma between this new parenting ideology and their pragmatic concern about their child's future career chances. As noted in chapter 2, and as the next section will further show, the solution for this dilemma often disregards children's own preferences.

EDUCATIONAL SERVICES AND PRODUCTS

Children's education is one of the primary areas in which Chinese family consumption has seen an extensive rise in recent decades. Completion of nine years of schooling has been compulsory in China since 1986 but education is not free; tuition and other fees for education at all levels can amount to hundreds of thousands of *yuan* per year depending on level, quality, and location. Despite attempts by the government to cap school fees, all types of educational expenses have risen incrementally since the 1990s. By the mid-2000s, for both rural and urban families, the cost of education had superseded housing as one of the largest budget items (Croll 2006: 188; see also China Daily 2005).

The increase in family spending on children's schooling is largely because the financing of education has been decentralized and privatized, with local governments, schools, and universities increasingly turning to fees to make good the shortfalls in central government funding (Croll 2006: 187). Over the past decade or so, under the ideological headlines of developing "a harmonious society" and "a new socialist countryside," former president Hu Jintao and his premier, Wen Jiabao, launched a number of policies aimed at reducing the rural–urban gap in China, including a commitment to provide free compulsory education for all rural children. In 2005, the government began eliminating tuition and book fees for primary and junior middle schools in the countryside and, starting from 2007, compulsory education (Grades 1–9) was made free for all rural children.

Despite these important initiatives, the reality is that many PRC schools, particularly in rural areas, simply cannot function without raising money to meet expenses that are not met by the local administration or governments at higher levels. While financial support for rural schools is supposed to come from county and township administrations, in some areas, local authorities lack funds for their own expenses, let alone for educating children (Wang 2007: 112, 116). As a result, education spending remains a primary budget item in many households. A recent Euromonitor survey indicates that in the five years prior to 2012, per capita annual disposable income in China rose by 63.3 percent, yet consumer expenditure on education rose by almost 94 percent (cited in Sharma 2013).

In rural impoverished areas, soaring educational costs have caused some parents to selectively invest in children's education based not only on the child's skills and aptitude, but also on gender. Statistical surveys of rural communities in the 1990s show that boys were more often sent to school, and that the school expenditures on a boy were larger than those for a school-going girl of the same age (Gong et al. 2005). As will be discussed in more detail in chapter 5, despite improvements, gender remains a major factor influencing the chances of rural children to attain nine years of compulsory schooling. Fewer girls attend school in rural areas and many drop out earlier than boys (Hannum and Adams 2007: 72; see also Ross 2006).

In the cities, where most families have just one child, caregivers do not face such dilemmas. They do, however, worry about the intense competition for entry into the key or better-quality schools. Periodically, reports in the Chinese media discuss the rising numbers of students who are admitted to better middle schools because they pay high fees rather than achieve sufficient examination scores. Parents who succeed in enrolling their children through this route consider the expense to be worth the satisfaction of having their only child study at a key middle school which has better teaching, resources, and facilities (Croll 2006: 188, 190).

Many caregivers also hire private tutors so that their only child can score high enough on entrance exams to senior middle school and later successfully pass the university entrance examination (*gaokao*) (Woerdahl 2010). Urban parents invest in private tuition of their only child not only in academic subjects but also in extra-curricular activities such as art, music, chess, and calligraphy. After-class academic and extra-curricular tutoring has now become almost a prerequisite for key school entry (Croll 2006: 193; Cockain 2011: 81). A recent survey found that nine out of ten children from urban middle-class families in China attend fee-charging after-school activities and that children are now being tutored for longer, starting younger. Tutoring used to begin a year or two before the university entrance exam; now it can start in middle school, primary school or even earlier (Sharma 2013). As entry to the best kindergartens and primary schools is fiercely competitive, city parents are eager to give their child the best possible start, even before they reach kindergarten age (Croll 2006: 192; Tobin et al. 2009: 33–4).

This expenditure can be seen as an "accumulation strategy": parents and grandparents invest in educating a child who will, ideally, generate dividends in the future (Woronov 2011: 83). To help meet the growing demand for quality in education, the government has encouraged private education at all levels, from primary school to universities. In the late 1990s, more than 60,000 high-fee privately owned educational institutions were reported to be offering education to some ten million students (Croll 2006: 193). A decade or so later, in 2008, the number had doubled, and private institutes constituted 20 percent of all educational and training institutes in the country. These institutions offer pre-school, primary, secondary, and higher education plus vocational and technical training, and enroll some 37.5 million students (Yeo 2011; Chen and Feng 2012).

The transformation of education into a market-supplied commodity in China is legitimated by a neoliberal discourse of competition, meritocracy, and self-determination (Crabb 2010). Exclusive private schools in China's metropolitan centers compete for the children of highly paid urban professionals, educators, entrepreneurs, and private and state managers. They have become adept at selling an idea of "distinction and cultural cachet" along with the national priorities of "education for quality" and "comprehensive learning" (*quanmian jiaoyu*). The private schools market the idea that the value of education is no longer to simply help children gain precious university places in a very demanding educational environment. It is also a ticket to participation in China's globalizing market economy. This message is particularly attractive to well-off families who plan to send their children to obtain education outside China at the tertiary level (Donald and Zheng 2008). Previously a luxury confined to the most privileged in China, foreign study has become more common among the swelling ranks of the middle classes and has even percolated to the lower urban classes. According to the Chinese Academy of Social Sciences, a third of Chinese students studying abroad in 2010 were from urban working-class families. This is a massive financial burden but some parents are willing to undertake it in order to give their child a shortcut to success (Sharma 2013).

Some Chinese caregivers express unhappiness with the growing financial burden on their families as well as with the mounting social pressure to enroll their children in numerous enrichment activities or hire private tutors to ensure the child's academic success. In practice, however, many parents, especially those from urban, middle-class backgrounds, continue to send their children to these activities for fear their only-child would lag behind his or her peers. As one Shanghai mother explained:

> I want to provide my child with the best education I can give her. Piano lessons are mandatory and [my daughter] must practice every day to get better....I didn't have this opportunity to learn the piano when I

was younger. Now, all the other children in this building play, and [my daughter] would be left behind if she didn't (cited in Nie and Wyman 2005: 330).

FOOD CONSUMPTION

As elsewhere in the world, Chinese caregivers are concerned not only about education but also about the health of their children. For urban families, the effects of the One-Child Policy exacerbate these anxieties. Companies selling food and nutritional supplements to infants and children have tapped into these concerns while relying on the powerful discourse of "scientific childrearing" to persuade parents to buy modern products such as infant formulas. The adoption of scientific childcare practices also has become a coping strategy for many parents regarding their food safety concerns, as caregivers in China rely on frequent health checks at hospitals to ensure that there is no food safety threat to their infants (Gottschang, 2000; Xu et al., 2006; Gong and Jackson 2013).

Older children, though, are exercising an increasing ability to dictate what their family eats at mealtimes and which snacks to buy (Chee 2000; Gillette 2000; Guo 2000; Watson 2000). In a recent ethno-graphic study of middle-class urban families in the city of Kunming, anthropologist Teresa Kuan (2015: 181) notes that during family meals, parents "have become accustomed to giving their child the best food on the table, and feel satisfaction simply in seeing the child eat something." For their part, children may place a great level of trust in their parents, who are perceived as the most credible information source about new food products. Like children elsewhere in the world, however, they are increasingly influenced by television commercials. Together with online ads and colorful packaging, these commercials now speak directly to Chinese children, bypassing parents in their attempts to appeal to a young market (see McNeal and Ji 1998; Fan and Li 2010; Yu 2014: 132).

There can be little doubt that economic reform has had a positive effect on the net nutrition levels of the Chinese population, children included, a fact that is evident in the increase in the height-for-age of PRC children over the past several decades. However, children's food consumption habits also reflect the growing socioeconomic and regional disparities in the country. Drawing on data from national nutritional and health surveys conducted between 1991 and 2007, a study by Yu and others (2008) reports that 35.1 percent of Chinese children between the ages of 3 and 17 consume snacks. However, the rate of 55.7 percent in urban areas is considerably higher than that of rural children (29.6 percent).

Meanwhile, data from national surveys of children's health conducted in 1979–2005 reveal that a third of Chinese school-aged children, particularly those hailing from urban poor or rural families, remain underweight (a level that has barely changed during three decades of rapid economic reforms). In contrast, as many as a quarter of 7–18-year-old urban boys, especially in the affluent cities of east China, are now overweight or obese. Whereas in 1979 there was little difference among the regions in the average weight and height levels of school-aged children, by 2005 both boys and girls were lightest in the country's poorer, western regions (Morgan 2014: 1033, 1052).

These figures suggest that China's economic development has failed some of the most vulnerable children in central and western provinces, where nutrition availability is often inadequate (Morgan 2014: 1033). While socioeconomic changes are part of the explanation for the disparities between children's food consumption in different regions, deep-seated cultural influences also interact with the effects of the population policy to encourage over-eating among urban boys. Traditionally in China, plump babies "were much admired as symbols of goodness and luck," while thinness represented "bad luck, illness and early death" (cited in Morgan 2014: 1065). The One-Child Policy has probably encouraged fatness among male urban children, because grandparents and parents – many of whom continue to associate fat with bounty and happiness – lavish gifts and food upon male singletons (Morgan 2014).

Urban girls, however, are less inclined to be overweight. In cities where many children are without siblings, a simple gender bias in household allocation of resources therefore does not explain the differences in weight; the increasing incomes of urban households would further reduce the likelihood of gender biases in the presence of mixed-sex siblings. A possible explanation is the influence on older urban girls of the media's promotion of a fashionable thinness that impels them to moderate their consumption of calories. As elsewhere in the post-industrial world, body dissatisfaction, concerns about weight, dieting fads, and eating disorders are on the rise in contemporary urban China (Morgan 2014: 1055–6).

Changes in children's lifestyles in the city also affect their body weight. Fewer children in Chinese cities now walk or cycle to school, and outdoors recreation has been replaced by indoor inactivity in front of electronic devices (Morgan 2014: 1065). The effects of the One-Child Policy once again exacerbate this trend for, as noted in chapter 3, many urban caregivers now prefer to keep singletons indoors to guard their physical safety or to ensure that the child devotes his or her afterschool hours to supervised study. Over the past decade or so, urban Chinese parents have become more aware of this problem, though many relate it not only to the sedentary labor of schoolwork but also to the ready availability of snacks and franchise foods (Anagnost 2008: 66).

One of the most telling indicators of China's consumer revolution has been the rapid proliferation of restaurants and the increasing percentage of household budgets ordinary families spend eating out. Dining out has quickly gained in popularity in China, accounting for 20 percent of the expenditure of urban households in 2004, compared with only 8 percent in 1994 (Morgan 2014: 1064). Children have played a central part in this trend. Studies conducted in China's urban areas, where dining out is more common than in rural areas, have found that children frequently choose the restaurant in which the whole family eats. With rising incomes and a faster pace of life, fast-food outlets are frequently the first choice of children (Davis 2000: 14; Yan 2000: 216–17; Zhang et al. 2014: 30).

As in many other parts of the world, children in China's large metropolitan areas have become loyal fans of Western fast food (Yan 2000: 210). Younger generations, who have experienced greater exposure to foreign cultures, also tend to be more prepared to try foreign foods and the consumption styles of other cultures (Zhang et al. 2014: 3). Global fast-food chains such as Kentucky Fried Chicken (KFC) and McDonald's have recognized the opportunity (Watson 2006; Yan 2000; Zhang et al. 2014).

A study of how KFC catered to Beijing customers in the 1990s shows, for instance, that children have played a key role in the localization of franchises in the city, influencing many of the changes in the company's business tactics (Lozada 2000). Children drew parents into these restaurants not only to eat fast food and "have fun," but also to "taste modernity" (Lozada 2000). An ethnographic study of McDonald's restaurants in Beijing by anthropologist Yan Yunxiang (2000) similarly discovered that while most adult customers did not particularly like the foods served at these restaurants, children were great fans, and parents and grandparents were willing to indulge singletons' desires. Beijing caregivers appreciated children's fondness for imported fast food because they believed that "eating a Big Mac and fries" can help prepare the child for a modern society. Or, as one Beijing mother explained: "I want my daughter to learn more about American culture. She is taking an English typing class now, and I will buy her a computer next year" (cited in Yan 2000: 212).

A more recent study by Zhang and others (2014) reveals that until the mid-2000s children (accompanied by adults) were the main customers of both KFC and McDonald's restaurants in the city of Nanjing.

The study observes that the restaurants have been popular among China's young as they allow even small children an opportunity to order their favorite meals, and represent a space to which older children can escape from the daily monotony of academic work. Western fast-food restaurants in China also offer a venue for conducting personal celebrations, particularly for youth and children, such as birthday parties or end-of-term parties (Zhang et al. 2014: 28; see also Yan 2000, 2006). As these studies indicate, the success of global food chains in China is not only attributable to the emergence of children as independent consumers, but has also contributed to their increasing empowerment and individualization.

TOYS AND LEISURE ACTIVITIES

While city parents will indulge their single child by taking him or her to fast-food restaurants, Chinese parents as a whole tend to be more cautious about spending money on toys. Since children's education is the highest priority for many parents and takes a large portion of parental incomes and savings, there is frequently little left for other child-oriented goods and services (Croll 2006: 196). Observations in Shanghai toy stores of the mid-2000s document that it is the smaller and cheaper items that were purchased even though the more expensive and imported toys attract the most attention for children. Toys are primarily seen as sources of enjoyment and recreation for children up to age seven years, but from seven to eight years of age, play gives way to learning and only toys and games that are perceived to be educational aids, or to develop children's creativity and hand-to-eye coordination, find favor with Chinese parents (Croll 2006: 180).

Associating their goods with "science, modernity, and foreignness," domestic toy companies, joint ventures, and foreign corporations are contributing to the production of new definitions of "child quality" in China (Jing 2000: 7; Greenhalgh and Winckler 2005: 242; see also Gottschang 2000). In major cities such as Beijing and Shanghai, schools are also introducing educational toys while parenting magazines feature toys and explain their educational value. Children of the rich and professional classes in the cities are now introduced to computing at an early age, but again it is the educational role of computers that is emphasized in promotional materials. Indeed, it is common for parents or grandparents in China to spend a chunk of their savings on a computer (Croll 2006: 181).

As noted, children in urban China frequently play indoors and under the supervision of an adult caregiver. In today's one-child families, parents' leisure time with their only-child has increased significantly and urban children in particular tend to rely more on their parents as companions and playmates. This has promoted equality in the parent–child relationship but has also restricted the interactions of singletons with other children (Feng et al. 2014: 23). The growing insulation of singletons within the home is related not only to parental concerns for the academic achievements of their only-child but also to recent transformations in China's urban landscape.

Until the 1990s, a majority of city families lived in relatively protected, closed-off compounds, constructed and managed by their work-unit (*danwei*). Even young boys and girls could play outside in the alley of the work-unit compound because parents knew that neighbors or members of local residents' committees would keep an eye on their children (see Naftali 2010a). The privatization of the labor and housing markets in the last two decades has dramatically changed children's living environments, however. As the shift to a market economy forced up prices of land, urban space became harder to obtain and new high-rise apartment buildings, separated from places of employment, began to replace the sealed compound housing structure of the former era (Gaubatz 1995: 34–5). The walls of existing work-unit compounds have been gradually dismantled or breached by newly constructed private businesses (Davis 1995: 2–3).

These architectural reconfigurations have had important implications for the social worlds and leisure activities of children. Increasing isolation in the new apartment blocks, where access to outside play spaces is impeded by lack of free time and the fact that most families live in high-rise dwellings contribute to children's seclusion within the home, where they can sometimes watch television, play computer games, and exchange Instant Messages with friends. Many parents also prefer to keep their child indoors because of the deteriorating air quality in Chinese cities and the increase in urban crime (Anagnost 2008: 66).

When urban children do spend leisure time outside the home, it is often in commercial venues: stores, amusement parks, and cinemas. Shopping has become a major form of leisure, with stores serving as a recreational setting where children socialize with their peers. During school holidays, older children are likely to visit the shops and amusement arcades on their own or in groups (Davis and Sensenbrenner 2000; Croll 2006: 186). Some children do engage in sports, travel, and camping. Others run newspapers, radio stations, and literary clubs or engage in environmental protection (Guan 2003b).

However, even in their younger years, school-aged children in China have less time for recreation than many of their counterparts elsewhere in the world. A national survey on children's leisure practices carried out in 1999 revealed that they are mainly busy doing homework assigned by teachers or parents. Playing with friends, participating in community activities, watching TV, movies and videos, and doing physical exercise were a lower priority (Chen 2006). In the 2000s, children's leisure time has lengthened as a result of the "education for quality" reforms, which include a reduction in schoolwork. As noted in chapter 2, psychological advice literature also advises Chinese parents to allow children more time to play and relax. Although some urban, well-educated caregivers are willing to heed this advice and to allocate more resources to their children's leisure and entertainment, together with poorer parents they are anxious to further their children's education (Croll 2006: 186).

Children's leisure time, particularly in urban areas, is therefore strictly controlled in order to maximize the time available for schoolwork and educative recreation, and to minimize distractions. For most parents, these distractions include television viewing, and in the past decade or so, also computer gaming and Internet surfing.

CONSUMPTION OF MEDIA PRODUCTS

Since the initiation of reforms and Open Door Policy in 1978, and particularly since the 1990s, China has seen an unprecedented development of children's media, including television, films, radio, newspapers, magazines, and new electronic media. Notably, however, most of children's media is distributed in cities and regions with more developed economies (Pu and Huang 1998; Chan and Cai 2009). Media ownership, exposure, and usage are higher among urban children than among rural children in China, particularly new media such as DVD, Internet and computer games (Chan and McNeal 2006a; see also Rosen 2003; Davey 2008).

The most predominant media consumption activity among Chinese rural and urban children is television viewing. The household penetration rate for television in China in the mid-2000s was already 120 percent (Chan and Cai 2009: 134). Notably, the arrival of television in ordinary urban homes around 1980 coincided with the implementation of the One-Child Policy. China's first generation of only-children can be said to have grown up in the absence of siblings but with the company of the small screen (Bin 1996). Until the early 2000s, however, there was a shortage of children's programs that featured music, fun, and entertainment. There were also very few programs that targeted the specific needs of teenagers such as development of social relationships and self-identity (Chan and Chan 2008). In 2004, however, in addition to the children's channel of China Central Television (CCTV), 24 provincial TV stations opened new children's channels (Croll 2006: 197). Today, hundreds of TV stations with national and local channels broadcast programs specifically aimed at children, from toddlers to teens, including cartoons, drama series, and games or variety shows.

Studies conducted in China in the late 1980s and early 1990s found that the great majority of parents claimed to exert control over how much television their children watched, without significant differences between social strata. The purpose of parental control over viewing time was to minimize the possibility of children being distracted from schoolwork (Bin 1996). In one study conducted in the 1990s, 52 percent of Chinese parents claimed that they only allowed their children to watch up to one hour a day of television, and 40 percent put the limit at two hours (Zhao and Murdock 1996: 206). In later studies, which also included children in rural areas, urban children reported their parents had concerns about excessive TV viewing. In contrast, a greater proportion of rural children had televisions in their bedrooms and ate meals while watching TV (Davey 2008; Sun 2009). Rural children also watched more television than urban children, and paid more attention to television commercials (Chan and McNeal, 2006b; Chan Kara 2009).

In the past decade or so, online activities have become another favorite pastime for children nationwide, especially in cities. According to a recent report of the China Internet Network Information Center (CNNIC), the number of Internet users in the country has now reached approximately 618 million, the large majority of whom are young people, with youth under 19 making up a quarter of all Internet users. A large-scale study conducted in seven Chinese cities discovered that 63 percent of children aged 12 to 18 have already accessed the Internet (China Internet Network Information Center 2014).

However, utilization of the Internet varies greatly from region to region. In more economically developed cities such as Beijing, Shanghai, and Guangzhou, the percentage of children using the Internet is relatively high; in underdeveloped cities, it is relatively low.

In the early 2000s, most Chinese children surfed the Web at home, at their relatives' or friends' homes, or at school, though the location where they accessed the Internet was related to the economic development level of their cities (Bu 2006). More recently, the share of young people who access the Internet via computers at school has dropped considerably, mainly because smartphone prices and the network service fees have dropped, enabling more school students in China to access the Internet via mobile phones at home or in public places. An ethnographic study conducted from 2005 to 2010 among middle-school students in Beijing and Shanghai demonstrated that the time students spent surfing the Internet far exceeded the time they spent consuming traditional media such as television, radio, newspapers, or magazines (Cockain 2012: 131).

Children were online for an average of approximately 17 hours each week, in contrast to about eight hours spent watching television programs or films. They also tended to consume television and film online, with sites such as *youku* and *tudou* coming to represent the typical viewing platform. Students who participated in this qualitative study expressed idealized views of the Internet, associating it with qualities often ascribed to communities, such as "belonging, sharing, and togetherness." The Internet was also seen as a space in which different kinds of self-expression were made possible in comparison to those commonly practiced offline (Cockain 2012: 132). A recent ethnographic study among students in a rural boarding school in Zhejiang Province similarly records how, despite repeated attempts of school staff to ban the practice, students frequently used their mobile phones to access the Internet, thereby expressing their new demand for individual space as well as their weakened trust in the school authorities (Hansen 2015: 62).

Although most Internet use occurs in the home or boarding school dormitory, some older children in the cities occasionally visit Internet cafés (*wangba*), typically when they want to play online games, activities which are not approved of by teachers and family members (Cockain 2012: 132). For many of these urban singletons, the Internet café represents a space in which they can find a sense of "freedom, relaxation, community, and equality" as well as "fun," which can be found hardly anywhere else in their lives (Liu Fengshu 2009).

The increase in Internet usage among Chinese children has been the source of much media and public concern in recent years. Excessive use of the Internet has been labeled as "Internet addiction," and the most dedicated users are depicted as "victims" and stigmatized as "addicts," while PRC experts connect addiction to crime. Most significant, however, is the portrayal of excessive Internet use as being an impediment to being a "good student" as defined by normative markers like examination success (Cockain 2012: 133).

Although perceptions of the potential threats and dangers of computer games, the Internet, and other communication media have become prevalent elsewhere in the world, such views are strongly held in China, while the more positive potential the media can provide, such as educational resources and a creative outlet, are often stated much less strongly (Cockain 2012: 133). Notably, parents, educators, and government officials worry not only about the frequency of media consumption but also about the contents of these media products and the sort of ideas and values they might instill in children.

CONSUMPTION, MORALITY, AND NATIONAL IDENTITY

Official rhetoric about children's media consumption often centers on the susceptibility of young Chinese to damaging content from abroad, and reference broader, long-standing concerns over the issues of youth "westernization," youth morality, and youth patriotism (Szablewicz 2010; Cockain 2012: 133). The Chinese state-controlled media carries many articles on the dangers of "Western" cultural influence on China, including the penetration of "Western values" through American TV shows and Hollywood films. Children's consumption of foreign media products has been criticized not only for fostering unhealthy desires for "foreign lifestyles" and "a loss of cultural identity," but also for developing "a culture of avarice, hedonism, and individualism" which has usurped "traditional," "Confucian" notions of frugality and collectivism (Cockain 2012: 45; see also Luo 2003; Yang 2006). In recent years, government and media critics have also targeted Japanese popular culture products, such as cartoons (*manga*) and animation (*anime*), arguing that these products portray unhealthy amounts of violence and obscenity, which are detrimental to the moral and psychological health of the nation's children (Ishii 2013).

In addition, many parents, particularly those born before the advent of economic reforms, believe children to be in need of protection from (and education about) consumption. While consumer society is seen to offer new opportunities for the capable child, parents also regard it as a threat to children's personality and potentially harmful to their moral qualities. Moreover, Chinese parents repeatedly raise concerns about their children growing up and adopting a more expensive lifestyle that they might not be able to sustain (Woerdahl 2010). Though they commonly see selfishness as a widespread problem among urban only-children, caregivers also blame themselves for their children's traits, and feel that they have raised their child in a way that did not foster caring for others (Kuan 2015: 181).

In a group interview I conducted in Shanghai in the mid-2000s, one grandmother pointed the finger at doting parents. "In our day, we didn't buy children any special foods or special clothes. There was nothing like that back then," she said. "We all thought that our children grew up okay, but when all is said and done, it seems that while we didn't pay enough attention to our own children, parents these days pay too much attention to theirs. No wonder that so many children today are self-centered and don't know how to respect their elders or seniors!"

Newspaper and magazine articles, television shows, and Internet blogs contribute to these concerns by highlighting popular anxieties associated with the looming "moral crisis" in the country, illustrated in problems such as a decline of social trust, pervasive corruption, extreme materialism, money fetishism, and a lack of altruism in social interactions (Xu 2014: 224). To counter these issues, state schools have sought to educate children in the proper ways of consumption as part of "moral education" classes at the elementary level. The textbooks, however, demand that children exhibit the moral qualities of the socialist era by tolerating hardships, expending focused and concerted effort, and demonstrating discipline, diligence, and constraint (Chan 2006). This type of civic consumerism stands in sharp contrast to the values of uniqueness, fun, and entertainment currently portrayed in children's media and in commercials, and appears oddly out of place in an age in which market discipline encourages "the playful construction of self through the immediate gratification of market goods" (see Donald 2005: 52; Woronov 2009a: 584; Greenhalgh 2011: 155).

An analysis of the major themes of children's television programs in the mid-2000s further reflects the ideological dithering that now characterizes the CCP's moral agenda toward children's consumption. On the one hand, the state-controlled children's media convey high aspirations for success, promotion of competition with peers, and the celebration of individual ability, in a reflection of the government's attempt to transform the nation into a modern consumer society. On the other hand, Chinese children's programs also try to teach submission to collective goals and authority, which are presented as "traditional Chinese values" (Chan and Chan 2008).

The appeal to the "time-honored values" of Chinese culture has also been a key theme in the government's ongoing "patriotic education"

(*Aiguozhuyi jiaoyu*) campaign. Implemented since the early 1990s through various media channels, organized discussion forums in military units, government agencies, state enterprises, research institutes, and neighborhood committees and villages, the campaign has also introduced a more pronounced "patriotic" curriculum and "patriotic activities" to the nation's schools. Beginning in primary school, Chinese students now participate in daily flag-raising rituals, visit "patriotic education bases," and are required to take part in military training courses on campuses and army bases (Zhao 2004; Vickers 2009; Wang, Zheng 2011).

A central site for the fostering of patriotic values to children is the Young Pioneers organization. A relic of the Maoist period, this national children's organization no longer focuses on identifying and excluding class enemies, as it did in the late Maoist period; indeed virtually all children are automatically inducted into the organization upon finishing first grade. However, at the institutional level, the Pioneers organization still has strong formal and ideological ties with the Chinese Communist Party (Woronov 2007b: 657; see also Chin 1988: 51–2). During the annual International Children's Day celebrations, for instance, Pioneer members carry and salute the national flag, take loyalty oaths to the Communist Party, and perform patriotic plays or soliloquies that they write themselves as paeans to the Party and the Chinese motherland. The climax of these performances is the long-held ritual tying of a red scarf around the neck of each of the first graders, to mark their entry into the group. The children learn that the red scarf is a "sacred symbol" that represents a corner of the national flag stained by the blood of the revolutionary martyrs. Each child also wears a red scarf to school every day, thus reiterating his or her link to the nation through the Pioneers, and "performing" the norms of national membership on a daily basis (Woronov 2007b: 658–9).

Though the practices of the Young Pioneers signify an attempt to link contemporary children to the history of the Communist Party and of a "timeless" Chinese nation, they also bear the marks of contemporary media culture. Woronov's (2007b) ethnographic study of Young Pioneers' activities in a Beijing primary school notes that one of the "special privileges" enjoyed by fifth- and sixth-grade Pioneer leaders was watching Japanese cartoons (dubbed into Chinese) in a special room the school had designated for Pioneer activities. The teacher in charge of the organization at the school explained that allowing children to watch these popular cartoons "was one way to make these [leadership] positions highly coveted among all the children" (Woronov 2007b: 659–60).

The teacher's statement reflects the Party's readiness to adapt to a more liberal, capitalist environment in order to remain relevant among the present generation of consumer-oriented urban children. In the course of the 2000s, the Chinese government has employed ever more sophisticated means, including animated films, computer games, and popular music videos, to make the messages of the "patriotic education" campaign more appealing to children (see Rosen 2008; Naftali 2014a). However, domestic, state-sponsored media productions often fail to compete with international, mostly American and Japanese, messages in the fight for popularity (Donald 2002). In the mid-2000s, these concerns drove the Chinese government to curtail the broadcasting of foreign animated programs on television and to encourage the development of Chinese cartoons and animation that "should embody the Chinese cultural spirit" as well as "socialist values" (cited in Ishii 2013).

Recent studies indicate that children aged 4–14 do watch Chinese animation. However, they continue to enjoy American animation as well. Japanese animation, which can now be downloaded or viewed through the Internet, remains highly popular among those older than 14. Even after the ban on foreign animation on Chinese television, a majority of adolescents continue to favor Japanese animation, and only a minority prefer animation from Europe, the US, or China (Chen and Song 2009; Ishii 2013).

The popularity of foreign media products among Chinese children notwithstanding, the assumption that increased exposure to such products has resulted in children's loss of cultural identity is debatable. Studies indicate that Chinese children, particularly those from well-off families in the affluent eastern cities, have become sophisticated media consumers. They may be fully competent in "their relationship to new knowledge in a new world" but they also retain and reiterate a sense of local and national identity (Donald 2004). Consumption of American TV programs has not led to significant identification with "Western" values and while Chinese adolescents may admire much of what they know of American society and culture, they are also highly nationalistic and can be critical of American motives and actions outside of the US (Dong 2002; Rosen 2003, 2008; Fong 2004a). Similarly, preference for Japanese animation has not been found to correlate significantly with pro-Japan attitudes among contemporary Chinese teenagers, even in the globalizing city of Shanghai (Ishii 2013).

The common assumption that Chinese children are becoming hedonistic also does not find empirical corroboration. Some studies (e.g., Chan and Hu 2008; Xu 2010) suggest that city children are more materialistic than their rural counterparts. Others note, however, that even urban children of middle-class families tend to associate ownership of a large number of possessions with qualities such as selfishness, while a child without many material possessions is regarded by his or her peers as more "hardworking," "smart," and "friendly" (Xu 2010). Such perceptions may be a result of the socialization children receive at home and at school.

In a perceived "immoral" era of money worship and hedonistic consumerism, adults in China often try to teach children the egalitarian value of sharing as a way to cultivate a sense of altruism among the so-called spoiled "little emperors" (Xu 2014: 237). However, teachers' and caregivers' own behaviors, including the use of *guanxi*, i.e., the practice of reciprocal gifts and favors in establishing personal connections, inevitably also affect children's moral attitudes and behaviors. For instance, in one Shanghai preschool located in a middle-class neighborhood, researcher Xu (2014: 237) found that parents tried in every possible way to cultivate a relationship with the teachers so that their only-child would be favored, or at least not ignored. They sent various gifts to the teachers in private; or invited teachers to have dinner with their family "as a way for the child to develop a personal relationship with teachers outside of the school setting."

The study further discovered that favoritism was present in the classroom, "as teachers felt indebted to some parents' favors and obligated to pay more attention to their children, e.g., assigning certain children better seats in the classroom or giving them a leading role in class" (Xu 2014; see also Kuan 2015: 133–5). Such practices were visible to the children – aged 2–6 – in subtle ways, and significantly shaped their social interactions with adult caregivers as well as their peers. Among the 120 children attending the preschool, many were observed spontaneously engaging in "strategic sharing" – extending favors so that others can help you – in their everyday interactions. On one occasion, a three-year-old who was celebrating his birthday by handing out pieces of cake to his classmates, approached his teacher and asked: "Hey, Ms. Xiaoru, didn't you see [the director]? Why don't you give her a piece of cake too? You know you should cotton up to your boss (*tao jinhu*)" (cited in Xu 2014: 222).

Such practices did not correspond to teachers' and caregivers' current emphasis on the importance of teaching children the value of altruistic sharing. However, they did match the norm of "pulling connections" ("*la guanxi*"), which dominates social interactions in China. Findings from studies such as this therefore suggest that Chinese children "are constructing their own moral universe," which may differ markedly from both the official, adult discourse of the need to return to socialist values and from widespread adult panic about raising a generation of essentially amoral, selfish children (Xu 2014: 224).

Though contemporary Chinese children know well from early child-hood that money is indispensable in life, some studies (e.g., Zhao 2006) indicate that many also maintain the values of diligence and thrift. In this sense, children's attitudes toward money and consumption may reflect their parents' and society's ambivalence toward these issues, as well as the discrepancies between the ideologies and practices of their caregivers and teachers.

CONCLUSION

Children's tastes and preferences have shaped the rise of consumer society in China (Tilt 2006). As the country shifts to market-driven capitalist enterprise, children and youth have become the emerging focus of the economy and constitute major players in a government-orchestrated "festival of consumption" (Donald 2005: 52; Greenhalgh 2011: 155). However, their growing consumer power is also cause for anxiety and unease among caregivers, educators, and government officials.

In many ways, China's consumer culture, in which children consti-tute key players, poses a challenge to the powerful role that the Chinese state seeks to play in the education of its youngest citizens (Tilt 2006). It also destabilizes intergenerational relations in the Chinese family. The shifting balance between individualism and collective responsibil-ity, the increasingly blurred line between parental care and indulgence, and the erosion of filial piety, are predominant themes in public debates about consumption by and on behalf of children in China (Zhao and Murdock 1996: 215). These debates and concerns are in turn trans-lated into ambiguous consumer socialization of children at home and at school, and to a common critique of excessive spending and media consumption among youth.

Chinese children appear to have internalized some of these mes-sages and exhibit relatively lukewarm attitudes toward materialism.

They do, however, appreciate that money is indispensable and, like their counterparts elsewhere in the world, many have become avid consumers of snacks, fast food, and global media products. They have enjoyed increased freedom and empowerment because of this revolution in consumption, and have also come to constitute important agents of social change in their own right.

As the discussion in this chapter has further shown, however, these processes have occurred unevenly among urban and rural child populations. Though contemporary Chinese children enjoy a material standard of living that has not been seen by any previous generation, those in relatively affluent metropolises such as Beijing and Shanghai are now experiencing a far more commoditized existence than many of their rural counterparts. The next chapter will further consider the distinctions between rural and urban children in China, while noting some of the negative effects of economic restructuring on the education, wellbeing, and social identities of children in the poorer parts of the countryside.

5 Children in the Countryside: The Effects of Economic Reforms and Parental Migration

While China has enjoyed spectacular economic growth overall in recent decades, the country has also experienced rising social and economic inequality, and the uneven conditions between eastern and western regions and rural and urban populations have led to a deteriorating development environment for many children residing in impoverished parts of the countryside. Historically, children in China's rural areas have faced substantial disadvantages in securing access to education, health, and welfare services. Since the 1980s, some rural households have experienced greater economic affluence and come to foster higher social expectations. Rural parents, like their urban counterparts, place their hopes in their children and many have been able to enlarge their resources for investment in children's education by migrating to cities and towns which have more employment opportunities. However, as rural family spending on educational and medical services has increased since the 1990s, poverty in the countryside has spread and parental migration to the city has had detrimental effects for children's care and education.

The present chapter explores this dialectic development by focusing on the effects of economic reforms and processes of large-scale migration on the lives and subjectivities of children in the countryside. It describes the main problems rural children face in areas of education and in their family and social relations, and pays special attention to the unique difficulties experienced by rural girls; by ethnic minority children who are over-represented within the poor rural population; and by rural children with disabilities or those whose parents have been diagnosed with HIV/AIDS.

A considerable part of the discussion will be devoted to the experiences of "left-behind" children, a new social category which represents an important segment of the child population directly influenced by the massive wave of peasant migration in China. Studies on the effects of migration worldwide suggest that the free movement of peoples in search of opportunity can affect inequality in diverse ways. Some argue that migration raises average income in the source region and reduces it in the target region. Other studies have found that migration can also be an engine of growth, working to enhance the dynamism of the target areas and so raise incomes there while maintaining or increasing inequality. In China, migration has not been seen to dampen the rural–urban divide (Riskin 2010: 93). Moreover, nationwide, less than 10 percent of rural migrant workers move to the city with their entire family. As a result, rural–urban migration is frequently associated in China with family separations, including between parents who migrate and children who are left in the care of grandparents or other guardians. As the discussion will show, prolonged parental migration has had negative effects on these children's schooling and particularly their emotional wellbeing. It has also impaired their relations with family members in crucial ways.

The central state and local governments in China have come to recognize and attempted to address these problems in recent years, but in many of the country's impoverished, rural regions, local authorities still lack the resources to implement these policies effectively. Under these conditions, and despite impressive achievements in expanding educational access in the countryside since the 1980s, China's rural children fall far behind their urban peers, and their social and personal development remains at risk. Unlike affluent city children in China, many rural children struggle to attain basic rights to welfare and education, and are therefore less able to assert their autonomy and their personal desires at home or at school.

RURAL SCHOOLING UNDER ECONOMIC REFORMS

Since 1978, China has made impressive gains in sending rural children to school. Moreover, economic growth, along with the impact of the birth control policy, has brought many rural families to the point where even a university education, although difficult, is possible (Huang et al. 1996; Kipnis 2001: 18). Despite these gains, the gap between rural and urban education in China has not disappeared and in some areas has actually widened since the 1980s.

Until recently, less than a quarter of the funds for education went to rural areas, even though more than half of the national population was considered rural (Postiglione 2011: 89). As noted in chapter 4, under the ideological headlines of developing "a harmonious society" and "a new socialist countryside," former president Hu Jintao and former premier, Wen Jiabao, started implementing a number of policies to reduce the rural–urban gap, including in education. In 2005, the central government pledged to provide free compulsory education for all rural children within three years and to invest more to increase rural children's access to higher education. The government began eliminating tuition and book fees for primary and junior middle schools, and from 2007, made compulsory education (Grades 1–9) officially free for all rural people (Postiglione 2011).

All these measures have helped alleviate inequality to some extent. Nevertheless, the basic infrastructure behind the uneven distribution of resources across the country has not been overhauled. Local governments of some rural regions have increased their education expenditure over the past decade, and dramatically improved their school facilities. However in other poor, rural areas, where local governments have no money to operate schools or to pay teachers' salaries on time, the quality of education continues to lag far behind that in the cities (Wang 2007: 112, 116; see also Kipnis 2011a).

The rural–urban gap is reflected in the structure of the education system itself. Most urban children are sent to kindergarten as early as three years of age, and by the time they enter the first grade at age six or seven, they have already learned simple reading, writing, and arithmetic, as well as singing, drawing, and dancing. In contrast, few children outside the cities have access to three years of pre-school (the last year being kindergarten). Early childhood education services in rural China are relatively expensive. Most are private; the government plays only a secondary role in their provision and the per capita investment is only a fraction of that being poured into higher levels of education. As a result, many families cannot send their children to pre-school, and rural children score much lower on standardized tests of educational readiness for school than their urban counterparts (Postiglione 2011: 89; Wang Dan 2011a: 161; see also Luo et al. 2012).

At age six, urban children begin six years of primary school, which is usually located in their neighborhood. In rural areas, because schools can be far from home and roads are unsafe for small children, some students do not begin school until age eight. Many rural children will attend a two- or three-year primary school in their village, then board at a six-year primary school in the township to complete their primary education. Until recently, schoolchildren in poor, rural counties were required to pay for boarding expenses, schoolbooks, and in some cases even for basic equipment such as desks and chalk. As educational costs have risen, many poor households have found it increasingly difficult to cover the costs. Even after tuition and fees were officially eliminated in the countryside in 2007, rural education has continued to suffer from poor-quality teaching and material infrastructure. Although some rural schools have qualified teachers, adequate facilities, and even libraries, others, particularly those in remote, mountainous regions, experience shortages of both workers and equipment. Teacher qualifications and salaries are rising but are often not enough to keep good teachers in the countryside (Postiglione 2011: 89–90).

Policies to develop innovative teaching styles, creative learning practices, and "all-round development" of students as part of the 1999 "education for quality" (*suzhi jiaoyu*) plan (discussed in detail in chapter 2), have often proved difficult to implement in the countryside. Whereas urban teachers try to add difficulty levels to the textbook content, teachers in some rural schools, particularly those in poverty-stricken areas, struggle to bring students to the minimum requirements of the textbook. Rural teachers in these areas therefore complain that the "education for quality" curriculum standards are set too high and the textbook schedule too fast for their students, making the goals of the program unrealistic (Wang Dan 2011a: 160, 163).

The "education for quality" plan also fails to address the issue of cultural bias. The contents of learning tend to focus on urban life, and school textbooks often emphasize the merits of "industrialized, city, and modern life," which causes rural children to feel alienated and to lag behind academically (Wang Dan 2011b: 90). Moreover, whereas children in urban areas have access to after-school and weekend classes in subjects such as English, computing, art, and music, rural students, especially those in poorer areas, spend more time on the core exam subjects of math and Chinese, while missing activities such as computing, oral English, or "creativity" classes. Without teachers who have expertise in such topics, most rural schools simply lack the resources to hold those classes (Kipnis 2001: 16; Hansen 2012: 166).

Under these conditions, illiteracy is still more widespread in rural areas than in urban ones, and although aggregated statistics from the Ministry of Education show almost universal compliance with the nine-year Compulsory Education Law, independent, survey-based studies regarding dropout rates in China suggest that the poorest rural areas have not yet reached the goal of nine years of compulsory education. Senior middle school – the last three years of a child's education which most urban children complete – is not compulsory in China, nor is it covered by the new scheme to develop "a new socialist countryside." In 1990, just seven percent of rural students completed senior middle school; today, the figure may be just over one-third. Even at the junior level, despite government figures suggesting full attendance, dropout rates are high (Yi et al. 2012; The Economist 2014).

Some rural children quit their studies before they reach senior middle school because of the cost of tuition. Including the cost of books, the bill for three years of study can easily amount to thousands of US dollars – more than a year's income for poorer rural families. Others quit because senior middle schools are often far from villages, so children have to travel long distances or board. Many rural teenagers choose to leave school because they can already find what they consider a decent job or because of a lack of confidence in continuing their education (Hannum et al. 2010: 145; Postiglione 2011: 90). As one youth in a northeastern Chinese village explained: "I didn't go [to school] after sixth grade. Not many did. On the TV now I hear people talk of education as an investment. For whom? Here it's like burning money, but it's for the living [not the dead], so why burn it?" (cited in May 2010: 905).

Many rural dropouts engage in paid labor, often under abysmal conditions. China has a demand for low-cost, low-skilled labor, which many employers meet with child labor in place of more expensive, less malleable, adult labor. China introduced a Minor Labor Law in 2002, which sets 16 as the legal juvenile age for employment and fines enterprises for each minor they employ. In addition, all persons employed between the ages of 16 and 18 are classified as "juvenile workers (*weichengnian gong*)" and are subject to specific legal protections, for example, being prohibited from working in mines or in other heavy industrial jobs. However, particularly in rural areas, large numbers of children under 16 engage in some form of work after dropping out of school early. Though precise statistics are hard to come by, various reports show that children under 16 years old, and especially girls, who are more in demand by employers due to their perceived docility, work in small enterprises in rural towns and villages, including small coal mines, brick factories, and weaving and clothing factories (China Labour Bulletin 2007: 5, 7).

Some rural children who fail the test to enter a regular senior middle school, and who may be too poor to afford a private school or extra studies, choose the route of vocational secondary schools. In theory, vocational education can serve as a plausible means for rural children to avoid agricultural work and to secure a future job that will provide more financial stability than farming. However, the training students receive in these schools is often not applicable to the work that they will do. The quality of teaching is low, and so is the status of vocational education, as it does not prepare students for entry into university, a coveted goal of many rural children and their families (Hansen and Woronov 2013; see also The Economist 2014).

Despite the prohibitive costs of schooling, rural parents continue to believe in the importance of education in creating "a modern society" and see it as a requirement to an individual's survival. A majority also want their children to leave the countryside, a wish which reflects not only the hope of relatively lucrative urban occupations but also a desire to shed the stigma of the "peasant" label (Kipnis 2001: 7; Kong 2010). While a university degree no longer guarantees a job, many rural parents in China still desire their children to go on to higher education (Kipnis 2011a; Hansen 2015). In the eyes of children who have managed to enter regular senior middle schools and are already follow-ing the prepared path to college, there is simply no other option. In a personal interview conducted in 2013, a teenager from a rural county in Henan Province explained the difference between the countryside and the city, and how, in his mind, he could exchange the lifestyle of one for the other:

They always say that the quality (*suzhi*) of Chinese people, especially those who live in rural towns and counties, is not very high, but let me tell you something. My mother's great-aunt was raised in a big city from a young age. She even went to university there. She is very different from my parents. Her family's life is nothing like ours. I remember visiting their home once in the city and seeing so many books there, not schoolbooks – extra-curricular books. Not like in our home. When my grandfather was very ill once, my great-aunt came back for a visit but her son refused to accompany her because of the poor conditions in our village. [...] Our lives are very different from those of children in the big city. We don't get to see so many things as they do. We don't go to museums or read books like kids in the city. But all this may change if I get to go to university.

As reflected in this boy's account, some rural youngsters do express resistance toward the labels imposed on them by the *suzhi* discourse, yet they "still engage with and implicitly accept the *suzhi* perspective, and the unequal power relations that it embodies" (Murphy 2004: 5). Moreover, this boy's hopeful statement concerning the possibility of changing his fate through university studies is unfortunately somewhat misplaced. Despite a constant expansion in the number of university places and the entry of large numbers of rural students into the university applicant pool, particularly in the 2000s (Wang et al. 2013), there is still much competition over places in higher education and the chances of entering university have not been distributed evenly throughout the system (Kipnis 2001: 20). In 2002–3, researcher Li Wenli found that approximately 32 percent of university students in China were from rural areas, compared with 68 percent from urban areas (cited in Hannum et al. 2010: 145). A decade later, the situation has not dramatically improved. A study by Wang et al. (2013), which uses a 2009 census of incoming freshmen from four tier-one universities in Shaanxi, Sichuan, and Anhui, concludes that despite the dramatic expansion in Chinese higher education enrollment rates since the late 1990s, rural students are still systematically under-represented in China's higher education system. This is particularly true of rural female and rural minority children. As the following two sections reveal, these child populations are also disadvantaged in terms of access to basic education.

GENDER DISPARITIES IN RURAL CHILDREN'S EDUCATION

While there is solid evidence of gender inequality in China's basic education system in the 1980s, recent literature shows mixed evidence on the state of girls' education in the early twenty-first century. Some studies in China and abroad suggest gender inequality is still severe in the country's rural areas; others report progress and suggest that the gap has been narrowing (Zeng et al. 2014). Certainly, gender remains a major factor influencing the chances of rural children of attaining nine years of compulsory schooling. Fewer girls attend school in rural areas and girls may drop out earlier than boys. Moreover, according to research reports from China's National Bureau of Statistics, there is still a disparity between men and women regarding the rate of illiteracy, average years of education, and the rates of starting and dropping out of school (cited in Hannum and Adams 2007: 72; see also Ross 2006).

Studies conducted from the 1980s to the 1990s reveal that in many of China's rural communities, boys were more likely to attend school and their education received more financial support than school-going girls of the same age (Zhong and Zhang 1996; Kipnis 2001; Chi and Rao 2003; Gong et al. 2005; Dong et al. 2008). Different parental expectations are often a key factor, reflecting traditional gender stereotypes and the idea that girl's schooling is a poor investment as she will marry and leave the family anyway. One mother to a 13-year-old rural girl who had stopped attending school after sixth grade explained:

"Why keep sending them on [to school]? She can talk and socialize. She'll be better off getting married" (cited in May 2010: 905).

Even when rural girls do attend school, the different gender expectations of their caregivers directly affect girls' ability to reach high academic attainments. A study conducted in villages in Shaanxi Province revealed, for instance, that rural girls often have to help with housework, while boys only participated in seasonal agricultural activities. Girls start working when they are very young, carrying water buckets with a shoulder pole, cooking meals, and taking care of younger siblings. Never-ending housework directly infringes on these girls' study time, and they have no way of guaranteeing that they will have time to study at home. Girls' safety also means that they are more affected by the remote location of schools (Dong et al. 2008: 67–8).

In contrast to these bleak reports, some studies indicate that gender inequality may be diminishing in some rural areas. Survey data from the Gansu Survey of Children and Families (GSCF), a multi-sited study conducted in 2000 and 2004 among 2,000 rural children aged 9–12 and 13–16, found that girls included in the sample did not face substantially greater access barriers to basic education than those faced by boys. Boys retained a modest enrollment advantage but among enrolled students in 2004, their advantage in educational aspirations was very small. The study also found that girls rivaled or even outperformed boys in academic performance and engagement (Hannum et al. 2009a). Most mothers interviewed for this project also expressed egalitarian views about girls' and boys' rights and abilities, at least in the abstract. However, the vast majority of mothers still expected to rely on sons for old-age support. Compared to boys, Gansu girls also faced somewhat lower (though still very high) maternal educational expectations and a greater likelihood of being called on for household chores (Hannum and Adams 2007).

Additional field studies conducted in rural Gansu from 2003 to 2005 indicate that, although parents sometimes viewed boys as having greater aptitude, they tended to view girls as having more dedication – an attribute parents perceived as being critical for educational success (Hannum et al. 2009a). These finding from one of China's most impoverished regions suggest that rural parents' educational attitudes and practices toward boys and girls are more complicated and less uniformly negative for girls than previously portrayed.

EDUCATION AND IDENTITY AMONG RURAL MINORITY CHILDREN

Another major dimension of educational inequality in rural China is the gap in schooling between Han Chinese and ethnic minority children. China's ethnic minorities currently constitute approximately 113 million or 91.5 percent of the entire population (National Bureau of Statistics of China 2011). Data collected in the 1990s and 2000s shows that children of ethnic minorities, many of whom live in rural remote areas, fall behind Han Chinese in educational enrollment and attainment. In the Tibetan Autonomous Region (TAR), for instance, less than 20 percent of the Tibetans had a primary education and few had much more than that by 1990. At the end of the twentieth century, illiteracy and semi-literacy in the TAR stood slightly above 50 percent, and enrollment in junior secondary school was below 25 percent (Postiglione et al. 2004: 195). Some minority girls, particularly from poor rural families, experience educational disadvantages associated with both their gender and minority status, and have lower enrollment rates than their Han or male counterparts. Rates of school enrollment for Han boys are roughly double those for girls from certain ethnic groups (Hannum 2002; Hannum et al. 2010; Sun and Xu 2010). Even among children who do stay in school, there is a discernible achievement gap in standardized exams in math and Chinese between ethnic minority children compared to the Han student population (Yang et al. 2013).

These abstract statistics reflect the dismal situation in many rural ethnic communities. A recent ethnographic study conducted among Miao and Dong minorities in Southwest China finds, for example, that over 30 percent of students attending middle school in the two village towns included in the study dropped out before completing ninth grade, often with tacit parental consent (Wu 2012a: 2). When asked why he had taken his daughter out of school when she reached eighth grade, a Dong minority father explained:

> We can't afford to keep her in school. Plus we need her to take care of the house chores and her little brother. And she is not really interested in school after all. [...] China already has too many talented people. Even college graduates have a hard time finding jobs these days, let alone our kids in the remote mountain village. The teaching quality here is poor, and we don't have social connections (*guanxi*) to help our kids get jobs. If I keep my daughter in school, she is not going to make it after all. She will still end up working in factories. So why waste the time and the money? We'd rather she started making money now. Besides, schooling makes her lazy and incapable of farm work (cited in Wu 2012a: 9).

This strong disillusionment with the net value of schooling has led a substantial number of minority children in this poverty-stricken area to "opt-out" from state compulsory education and to embrace work as a more realistic path to social mobility (Wu 2012a). As further indicated by this man's statement, the gap between ethnic minority and Han children can be attributed in part to the fact that more ethnic minority children live in rural areas and in the country's western regions, areas that are relatively poor and suffer from low-quality educational infrastructure.

However, this is not the only factor that contributes to low achievements and high dropout rates among rural minority children. A growing number of studies show that cultural, religious, and linguistic differences make it difficult to increase the enrollment and retention rates of children hailing from ethnic minority regions (Hannum 2002; Hannum et al. 2010; Sun and Xu 2010; Hansen 2012; Wu 2012a).

China's 55 minority groups live in 116 designated ethnic autonomous areas, which cover half the country. These regions are authorized to develop their own educational programs, including levels and types of schools, curriculum content, and languages of instruction. In minority areas, the state has to ensure that education promotes access and equality, economic development, cultural autonomy, and national unity. Minority education is supposed to reflect the cultural diversity of China's minorities and improve ethnic relations. It should "make schools more attractive to ethnic communities," promoting a "harmonious multiculturalism" (Postiglione 2011: 91–2).

Though multi-ethnic diversity is a prevalent theme in government propaganda, in reality ethnic mixing is not highly encouraged in PRC state education. Ethnic cultures are celebrated at national events but cultural diversity in schools and wider social settings is carefully managed. State schools are challenged by the responsibility to conserve ethnic minority cultures within a national context that places a premium on Han Chinese cultural capital. Much of the content of school curricula, textbooks and teaching materials used in rural ethnic minority regions would be more familiar to urban schoolchildren of Han Chinese ethnicity than to the ethnic minority children who reside in these regions. While schools in minority areas are supposed to employ bi-lingual education, there is often a shortage of teachers who can teach in the native languages of the minorities. In many areas, ethnic minority cultures and, in particular, minority languages become truncated or even eliminated, a policy that negatively affects the education of ethnic minority children (Postiglione et al. 2004: 197–8; Lin 2008).

A pioneering ethnographic study held among Naxi and Tai communities in Yunnan Province during the 1990s further discovered that state education fosters in some ethnic minority students a perception of themselves as members of a "backward minority." The school had denied the usefulness (sometimes even the existence) of the minorities' languages, histories, religions, forms of education, customs, values, and ethics (Hansen 1999: 160). Rural Han children are also described as "backward" groups whose quality (*suzhi*) the state education attempts to enhance. Nonetheless, there is inevitably an ethnic dimension to the description when it is applied to minority groups whose "backwardness" is frequently explained as a product of cultural deficiencies. Often the languages, cultural practices, and economic life of ethnic minorities are described in texts, media, and oral communication as obstructing the development and modernization of the areas they inhabit. Many rural minority children absorb these messages and have to disassociate themselves from their cultural heritage in order to be academically successful in Chinese schools (Hansen 1999: xiv, 161). Others become alienated and may lose interest and motivation to work at their studies.

This dilemma is well illustrated in Wu's (2012a) study of Miao and Dong ethnic minority children. State schools in the rural areas included in this ethnographic study promote a modern curriculum that is "urban- and outward-bound." Replete with "secular-rational knowledge," the curriculum aims toward "the quality (*suzhi*) citizenry: patriotic and productive, technologically savvy and problem-solving" (Wu 2012a: 15–16). It leaves little room, however, for the teaching of alternative knowledge and skills such as singing, embroideries, and virtuosity in indigenous instruments – skills that were traditionally highly valued among members of these ethnic groups as channels for transmitting ancestral history in an indigenous language that lacks a writing system. Yet the Han-dominated school discourse regards such folk practices at best as symbolic pastimes partially revitalized by tourism. The result is a strong disconnect between the contents of schooling and the actualities of minority children's lives which might in some cases drive families to opt out of the state education system (Wu 2012a).

Due to this disconnect, some minority parents prefer to enroll their children in private schools, including religious schools in monasteries. Such practices may allow children to maintain their ethnic and cultural identities, but the chances of social mobility may be even more limited compared to those of their peers in public schools of either minority or Han descent. Children may learn their language and heritage in these private institutions, but lag in Chinese language acquisition necessary for their advancement to higher education and to career success later in life (Sun and Xu 2010: 45; Postiglione 2011: 93; Yang et al. 2013).

Indeed, the Han-Minority achievement gap is found to be largest among minority students whose primary language is not standard Mandarin (*Putonghua*) (Yang et al. 2013). Upheld as the "language of independence and sophistication," Mandarin is juxtaposed in government and educational discourse with the minority languages that are considered parochial tongues holding minority children back. Minority students, many of whom hear Mandarin for the first time in school, find it difficult to think and converse in the official language, the main medium of instruction from kindergarten onwards for all subjects (Wu 2012a: 17). A rural student of the Naxi minority in Yunnan Province related the problems she encountered upon entering school:

When I was born, people around me spoke the Naxi language all the time. With the guidance of my grandparents, I learnt the […] language. […] In my primary school, the Naxi language was the medium for instruction. Later, I gradually learnt the concept of ethnic group, and I gradually became aware that I was a Naxi.

At the beginning of Junior Secondary, many classmates spoke Chinese. I had a language barrier and I felt very uncomfortable. After a long period, I gradually learnt Chinese. My pronunciation of Chinese was not good. Sometimes, I could not avoid being ridiculed by "Han Chauvinism." I felt that I was discriminated against, and was depressed […] (cited in Yu 2009: 79).

This girl's account conveys the adverse effects of a Mandarin-centered education on the ability of minority children, in particular those who speak a different language, to attain high academic achievements. Han children who speak local dialects are also required to learn *Putonghua* and may face similar difficulties at school. However, for minority children, such language barriers may also impinge upon their ability to construct a coherent sense of social and national identity.

With the universalization of mandatory state schooling, the rise in ethnic tourism, and the increase in television viewing even in the country's remote rural regions, fewer and fewer children in ethnic minority areas can still claim proficiency in folk cultural practices and even their own languages. Many express "an intense desire for acquiring Chinese literacy and the mainstream form of *suzhi* [quality] to function in the larger society" (Wu 2012b: 673). Minority parents, especially cadres, teachers, and business people, often prefer to send their children to Han, rather than to minority schools since Han schools have better facilities and well-trained teachers. Yet, even though Han schools may provide minority children with access to the majority language and culture, integration and access to them are in some instances more illusory than real. In interviews with Uyghur primary school students in the Xinjiang Autonomous Region, children reported that although they had "some Chinese friends," they usually did not mix with Han Chinese students outside the classroom or school sites. Instead, they played with Uyghur friends after school. The language they used during their playtime was Uyghur, with a majority of students watching Uyghur films or Chinese movies with Uyghur subtitles (Tsung 2014: 173, 175).

Even though minority languages, lifestyles, and ways of knowing the world are viewed as "backward and obstructing social progress and quality (*suzhi*) acquisition" (Wu 2012b: 673), they continue to serve as a significant force in shaping minority children's social identification. The disavowal of minority cultural practices by teachers and school curricula therefore contributes to these children's social exclusion and their estrangement from school. Ultimately, it also denies them a place in China's national collectivity.

SCHOOLING, DISABILITY, AND ILLNESS

Children with disabilities are China's "largest minority" (Mcloughlin et al. 2005). According to recent figures, China has 25 million people with physical disabilities, followed by those with hearing, multiple, visual, mental, intellectual, and speech disabilities. There is currently no data on those with autism (cited in Human Rights Watch 2013). The number of Chinese infants with birth defects has recently risen to an average of one million per year and the total number of those afflicted increased by 40 percent from 2001 to 2006. Various studies have linked the rise of birth defects in China to worsening environmental pollution, particularly chemical waste pollution and toxic emissions, as a consequence of the country's scramble to develop its economy (Apter 2014: 8).

Government reports state that 75 percent of people with disabilities live in rural areas; over 40 percent are illiterate, and 15 million live on less than a dollar a day in the countryside (cited in Human Rights Watch 2013). Because of economic restructuring and diminishing health and welfare subsidies, couples in China have been forced to bear the rising, and oftentimes crushing, medical costs of raising a disabled child entirely on their own. Growing numbers of parents in the country's impoverished, rural areas have been unable to cope with this burden, and many have resorted to abandoning their disabled and ill offspring. Alongside girls, disabled children now over-populate China's state-run orphanages (Apter 2014: 9–11).

Rural disabled children who do remain in the care of their families often struggle to receive a basic course of education. China's Compulsory Education Law, passed in 1986, was the first PRC legal code ensuring that all children, including those with disabilities, had the right to receive a free nine-year education. Since then, a series of laws and ordinances promoting the rights of people with disabilities have been promulgated. According to the National Survey on the Status of Disabilities (NSDD) conducted in China in the mid-1980s, approximately six million school-age children were in need of special educational services; only 55 percent received them, however (cited in Mcloughlin et al. 2005: 276). The situation has improved over the last two-and-a-half decades, and by the end of 2012, compulsory education covered 71.9 percent of disabled children in the country, compared to 99.5 percent of eligible children without disabilities who were in primary education (Xinhua News Agency 2014a). As an official from the Ministry of Education recently admitted, however, the country's "special education work in general is still at a low level and suffers from regional imbalance" (cited in Xinhua News Agency 2014a).

Despite the fact that over 80 percent of children with special educational needs reside in rural areas, the majority of special schools are located in large cities, often the capital cities of provinces, which are inaccessible to children with disabilities in the remote countryside. Rural schools that attempt to educate children with severe disabilities are also more likely to provide limited services, if at all. For the most part, children with more severe or multiple disabilities are excluded from what is referred to in China as "Learning in Regular Classrooms" (i.e., mainstream education). Many rural children with severe disabilities simply do not attend school (Mcloughlin et al. 2005: 278, 280; Deng and Poon-McBrayer 2012: 120).

Public recognition of the issue of special education is far from wide-spread in China. Chinese society regards learning as acquiring academic knowledge and skills. However, serious doubts remain in the minds of many people as to whether children with disabilities have the capacity to learn. For children with disabilities living in rural areas, parents are often reluctant to send their children to school because they do not perceive the incentive of a better life or enhanced employment prospects for their children resulting from schooling. Developing self-care and living skills are frequently considered family responsibilities and not the responsibility of the school (Mcloughlin et al. 2005: 279; see also Ellsworth and Zhang 2007; Deng and Poon-McBrayer 2012).

Parents' illness may also affect the education of children from economically vulnerable families, many of whom reside in the countryside. Rural children with a sick father are less likely to be enrolled than others; prior parental ill health is associated with lower household educational spending; and sick parents are more likely to report borrowing for their children's education. Children with ill mothers are more likely to be absent and to work longer in the household, and children with both ill mothers and sick fathers are more likely to work for wages (Hannum et al. 2009b).

The increasing number of HIV/AIDS cases in the Chinese countryside have had particularly negative consequences for children's education. A study conducted in 2006 in a village in central China, where many residents were infected with HIV/AIDS through unhygienic blood collection procedures, examined the effects on children aged between 8 and 17 who had lost one or both parents to AIDS. Many of these children had experienced increased responsibilities in housework and caregiving for family members, including younger siblings, parents with illness, and for elderly grandparents (Zhang et al. 2009). Other studies (e.g., Xu et al. 2010) show that rural children whose families have been affected by HIV/AIDS also suffer from physical fatigue, psychological fear, and anxiety, and possess lower levels of self-esteem. While children's participation in family caregiving does contribute to their personal growth and emotional maturity, these children also show greater tendencies to drop out of school, repeated absences, and an inability to concentrate in class.

PARENTAL MIGRATION AND THE EMERGENCE OF CHINA'S "LEFT-BEHIND" CHILDREN

A final factor that shapes rural children's wellbeing and educational attainment is parental migration. Over the past two decades or so, rural out-migration has kept pace with the increasing demand for labor in China's expanding urban areas. However, due to financial constraints and the dual (rural or urban) household registration system (*hukou*), farmers face many difficulties when they migrate to cities. They have no recognized legal status there, limited access to public services, and are unable to afford decent housing, transportation, and educational costs. For these reasons, many migrant parents choose to leave their children behind, entrusting their care to family members or other persons in the village and creating a new, vulnerable group of children, referred to in Chinese media and academic literature as "left-behind children" (*liushou ertong*) (Ye et al. 2010: 253–4; see also Meyerhoefer and Chen 2011; Murphy 2014b).

The definition of "left-behind" populations in China is unclear. Should the term refer to children with both parents in the city or only one? Should the children be aged under 16 or 18, or even under 21? How long should peasant workers migrate out before their children are counted as being "left behind"? Three months or six months or even one year? Despite the difficulties of terminology, studies suggest that out-migration has created numerous split families in China. Some estimate the numbers at 47 million wives, 45 million elderly, and approximately 58 million children who are left behind, and who make up about 23.8 percent of all rural children. Of these, at least 23 million children are currently of school age (Ye et al. 2013: 1119; Xinhua News Agency 2014b; see also Jia and Tian 2010).

According to a recent survey by the China National Institute for Educational Research, 56.4 percent of left-behind children are raised by grandparents, and 4.1 percent live with other relatives; 0.9 percent with unrelated persons, and some care for themselves, becoming virtual orphans (Ye et al. 2010: 254). A pioneering study that compared left-behind and non-left-behind children in villages in four provinces revealed that in many cases, it is fathers who migrate while children are left in the care of mothers or grandparents. Fathers are also away for longer periods if their work is far from home (Ye et al. 2011). The gender of the child can also play a role in the duration of the parents' migration; one study found that parents of a boy tend to reduce the period of their migration (Démurger and Xu 2013).

Since the mid-2000s, extensive media coverage in China of the plight of these left-behind children (hereafter LBC) has exposed individual cases of abuse, suicide, and accidents (Ye et al. 2010: 254). In recent years, a growing number of academic studies in China and abroad have also started to examine the unique problems LBC face in different areas of life. The next two sections will discuss these problems in detail while presenting the available data on the effects of parental migration on children's education, social relations, and emotional wellbeing.

THE EDUCATION OF "LEFT-BEHIND" CHILDREN

Whether parental migration has a negative impact on the education of rural children is a contentious issue among scholars. One view suggests that it has no major effect; another claims significant negative consequences. Studies which support the former view argue that there is no distinguishable difference in study performances between left-behind and non-left-behind children (Ye et al. 2010: 255–7, 271). A survey by Chen and others (2009) conducted in Shaanxi province, one of China's poorest areas, examined changes in school performance before and after the parents of 1,649 students out-migrated. To their surprise, the researchers found that there was no significant negative effect of parental migration on school performance. In fact, educational performance improved in migrant households in which the father out-migrated. The study also indicated that the effects of migration on children's school performance were not systematically different for wealthy households. Neither were the effects different across households that have one or more than one child.

Another study, which drew on ethnographic work conducted in a village in Jiangxi Province, also found that parental absence due to migration has had no significant influence on children's school learning (Liu Zhijun 2009). The researcher explains these findings by the fact that parental experiences from outside and the pursuit of income may be conveyed in stories and attitudes to children, which may in turn affect children's worldviews. Some LBC understand their parents' hardships and their expectations of them. They see these as a reason to study hard and reach university to find a good job so that they can reduce their parents' burden.

In contrast, other studies have noted a deterioration in LBC's enrollment and academic attainments. Data from the 2005 survey of 1 percent of the population and the "Report on Left-Behind Children in Rural China" conducted by the All-China Women's Federation in 2008, reveals that the majority of LBC attended school at a rate of 92.58 percent for boys and 92.01 percent for girls. However, LBC were still less likely than other rural children to attend school (cited in Gao and Wilson 2010). A sample survey undertaken in 2004 by the Xinhua News Agency and the Education Department of a county in Sichuan found 48 percent of LBC had poor educational achievements, and another 40 percent had below average performance. A further tendency was for a large number of left-behind primary school students to go from being "good students" to "average" and then "bad" following parental migration for work (cited in Ye et al. 2010: 256; see also Lee 2011; Wen and Lin 2012).

Parental absence due to out-migration can negatively affect children's education in several ways. In poor communities, delayed submission of tuition fees is normal for both left-behind and non-left-behind children, though for LBC the delay is usually greater. They must wait for their parent's return to the village before they can pay the school. This causes stress and is often felt as a stigma with an accompanying loss of dignity and confidence. In some cases, exceedingly high expectations on the part of migrant parents can actually demotivate children, alienate them from their parents, and intensify the strains that parental absence already places on the parent–child bond (Murphy 2014b). Others see their parents making money despite their lack of education and seek only to finish school and find a job (Ye et al. 2010: 268, 271; 2011: 94–5).

Studies of different types of migrant families indicate that the child's age and gender and the identity of the migrating family member can shape children's schooling experiences in crucial ways. Children left behind by migrant mothers, but not fathers, are most disadvantaged in terms of health, behavior, and school engagement (Liang et al. 2008; Chen et al. 2009; Wen and Lin 2012). Some studies further note that fathers' migration reduces school enrollment by sons, but has significant positive effects on the academic outcome of daughters (Leng and Park 2010); and that younger children are especially susceptible to the disruptive effects of parental out-migration (Lu 2012).

The academic conditions of LBC looked after by sisters or brothers are at the most risk. These children must fend for themselves, and their lack of supervision makes it more likely for them to be late for school, have poor attitudes to study, play truant, and fail to submit assignments (Ye et al. 2010: 271; see also Liang et al. 2008). As noted, more than half of LBC are left under the guardianship of grandparents, an option usually considered the best. However, the education of these children also suffers. One rural teacher who worked in a poverty-stricken area in southwest China explained:

> Children don't do homework at home. I have already added an extra class in the afternoon for them to finish their homework before going home. Their parents don't care. Most moms and dads have left home for work in cities, and the children have been left with their grandparents. The grandmothers and grandfathers cannot help at all with the children's coursework.

This teacher's complaint reflects a common issue among LBC cared for by grandparents. Many of the grandparent generation in the countryside have no formal education at all or have only primary education. They are unable to help their grandchildren with homework and can afford only to take care of children's physical needs (Ye et al. 2010: 268; 2011: 50; Lee 2011; Lu 2012).

In contrast to urban singletons who, as noted in previous chapters, are often exempt from household duties, all rural children have to undertake household chores. By the age of seven or eight, many have to shoulder adult roles such as cleaning and cooking or looking after younger siblings. Later, children are expected to help out on the farm and perform light agricultural labor (Wu 2012a: 14). When one or both parents migrate to the city, the remaining parent or other guardian must take their share of work. Under excessively heavy workloads, children who are left behind usually have to share some of the burden. Left-behind girls often help the most (Ye et al. 2010: 268; 2011: 61; Chang, Dong, and MacPhail 2011; Meyerhoefer and Chen 2011).

Many children show an understanding of their need to help. However, the increment in the frequency and intensity of work both at home and in the fields limits not only their playing and relaxing time, but also the time they have for study and for enjoying the afterschool resources offered by schools (Ye et al. 2011: 62–3; see also Liang et al. 2008). Ironically, the importance many rural parents give to education and its cost is often cited as a prime reason for migrating. The paradox, however, is that while many rural parents can now afford to send children to school, schoolwork can suffer in the absence of parental support and supervision (Lu 2012; Murphy 2014b).

THE EMOTIONAL WELLBEING AND SOCIAL RELATIONS OF "LEFT-BEHIND CHILDREN"

Parental migration can affect not only children's education but also their physical and emotional wellbeing as well as their relations with the absent parent/s, their caregivers in the countryside and their peers. Parental migration may make some LBC physically better off as their households can afford more items of clothing and more nutritious food (Ye et al. 2011: 57, 67). But the biggest difference between LBC and non-LBC is emotional.

Children left behind with their mother have more opportunity to communicate their feelings than children left with other guardians. However, the extra workload forced upon the mother, even when she can pay for help and exchange labor, inevitably affects the patience, time, and energy she has available to listen to her children. Mother–child communication tends to be brief and superficial and these children are more readily scolded and punished than non-LBC. In the few cases in which fathers are left to do the caring, children on the whole were less cared for and exhibited more behavioral problems and emotional disturbances compared to others (Ye et al. 2011; see also Ye et al. 2010).

Children left behind with grandparents often lack effective communication with their elders and feel that their grandparents do not understand their needs. Moreover, elderly grandparents struggle to meet the emotional needs of children when there is less time for care and no one to share the burdens of that care. Some grandparents provide grandchildren with endless love and spoiling indulgence. They feel sorry for the children because of the absence of their parents, try to satisfy whatever they demand, and protect them even when they misbehave, a degree of indulgence that can cause behavioral problems. Some children disobey their grandparents, contradict them, or keep silent with their elders (Ye et al. 2010, 2011; Silverstein and Cong 2013).

Guardians who are relatives, friends, or neighbors may attend to children's physical needs but do not communicate with them as parents would. Children looked after by sisters or brothers or who must take care of all their own needs (study, household chores, and so on) are at most risk of becoming exhausted physically and emotionally. Those cared for by relatives, usually an uncle or aunt, or by neighbors are often uncomfortable and do not feel at home (Ye et al. 2010, 2011).

The absence of one or both parents leads to feelings of loneliness and insecurity and, in general, LBC are found to be less happy than other children. They are not as free to play and they feel more acutely the pressures and worries about household life and their parents' health and safety. Some experience their family life as less lively and interesting compared to non-LBC children. Many express envy of the more complete family life of non-LBC children and long to live together with their parents in the countryside or in the city. However, they often repress these thoughts and feelings (Ye et al. 2010).

Many LBC have little opportunity for real contact with an absent parent and, although they understand the need for the parent to leave, they can become alienated psychologically from the migrating parent due to the long periods of separation. The long distances and prohibitive cost of travel often mean that many migrant parents visit their children only for the Chinese New Year or Moon Cake Festival, for family emergencies, or at peak agricultural periods when their labor is needed by wives or aged parents. In general, however, migrating parents spend only short periods with their children. A few days interacting with them cannot compensate for the missing care and affection or lack of communication that prevailed when they were away. As time goes on, some LBC become indifferent to their guardians' attempts to communicate with them. Others feel they have been abandoned (Ye et al. 2010: 254, 267, 271–2; see also Jia and Tian 2010; Liu et al. 2010; Hu et al. 2011).

The social ties of LBC also change after their parents migrate. Many become distanced from their parents psychologically and grow closer to other contacts. When confronted with difficulties or troubles with their studies or in life more generally, young LBC children are more likely to turn to teachers for help than other children do. As they grow older, the peer group becomes more important for them than for other children. LBC often seek help from their friends since, although guardians may care for material needs, they ignore or are ignorant of the need for emotional security (Ye et al. 2010: 256–7, 270).

The lack of moral guidance from parents during the crucial period of growing up can also affect children's social nature. LBC have been found to display poor social skills, poor self-reliance, and low self-esteem, as well as a lack of enthusiasm for participating in school collective activities. They may be easily influenced by anti-social modes of behavior that can lead to delinquency. Due to a lack of parental control and education, these children may also develop poor health habits, such as smoking (Lee 2011). Some become addicted to electronic games or involved in extortion and drug taking. Others suffer from depression in rates which are higher compared to non-LBC or migrant children living with their parents in the city (Ye et al. 2010: 256–7; see also Liu Zhijun 2009; Jia et al. 2010; Leng and Park 2010; Liu et al. 2010; Guo et al. 2012).

In some cases, children's feelings of abandonment and helplessness can lead to tragic consequences. A recent report by Xinhua News Agency relates, for instance, the story of nine-year old Xiao Lin, whose divorced parents had been working away from their village in Anhui Province for years. According to witnesses, the boy went to school to pick up his academic report alone, while most of his schoolmates were accompanied by their parents, and "looked a bit disappointed by his scores." Lin's mother had phoned home that night, saying she would not be home for the Lunar New Year, the second year Lin was not going to see her. Later that night, the boy killed himself in the toilet, just days away from Spring Festival. He left no note. According to the same report, a day before Lin killed himself, two "left-behind" girls aged nine and ten in central Hunan Province "secretly took a train to meet their parents in Zhaoqing City in southern Guangdong Province." And in November of the same year, an 11-year-old boy from Hubei Province "went to look for his parents in Beijing with less than 100 yuan (US$16.5) in his pockets that he had saved up. The boy was sent home by police" (ShanghaiDaily.com 2014).

The lack of family closeness and protection also places left-behind children at a greater risk from the dangers of sexual assault, child abduction, and child trafficking (Ye et al. 2010: 254; Shen et al. 2013: 37; see also Cunningham 2014). The phenomenon of trafficking in humans, and particularly children, re-emerged in China in the early 1980s. In 2004, for instance, 41 percent of all recorded trafficking incidents in China involved children, and it is estimated that 70,000 children are kidnapped in China every year and traded on the black market for adoption or forced labor (cited in Shen et al. 2013: 32). Rural children left in the care of old and weak grandparents, older siblings, or who are required to fend for themselves, form a major target group for these criminal activities (China Labour Bulletin 2007: 7).

Local governments in some of China's provinces have been proactive in addressing the problems of rural LBC. Initiatives include organizing parent–teacher contracts outlining the needs of children and the transfer of guardianship; providing teacher mentors for children; setting up activity centers for LBC; and organizing parental schools and seminars on communicating with children affected by migration. Some local authorities have teamed up with various non-governmental organizations (NGOs) and private enterprises to offer free lunches to LBC. Others have instigated army-and-police joint defense measures to increase the security of these children, and have compiled a system of files and contact cards for children who have disappeared or are presumed kidnapped and sold (Chan Aris 2009; Ye et al. 2010: 254, 272; 2013: 1131–2). However, local governments in many of China's impoverished, rural regions continue to lack the human and financial resources needed to effectively implement these policies and programs, leaving LBC in these areas in a particularly vulnerable position.

CONCLUSION

As this chapter has shown, the rise in incomes, inequality, and educational costs in recent years has had mixed consequences for the lives of rural children in China. On the one hand, the level of education in rural areas is increasing rapidly and a large majority of rural children aged 7–16 (the age of compulsory schooling) are now enrolled in schools (Hannum et al. 2010: 143). The number of rural children excluded from primary and junior middle schools has also dramatically dropped – an accomplishment that should not be minimized.

On the other hand, exclusion from education before the age of seven continues to exist and is almost entirely a rural problem. Among the children who remain locked out of access to compulsory education, the vast majority are rural and many are children of ethnic minorities residing in China's poorest western regions. Access to secondary schooling has risen in the countryside, but the gap between rural and urban access remains (Hannum et al. 2010: 143–4; Hansen 2012: 166).

Although gender inequality in educational attainment has narrowed over the past several decades, it still exists, particularly in the countryside. While Chinese girls face no significant gender inequality in urban areas, and a majority can now attain nine years of compulsory education, they still face inequality in rural areas, especially when they reach senior middle school or beyond (Zeng et al. 2014). As this chapter further shows, parental migration has not helped to alleviate the rural–urban gap in children's education, and in some respects has even exacerbated it, while negatively affecting children's personal and social wellbeing.

The Chinese government certainly recognizes the severity of these problems, and over the last decade has introduced a raft of policies, laws, and regulations to provide better care for rural children, especially girls and minorities, and to reduce inequalities in areas of child welfare and education. The CCP's new leadership, headed by President Xi Jinping and Premier Li Keqiang, has recently reiterated its commitment to improving conditions in the countryside, while vowing to increase by at least 10 percent the number of rural students from poor areas enrolled in key universities. According to official reports, since 2010, the government has also invested 61.8 billion yuan (US$10.1 billion) into improving schoolhouses and educational facilities in rural areas, including those populated by ethnic minorities (Xinhua News Agency 2014c). In early 2014, it was further announced that a new plan to ensure that at least 90 percent of children with visual, hearing, and intellectual disabilities enjoy free primary and middle school education would be implemented by the end of 2016 (Xinhua News Agency 2014a, 2014c).

These are important steps, which may improve the life conditions of rural children in the country's most impoverished areas and allow them to exercise their basic rights to education and to growing up in a healthy, supportive environment. Like their peers in the city, Chinese rural children have been accorded various new rights under the law, and receive encouragement to foster their autonomy and individuality. But their ability to exercise these rights and to fully develop their individual potential remains relatively limited, in large part due to uneven structural conditions rather than to "backward" peasant thinking or their "low *suzhi*," as government and media discourse claim. Recognizing the limitations facing them, many rural children dream of escaping the countryside and constructing new identities for themselves through university studies or a lucrative city job. As the next chapter will indicate, however, rural children who have migrated with their parents to the city have not necessarily fared better than those in the countryside.

6 | China's Migrant Children: Opportunity and Exclusion

Over the past three-and-a-half decades, China has transformed from a relatively immobile society to one in which more than 10 percent of the population are migrants. Although the country's mobility rate is still low compared to that of advanced industrial economies, the sheer size of the migrant flows and their consequences have already affected economic growth and urban development (Fan 2008: 65). According to official statistics, the level of China's urbanization reached 53.73 percent at the end of 2013. However, at least 245 million of the country's urban residents lack urban registration records (*hukou*) (National Bureau of Statistics of China 2014), and some put the number of this "floating population" of internal migrants as high as 260 million (UNDP China 2013: 1).

Internal migrant workers now comprise about one-third of China's labor force. Since the 1980s, they have been streaming into urban areas seeking employment and a better life. Their cheap labor has fueled Chinese economic growth over the last several decades but their rural residency papers have prevented them from accessing the social services that urban governments provide to local city dwellers (Ming 2014: 5). As discussed in chapter 5, a majority of migrant parents have therefore chosen to leave their children in the countryside where they are entitled to state-sponsored education, health, and social services. Since the 1990s, however, increasing numbers of migrant workers have elected to bring their children with them or to raise their city-born children in urban areas. The presence of large numbers of migrant children in the cities, especially children without local *hukou*, has created major problems for these children and their families.

This chapter considers the unique difficulties that migrant children face in the cities, as well as their perceptions of these difficulties, their expectations, and their social identities. As the discussion will show, the migration experience has opened new educational opportunities and more avenues for carving out new identities for some migrant children. However, the restrictions from both the *hukou* system and the urban educational system discriminate against migrant children (Liang and Chen 2007; Chan Aris 2009). One immediate difficulty facing migrant families (regardless of children's place of birth), concerns the public, particularly compulsory, education of their children who often face higher tuition fees and exclusion from public schools. Migrant girls, in particular, suffer from lower school enrollment, lower educational attainments, and higher rates of child labor.

The migration experience has also exposed children to the negative social stigmas of permanent urban residents who frequently consider these children to be of lower "quality" (*suzhi*) compared to those of urban descent (Woronov 2004; 2009b; Chan Aris 2009). As the discussion will demonstrate, such attitudes have had damaging effects for migrant children's emotional wellbeing and social identities, and have made it hard for them to feel "at home" in the city or to assert their individual interests and desires at home and at school.

CHILDREN AND INTERNAL MIGRATION IN CHINA

The first large-scale movement of laborers from the countryside in the late 1980s and early 1990s consisted almost entirely of single adults; either men entering the service or construction industries, or young women going into service or factory work (Davin 1998; Solinger 1999). As China industrialized and the urban–rural income gap grew in the mid-1990s, more migrants have chosen to switch to urban employment entirely and to move their households to urban areas (Woronov 2009b: 96). This trend has become more dominant in recent years. Exact statistics of the numbers of migrant children now living in China's urban areas are difficult to come by because not all are registered with local authorities. Some estimates, however, put the figure at more than 22 million migrant children aged 14 years or under, accounting for approximately 10 percent of the national population of children within this age range (Wang 2008; Woronov 2009b; Lan 2014; Ming 2014; Xiong 2015). Two of China's largest cities, Beijing and Shanghai, now have about 450,000 and 500,000 migrant children, respectively (Luo 2013; Ming 2014: 5).

Parents' decision on whether to leave their children behind in the countryside or take them to the cities is often shaped by regional variations in costs and benefits (Wang et al. 2008). There are indications, however, that the gender of the child plays a role in the decision. According to a 2013 study by the All-China Women's Federation, the sex ratios of migrant children varies when divided by different age groups, especially when compared with those of "left-behind" children. For kindergarten children and those in compulsory education, the proportion of boys is higher in migrant children than in "left-behind" children. In contrast, for children who were at a post-compulsory education age, normally older than 15, the proportion of girls was greater among migrant children. These findings suggest that rural parents practice gender selection when deciding whether to migrate with their children (cited in UNDP China 2013: 22; see also Connelly et al. 2012).

Another significant factor in the decision to bring children to the city is whether the husband and wife are able to live together. Those who cohabit are highly likely to take their children to their city of employment. As China's migrant population ages, couples from different provinces who meet in their urban employment locations are also increasingly common. Because they do not share a rural hometown, many choose to raise their children locally in the urban areas. Finally, the option of leaving children behind in rural hometowns is also contingent on the availability of caregivers in the countryside, usually the grandparents. For some migrant households, however, the grandparents are themselves migrants working in the cities, another factor leading young rural migrants to move with their whole families (Wang et al. 2008; see also Ming 2014: 15).

The migration process in China is often serial and even cyclical, with family members following each other between their hometowns and cities (Connelly et al. 2012). Migrant children, on average, arrive in the city at the age of six, the official age for starting formal education, but their numbers tend to decline with age (Wei and Hou 2010). The trend of reverse migration (moving back to the countryside) is most significant when migrant children reach grade seven (Lan 2014: 243–4; Ming 2014: 10; see also Woronov 2009b). This pattern is a product of migrant children's lack of local registration (*hukou*) status. Children to migrant parents who were themselves born in the city or those who have spent more than half their lives in cities are often still registered as peasants on their *hukou*. Some do not have a *hukou* registered anywhere, because their migrant parents living in the cities have had more than one child in violation of the One-Child Policy. As the next sections will show, the lack of urban *hukou* shapes migrant children's schooling experiences in the city, creates considerable barriers to their educational attainments and their chances of future mobility, and molds their social identities in crucial ways.

MIGRANT CHILDREN'S EDUCATION

The educational challenges faced by migrant children in the cities are formidable. Until the mid- or even late 2000s, children of migrant families could only attend urban public schools if they paid exorbitant "sponsor fees" (*zanzhu fei*). These fees were commonly tens of thousands of RMB at a time when an average migrant worker was only making a few hundred RMB a month (Ming 2014: 27). Even if their parents could afford the fees, some migrant children, especially those who are also disabled, found the doors to state schools closed to them entirely (Froissart 2003).

In 2003, China's State Council urged local governments to take responsibility for the provision of nine-year compulsory education for migrant children without charging discriminatory tuition fees. However, most local governments ignored their responsibility to guarantee equal education for migrant children, believing any such concessions would harm the quality of education in their jurisdictions (Wang 2007: 115). In 2008, the State Council again demanded that all local governments comply with the Compulsory Education Act, and provide free and accessible compulsory education for all migrant children with valid documents (Lan 2014: 249).

Since then, official statistics do indicate a rise in the proportion of migrant children admitted to public schools in some cities (Pong 2015: 65–9, 130). However, city public schools often lack the spaces to satisfy the demand of all migrant students without additional government investment, which leaves room for the schools to continue charging migrant families illegally. In addition to levying high fees, local governments and schools also use paperwork to limit migrant children's access to public schooling. Each school has a quota for the number of migrant children it will admit, and migrant parents have to seek out schools on their own and compete for available slots. As a student's registration at primary school is not linked to his/her registration at secondary school, it is especially difficult for migrant children to gain entry to public junior middle school (Wang 2007, 2008; Woronov 2009b).

Migrant children have also not been allowed to take the public senior middle school entrance examination in their host cities, effectively barring them from attending local senior middle schools regardless of their academic performance or the number of years they have lived in the city (Lan 2014: 258; Ming 2014: 9). In recent years, some large cities have opened another route for migrant children wishing to continue their education in the city. Starting in 2009, for instance, migrant children in the city of Shanghai could enroll in public vocational schools. However, only a limited number of subjects, such as hotel management, cooking, hairdressing, car repair, and electroplating, are available for migrant students (Lan 2014: 260; see also Woronov 2011; Hansen and Woronov 2013).

The labor market opportunities and future chances for the upward mobility of migrant children have been further blocked by the *hukou* restrictions of the college examination system. Until 2013, these restrictions had officially barred even those migrant children who managed to attend senior public middle schools from taking the college entrance examination (*gaokao*) in their place of residence (China Daily 2014). The policy to exclude non-locals was originally intended to ensure fairness in the higher education system, as each province has different cut-off scores; in the past, many students took the *gaokao* in provinces where these scores are lower. However, the policy has effectively robbed migrant students of the chance to take the *gaokao* where they live and go to school, disrupting and often blocking their passage through the education system (Lan 2014; Ming 2014).

Due to these structural barriers, since the 1990s, large numbers of migrant children in Chinese cities have been attending private, profit-driven schools operated by migrant entrepreneurs for migrant students only. This trend has continued even after the government's introduction of new policies, laws, and regulations meant to make public education more accessible to migrant children. According to recent reports, about one-third of the migrant students in Beijing and one-half of those in Shanghai enroll in migrant schools, while a minority are placed in state-subsidized private schools for migrant students (Lan 2014: 249, 253; Ming 2014: 5, 9, 28; see also Woronov 2009b; Pong 2015). As the next section will show, many of the private migrant schools are unlicensed and supply students rudimentary knowledge and education. They may offer children a supportive environment but fail to integrate them into local urban life.

CHINA'S PRIVATELY RUN "MIGRANT SCHOOLS"

Recent studies of the privately run migrant schools reveal that conditions in these schools are generally very poor. While it is legal to operate schools outside the state sector, completing the necessary transactions to be officially registered with government education authorities can be arduous and expensive, and many migrant schools are not formally registered (Woronov 2009b: 98). Some schools have rented space from standard government schools and thus have had access to their facilities but most exist in much more tenuous circumstances. Migrant schools are sometimes housed in abandoned warehouses, dilapidated buildings or even open land. Facilities are largely rudimentary at best, with many lacking even blackboards or chalk. Some have no playgrounds, others no running water. As many as 50–80 students may huddle in one classroom with poor lighting, and sometimes one teacher teaches several classes in the same room. Local authorities have repeatedly shut migrant schools for violating health, fire, or other regulations (Kwong 2004: 1083; 2011: 877; see also Chan Aris 2009; Lan 2014; Ming 2014; Pong 2015; Xiong 2015).

Teachers' qualifications, the structure and contents of the curriculum, and students' attainments in the private migrant schools also differ from those found in city public schools or in rural areas. For instance, in the migrant primary school studied by Woronov (2009b: 101–1) in Beijing, teachers – often young migrant women who were vocational middle-school (*zhongzhuan*) graduates – taught all the lessons in the curriculum; in standard Beijing public schools, each subject was taught by a different teacher. Different age ranges were grouped together and the students did not follow a disciplined schedule. The migrant school also did not offer children access to computers or to the extracurricular enrichment programs, such as chess, calligraphy, or martial arts, which are extremely popular in Beijing public schools.

Another recent study on migrant schools in the city of Shanghai similarly found important differences in the learning environment provided by privately run migrant schools and city public schools. Whereas the pictures and slogans posted on the walls of the public school emphasized values such as student autonomy and self-discipline in conformity with the dictates of the "education for quality" program, the walls of the private migrant school lacked these messages. They only displayed the school administration's notices about school fees, lunch and transportation charges, and various regulations regarding student safety, reflecting the migrant school's stress on student compliance with authority (Xiong 2015: 171).

Children who attend migrant schools do acquire basic knowledge and language skills (Kwong 2006: 172). However, their achievements in subjects such as Chinese and mathematics are often lower than those of city children or migrant children attending urban public schools (Wang and Holland 2011; Chen and Feng 2012; Yao and Hao 2013). A recent study by Fang and others (2012) compared the academic performances of students in Beijing migrant schools and in poor rural public schools in Shaanxi Province. The researchers discovered that, although the migrant students in Beijing outperformed students in the rural public schools when they arrived in the city, they gradually lost ground to rural students due to the poorer school resources and teachers in the migrant schools.

Some studies (e.g., Kwong 2006: 172) suggest that the children attending the migrant schools are relatively mature and highly motivated, interested in their studies and exhibit curiosity about the world around them. Others, though, have shown that children attending migrant schools tend to be more pessimistic about their academic futures and less motivated to excel in their schoolwork. Many opt to abandon their educational aspirations once they discover that there is no chance of furthering their studies. Compared to their peers in public schools, a greater proportion of these students also hope to find work immediately after graduating from junior middle school (Xiong 2015: 171–2).

Despite their low standard of teaching and poor facilities, the migrant schools do enjoy one obvious advantage: they have been able to provide an education where the local government in the city has failed to do so. The schools also function as community centers and as informal social welfare institutions for migrant families (Hou 2002; Kwong 2004; Yan 2005). Some provide transport to and from school, and others keep the children in school until the parents pick them up after work. If the family moves away, the schools often refund unused tuition (Kwong 2004; Woronov 2009b).

Many migrant parents therefore tend to report satisfaction with the migrant schools (Woronov 2009b: 107; see also Kwong 2006). Children, especially in the lower grades, also say that they are "happy" in these schools because they are located in their migrant community and feel they are among "their own people" (Kwong 2011: 877). This sentiment reflects the fact that despite a considerable lack of resources and their inability to prepare children for middle school due to a lack of proper certification, migrant schools do offer important advantages over city public schools (Woronov 2009b: 108; Pong 2015: 134). These advantages are not only financial but also social, as migrant children often face considerable discrimination even when they are allowed to attend city public schools.

MIGRANT CHILDREN'S EXPERIENCES AT THE PUBLIC SCHOOL

Public schools enjoy state funding, better teachers, and better physical facilities than the privately run migrant schools. However, migrant children who attend city public schools often experience spatial segregation and suffer from a hostile environment that does not allow them proper study. As discussed in chapters 2 and 5, the powerful public discourse on *suzhi* (quality) marginalizes Chinese peasants as an underclass because of their alleged lack of "cultivation." This discourse also serves to justify differential treatment toward migrant children who live with their parents in the city (Woronov 2009b; Lan 2014: 247).

Teachers and administrators at the public schools are often reluctant to accommodate students from the countryside because of their supposed "low quality" (*suzhi tai di*). When used in relation to migrant children, this expression may refer not only to the mediocre academic level of children, attributable to the state of the rural education system, but also to what city teachers regard as an inherent "flaw" of the migrant children due to a considerable "backwardness in their process of civilization" (Froissart 2003). Teachers and staff at public schools which do admit migrant children may also be more inclined to impose "*suzhi* cultivation" even on migrant children who were born in the city or who had limited exposure to rural hometowns or migrant schools (Lan 2014: 262).

In some public schools, migrant children find themselves lumped together in separate class sections and not permitted to study with urban children in the same classrooms. In other cases, migrant children are confined to a leased territory with second-class facilities, equipment, and resources. Their teachers, many of whom had transferred from closed-down privately run migrant schools, receive substantially lower salaries than the teachers at the regular public school (Wang 2007: 114; Lan 2014: 252).

Some city school administrators defend such segregation by claiming that they "protect migrant children's self-esteem." More importantly, however, local city parents view schools that accept a substantial number of migrant students as compromised in the competitive race for academic results, and may pressure public school staff to separate the children. Teachers, who are evaluated on the progress of their own students but not on the performance of the migrant children, often oblige (Wang 2007: 114; Lan 2014: 252–3). Some urban teachers put pressure on the school principals to expel the migrants (Froissart 2003). Others unconsciously deliver the message that local students are superior to rural migrants. In a revealing ethnographic study conducted by Holly Ming (2014), one eighth-grader living with his migrant parents in Beijing told the researcher:

> [T]here was a teacher who was irresponsible towards us non-local students. That is, in general, when we attended class, no matter how attentively we listened to his teaching, he would not look at us even a bit. It was as if he did not want to look at us. Then, when we had exams, you know? Sometimes he didn't even care looking at our examination results (cited on p. 70).

As shown in this boy's account, some teachers in the city public schools simply ignore the migrant children. Although there are city teachers who associate migration with modern moral values and with an adventurous, entrepreneurial spirit of capitalism, many others reinforce a hierarchical and moral distinction between urbanity and ruralism (Lin 2011). As a result, many migrant children have lower educational attainments than local students, an outcome that only reinforces the stereotype that rural children are "unintelligent" (Koo 2012; Lan 2014).

Outstanding migrant students often do not receive the appropriate credit. They cannot be nominated as "three-good students" (good in academic work, character, and physical ability), a coveted honor for Chinese students. Some may be good enough to represent their schools in local competitions, but as non-locals they have to compete using the names of local students. They cannot take part in extracurricular

activities and cannot become members in the national children's movement, the Young Pioneers (Kwong 2006: 170).

The treatment that urban parents, and some teachers and school
administrators, give migrant children has inspired local students to
treat them in a similar way. Even when they attend the same school,
urban students continue to underscore differences in culture and status
between themselves and migrant classmates (Lan 2014: 262). In the
lower grades, some local students see migrant children as inferior and
ostracize them during play (Kwong 2011: 876). Older students may
be concerned about migrant children becoming their future "competi-
tors." One eighth-grader who was one of the top students of her cohort
in a Shanghai public school that admitted migrant children related:

> [T]here are very good students even among the non-locals. We are not
> like them, but it is a good thing that the teachers educate them. The
> thing that is not so good about it is that we face more competitors. They
> should return to their hometowns for high school, but they could still
> get into colleges in Shanghai if their grades are good enough. We might
> face the migrant students in the future. … They can jump out and
> become our competitors. We have the same starting line, and we are
> racing forward together, like athletes – we would face the same finishing
> line (cited in Ming 2014: 180).

This girl's views reflect the ingrained and widely held sense of entitlement among many local city children to the privileges they enjoy (Ming
2014). They further indicate local children's skewed sense of fairness
over college admissions. In reality, competition for spots at China's top
universities is less fierce in Beijing and Shanghai than it is in China's
rural provinces. Under China's intensely competitive university entrance
exams, each province and the major cities, such as Beijing and Shanghai, devise and score their own exams. Students indicate the universities and colleges to which they want to apply, and their test scores are

used to allocate spots, with the central authorities setting quotas indicating the number of applicants schools should admit from each area. Because the elite universities located in the largest cities reserve more spots for students with a local *hukou*, the lowest qualifying score for a local test-taker may be vastly lower than the score required from rural student or a migrant student hailing from provinces such as Henan or Jiangsu (Buckley 2015).

Despite these structural barriers, migrant children enrolled in city public schools tend to believe that their life opportunities can be affected by knowledge. Those in the lower grades often show greater willingness to study hard and achieve better results compared to children attending privately run migrant schools (Xiong 2015: 167). However, the academic performance and morale of these students tend to deteriorate as they move through each grade in public middle school and become more aware of their slim chances to enter a public senior middle school in the city (Ming 2014). Many believe that only migrant students without educational futures stay in the city, and those who stay would have no educational future. As a result, they give up working hard for academic achievement even before junior middle school graduation. As one ninth-grade migrant student explained:

> When we were in seventh grade, we still studied hard. ... Because we were simpler then, so were interested in learning still. That changed in eighth grade. [...] When I got into eighth grade, I did not behave as well ... I became very realistic. Since I really could not take the high school entrance examination, [...] I did not want to waste my efforts anymore. Since there is no chance to get in a high school, there is no point to work so hard. [...] My classmates think the same too (cited in Ming 2014: 120).

Like this girl, many migrant children are reduced to choosing either to stay in the city with their families, but give up the possibility of a university education in the future, or return to the countryside without their parent/s. Migrant students who perform best academically and who have the greatest family resources are often sent back to their hometowns during their middle school years or even earlier. But they too face educational obstacles due to the use of different syllabi and textbooks. Most of these returned migrants do not attend a senior middle school of their choice, one that would give them a reasonable chance of entering university upon graduation (Ming 2014: 11; see also Lan 2014: 259; Xiong 2015).

Children who do not perform well academically may enroll in vocational city schools. However, such schools often channel migrant children into exploitative and oppressive labor conditions (Lan 2014: 260; see also Woronov 2011; Hansen and Woronov 2013). Those who hail from relatively poor families may stay in the city but drop out of school altogether to engage in paid labor or to help their parents earn money.

MIGRANT CHILD LABOR

As factory suppliers and local enterprises have competed to lower the costs of their just-in-time production and raise the quality of their products, China has seen an increase in incidences of child labor, particularly since the 1990s. There are no official statistics on child labor in China but estimates put the number of child workers at between 10 million and 20 million (Pun 2005; see also China Labour Bulletin 2007). A significant proportion of China's child laborers (defined as those under 16 years of age) are rural migrants who take part in light mechanical work and labor-intensive manufacture of products such as toys, garments, and plastics (Pun 2005; Liang and Chen 2007: 29; Liao and Hong 2011). Data from the 2002 China Nine-City Survey of Migrant Children, which studied 7,817 children, indicated that child labor was relatively high among the migrant population with as many as 15 percent of the children working in one city. The survey also showed that migrant girls aged 12–15 were more likely to be engaged in paid labor than boys of the same age (Liang et al. 2008).

As noted in previous chapters, the Chinese government has become more aware of the issue of children's rights, and since the 1990s has promulgated a series of laws committed to protecting minors' interests. However, labor regulation is not effectively enforced. Because child workers lack basic legal knowledge and an awareness of their rights, they are often unable to make demands on their own behalf regarding wages and working conditions. They have little understanding of legally mandated work times or local minimum wage standards. Afraid of being caught and losing their job, children also collaborate with their employers when faced with government inspections (China Labour Bulletin 2007: 12, 14–15).

Many migrant children who are not wage earners still engage in unpaid labor to assist their parents and older siblings. They perform household chores or help their families to operate small factories, workshops, grocery shops, restaurants, and so on in the city (China Labour Bulletin 2007: 6). An ethnographic study of migrant children in Beijing documents that some migrant children attended school during the week, but parents' busy work schedules meant that the children rarely went to parks or other recreational spaces in the weekend (Woronov 2009b). Instead, they worked as babysitters for younger siblings or nieces and nephews, cooking and cleaning, and helping to sell fruits and vegetables in the market. While many migrant families included in the study sent their 11–12-year-old children back to their home villages to continue their education after the primary school level, other children remained in Beijing with their parents and started to work full-time as unskilled laborers.

Most of the Beijing and Shanghai migrant students interviewed in a study conducted by Holly Ming in 2014, similarly reported helping their parents with household chores or even income-generating tasks, especially in households that owned small businesses. While migrant and local students in the two cities spent roughly the same amount of time on homework, migrant students in Beijing and Shanghai spent 71 percent and 36 percent more time, respectively, on household chores than did their local peers (p. 63). Both migrant parents and their children attributed migrant students' helpful behaviors to their life experiences: their rural backgrounds and the serial migration process. For instance, an eighth-grader who had moved to Beijing three years earlier explained to the researcher that she was in charge of cleaning their house because her parents had to go to work. "I started helping with housework when I was about 12, before I moved over from my hometown," the girl related, "[b]ecause our hometown is a rural village, our father required us to start helping out earlier. That is why he taught us to cook for ourselves, and other tasks" (cited in Ming 2014: 65).

As indicated by this girl's account, the unstable, unpredictable job conditions of many migrant families in China have led to children's early maturity, immense gratitude for help offered, and a desire to be helpful to their parents. Frequently, however, this desire comes at the expense of schooling. In extreme cases, the failure to educate migrant children results in children living on the streets. The Ministry of Civil Affairs has estimated that in the mid-2000s China had over 152,000 street children, most in urban areas (Liang and Chen 2007: 29; see also Cheng and Lam 2010). Some homeless children turn to the selling of fake goods, scrap collecting, or performing in crowded areas, such as railway stations, markets, and public squares, to subsist (Apter 2014: 13). Others engage in begging or street crime. These street children, many of whom are boys hailing from migrant or disharmonious families, are at a particularly high risk of falling victim to child trafficking for labor or sexual exploitation.

According to statistics from Guizhou City, for instance, the vast majority of more than 200 trafficked children reported in 2001 were from migrant families. In addition, from January 2002 to May 2004 of 352 missing children at the age of one to seven, 99.4 percent were children of migrant families. Statistics from Beijing, Shanghai and other large cities reveal similar trends (cited in Shen et al. 2013: 37, 40–1).

In response to the low school enrollment, high dropout rate, and increasing instances of child labor and street children among migrant populations, some officials have accused migrant parents of ignoring the educational interests of their children when they move with them to the city. Local city residents also frequently blame the migrant children's parents for having little interest in or respect for education (Woronov 2009b: 109). Such accusations are far from true, however, as studies find that many migrant parents have high aspirations for their children. They see education as inherently good and a way to allow their children to climb the social ladder and leave the migrant community (Kwong 2006: 171; see also Ming 2014). One survey found, for instance, that 62 percent of migrant parents would like their children to receive a college education or higher (Chen and Liang 2007: 129).

Parents who harbor such aspirations have been found to protest and petition against urban discriminatory educational policies (Pong 2015: 156–7). Others cling to the hope that the policies might change in time for their children's senior middle school enrollment. Many are prepared to take drastic measures or pay exorbitant sums so that their children could attend a public senior middle school, but few are successful (Ming 2014: 10–11). Migrant parents have little local social capital and find it difficult to locate the necessary information and navigate the process of school selection, which often requires reliance on *guanxi* (personal networks). Migrant parents also earn less than local parents, and have more erratic and unpredictable income streams. They seldom have the time or knowledge to help their children with schoolwork beyond verbally emphasizing the importance of an education (Lan 2014: 253; Pong 2015: 156). Faced with such difficulties and the formidable structural barriers that block children's progress in the education system, some poor migrant parents have little choice but to send the child to work.

MIGRANT CHILDREN'S IDENTITIES AND SOCIAL RELATIONS

Rural parents' decision to take their children with them to the city rather than leave them in the countryside often rests on the belief that children will be emotionally better off living with parents than under the ineffective watch of grandparents or distant relatives (Woronov 2009b). However, as parents work excessively long hours in arduous jobs, leaving little or no time for their families, some migrant children have been found to suffer from psychological problems, including separation anxiety, depression, and Internet addiction (Chan Aris 2009; Fu et al. 2009; Guo et al. 2012).

Others become embittered and deeply frustrated because of the structural barriers and cultural exclusion they experience in the city. Some migrant children, especially those who have spent most of their lives in cities, may harbor very different career aspirations and quality of life concerns compared to their parents. Contrary to the perceptions of some city-dwellers, children of migrant workers are often unwilling to take the type of low-skilled jobs usually accepted by their migrant parents. Instead, they show preferences for white-collar and professional jobs. At the earlier grades, migrant children's dream jobs are often similar to those of their local peers in the cities. They want to become professionals, academics, pop stars, Olympic athletes, and so on. However, the expectations of migrant children and local city children increasingly diverge as they grow older and confront the realities of the dual-track education system (Ming 2014; Xiong 2015). Migrant children who attend vocational schools often recognize that the education they receive is inferior or even illegitimate (Woronov 2009b: 108; Hansen and Woronov 2013: 246). They and others resent the unfairness of the situation and report feeling like "second-class citizens" in their own country (Froissart 2003; Woronov 2009b).

This sentiment is also a product of children's marginalization by permanent city dwellers. Some city people consider all migrant newcomers "rough, ill-mannered and rude; dirty and oblivious of the simplest rules of hygiene" (Kwong 2011: 873). Worse still, they are blamed for the traffic congestion, damage to the cityscape, and thefts and crimes in the city. Migrant children often share the blame and become targets of prejudice and discrimination (Lan 2014: 256). A seventh-grader from a migrant family who attended a public school in Shanghai described his experience:

> I used to have some local classmates. I like to hang out with migrant friends more because the parents of locals did not welcome migrant children to play with their children. The Shanghai locals always feel that is dangerous for their own children to play with migrant children. Sometimes they did not even let us enter their houses. They were worried that we would steal their things [...]. No one has ever lost anything because of migrant children playing at their houses, but the local parents have this stereotype. I do not like it. I think you should trust others (cited in Ming 2014: 74).

Though this student added that he had only experienced discrimination by the local parents, never their children, in this prejudicial climate, close proximity between migrant and city children in the public school often only reinforces these stereotypes (Kwong 2006: 170). In mixed schools and classes, social segregation shadows the daily encounters between migrant children and urban students. Boundary marking is especially salient when imposed upon those migrant children who were born in the countryside and who display marked differences, such as dark skin or hometown accents and dialects. Therefore, some migrant parents encourage children to discard apparent markers of cultural differences associated with their hometown (Lan 2014: 256, 262).

In the more amicable climate of the privately run migrant schools, children do share a sense of camaraderie but attending such schools does little to socially integrate the migrant children into the urban community. Most migrant workers in the cities already live in segregated neighborhoods and seldom venture into the city centers. Children who attend migrant schools therefore do not have an opportunity to mix with local children, learn the subtleties of urban culture, or share an identity with the city children (Kwong 2006: 172; see also Woronov 2004). Instead, they develop a sense of identity with other migrant children of different ethnicities from all over the country, and their reference group boundary expands beyond their home regions. They learn each other's dialects, customs, and habits, but their circle is still confined to the migrant community, and they see themselves as a pariah group (Kwong 2006: 172).

Migrant children's social circle is a good indicator of their exclusion and marginality. In one study, 65 percent identified another migrant child as a close friend and another 23.9 percent pointed to a migrant child in their neighborhood. None picked a local student in the public school they attended (cited in Kwong 2011: 876; see also Ming 2014: 10). While most migrant children say they want to stay in the city, many feel unaccepted and report identification with their home provinces rather than the city, even if they personally have few historic or sentimental ties to the countryside (Kwong 2011: 879; Ming 2014: 10). Migrant children who were born or raised most of their lives in the city are often caught in a state of "in-between-ness" in that they are labeled as peasants in the city but regarded as urbanites by villagers back home. The children see themselves as members of their home regions, but would have difficulty fitting into their home communities and have no intention of living there. This leads to feelings of deep ambivalence and confusion about their identities (Kwong 2011: 881; Lan 2014: 258; Ming 2014: 12; see also Woronov 2009b; Geng et al. 2012).

Many migrant children see themselves as a group apart from the city children, inferior in some ways but superior in others. City children may "speak better Chinese" and "are more knowledgeable"; they "have money, houses, bicycles, computers, and cars," things the migrant children would like to own too. However, the migrant children also see their urban peers as "sheltered, spoilt, and snobbish," while they themselves are "honest, tough and hardworking" (cited in Kwong 2011: 879; see also Kwong 2006: 171). Some adopt a strategy of distance in response to the hostile manner of their local classmates (Lan 2014: 255).

One migrant child confessed that she "hated" urban people, as they were unfriendly towards migrants in Beijing. In the schools for migrant children, she noted, "all the students were from the rural areas" and therefore "felt equal to each other" (cited in Wang 2007: 114). A migrant student who had arrived in Shanghai from Anhui Province at the age of three, and who was admitted to a public junior middle school based on her outstanding grades, described the social obstacles that prevented her from fitting in with the local children:

> It seems that we *waidiren* [people from outside locales] are not as rich as them, so they like to hang out with locals. Every time we go out, locals and *waidiren* group separately … I watch them saying to each other, "let's go out." They never ask us *waidiren*. I hear them saying how much money they will bring and we have no such money. […]
>
> Some classmates call us country bumpkins (*xiangbalao*) […] I just pretend I didn't hear it … I watch them like I am watching a play […] Now I think *waidi* students are better. We have a common language. We are all *waidiren*. Nobody looks down at one another (cited in Lan 2014: 255).

The same girl did occasionally attempt to debate the definition of *suzhi* (quality) with the local children by telling them, for instance, that they may "have KFC fried chicken and piano," but her father "can play *erhu* (two-stringed Chinese fiddle) and *kuaiban* (traditional Chinese rap)!" (cited in Lan 2014: 256). However, such attempts may only serve to reinforce this girl's – and other migrant children's – separate identity as "outsiders" who do not share the same lifestyles and cultural identities as city people.

While migrant schools can offer migrant children an environment that is more socially inclusive, a recent study by Xiong (2015) documents that higher-grade students in the migrant schools can also develop a sense of alienation toward the teachers and staff in these privately run schools. As they grow older, migrant students see the knowledge they gain at the migrant schools as useless and have no belief that it can alter their destiny or situation. Many lack respect for the teachers' authority and believe that the staff are "only interested in making money" (cited in Xiong 2015: 176). These feelings drive some children to become gang members. Indeed, almost every private migrant junior high school examined by Xiong (2015) in the city of Shanghai had such a small "gang." The researcher found that members typically had a strong sense of honor regarding their own classmates, so they generally did not bully them. Instead, they tended to take issue with students in other classes with whom they were uncomfortable. The gang members were also sharp-tongued and liked to challenge the teachers' authority (Xiong 2015: 177). It is possible to see this development not as resistance directed against the current system but as an adaptation to the external environment and the system's bias, but the result is still the social exclusion and academic failure of migrant children. This failure, in turn, becomes a "self-fulfilling prophesy," and largely reinforces the inequalities in the system (Xiong 2015: 181).

CONCLUSION

For the first time in history, China has more citizens living in cities than in rural areas. The country's rapid urbanization is a product of the diminishing significance of the household registration system (*hukou*), the disintegration of the planned economy and the privatization of education, health, and social services. As this chapter has shown, however, the *hukou* system still contributes to stratified citizenship in China, and, in general, children who come from the countryside remain second-class citizens in the city. The low quality of education in private migrant schools and the tracking of many migrant children into public vocational schools inevitably leads these second-generation migrants to employment in blue-collar jobs, such as factory workers, hotel service staff, cooks, and salespersons (Xiong 2015). The result is a reproduction of social inequality and the low status of migrant children.

Over the past decade or so, China's central government has repeatedly issued policy directives stating that the education of migrant children is the host cities' responsibility, but provinces and cities have adopted the policy at their own pace and using different measures, with varying success. When it comes to providing social security and various services to migrants, there is a discernible gap between central government and local government practices and priorities (Pong 2015). While inclusive education is beneficial to the nation as a whole, local governments find it politically unpopular and/or financially unfeasible to use the local education budget to educate migrant children or to expand access to urban schooling (Ming 2014: 7). The suggestion that urban schools could be open to any child who wished to enroll remains deeply abhorrent to many urban Chinese who believe that such a policy would lead to the total evacuation of the countryside, "bringing all of China's peasants into the cities" (Woronov 2009b: 111).

The only long-term solution to these problems is wide-ranging and systematic reform of the social welfare system and ultimately the abolition of the *hukou* system, which has existed since the 1950s. This, of course, will not happen overnight or, realistically, within the next decade. In July 2014, the Chinese State Council issued a circular on the "end of the *hukou* (household registration) system," which promises a unified system for both urban and rural populations. The plan is to remove registration limits in townships and small cities, relax restrictions in medium-sized cities, and set qualifications for big cities. However, recent reports suggest that much of the policy itself is neither new nor likely to benefit most current and prospective rural–urban migrants, especially in the country's large metropolitan areas. Real progress will require corresponding changes to the way pension, education, and healthcare benefits are distributed in both rural and urban regions. Such reform will be difficult and costly, and remains a long way off. Moreover, as long as land rights are tied to the rural *hukou*, many rural migrants may be reluctant to part with their rural identification, which functions as a safety net (Goodburn 2014: 1–2; Wang 2014).

Interim solutions may include compensating city schools in proportion to the number of migrant children admitted, and increasing financial investment in education to alleviate the pressure on local governments in regions with large amounts of migrant children (Gao and Wilson 2010). Opening exam opportunities for migrant workers' children may be another important step. In 2012, Beijing and Shanghai announced that starting in 2014 they would allow migrant children who qualify according to a points system to enter local senior high schools or vocational schools and to take college entrance exams locally (Luo 2013; Lan 2014: 263). These are, of course, important steps, but they fail to recognize and address the issue of migrant children's social and cultural exclusion. Only when city residents and their children see migrant children as equals will those children be able to assert their right to education and realize their personal dreams and ambitions to the same extent as their local, urban peers.

Conclusion: Chinese Childhood in the Twenty-First Century: Current Trends and Future Directions

Chinese childhood has undergone a major transformation in recent decades. The country's re-integration within the global market economy; the increasing flow of people, products, and ideas across China's borders; and the demographic shifts caused by the One-Child Policy have led to the emergence of new notions of childcare, child agency, and child vulnerability. These developments have contributed to an increase in the perceived emotional value of children and their growing empowerment within the family and society. Compared to previous generations, many Chinese children are now encouraged to develop their individuality and many are also becoming more adept at asserting their personal wishes and interests in the spheres of consumption, schooling, and family relations.

As this book has attempted to show, however, these developments have given rise to ambiguity, criticism, and even resistance on the part of teachers, caregivers, and government officials in China. Moreover, the manifestation of these changes among child populations of different genders, ethnicities, and socioeconomic backgrounds has been far from uniform. Economic restructuring processes, the rural–urban mass migration, and the One-Child Policy have not necessarily improved the lot of all boys and girls in the country. By any measure of living standards, contemporary Chinese children are far better off than their parents were at their age. But unlike previous generations, they have few siblings or none at all. Growing up in the transition to a market economy, many children are surrounded by a new prosperity and an emerging culture of consumerism but their lives have become increasingly regimented. Others suffer from growing social inequality.

The experience of childhood in contemporary China is therefore highly heterogeneous and is characterized by notable tensions. In this concluding chapter, I outline the central contradictions that have emerged from the discussion in the previous chapters, and note their implications for the lives and subjectivities of children across the country. I conclude by identifying a number of issues that have so far received scant attention in the literature on Chinese childhood but which are, nonetheless, crucial for our understanding of what it means to be a child in China today.

GOVERNING CHILDREN IN CHINA: BETWEEN AUTONOMY AND OBEDIENCE

As the first two chapters in this volume have shown, the growing empowerment and individualization of Chinese children within the family and society is one of the most important developments of the modern era. The roots of this process can be traced back to the early decades of the twentieth century, when Chinese educational reformers and political leaders sought to transform the status of children and youth from subordinates to active agents in order "to save the nation" from foreign aggression and internal decay. As the discussion in chapter 1 demonstrated, the empowerment and improved care of children, especially girls, was also the mainstay of government policies in the Maoist period. The CCP systematically sought to overhaul the patri-archal family system and to turn children of both genders into "modern, socialist persons" who would actively contribute to the building of a just society. In the process, children in China were increasingly reconstituted as individuals separate from their extended family group. Thanks to the expansion of the mass schooling system and the widespread dissemination of official media products geared toward the political socialization of the young, PRC children were also subsumed, however, under the collective interests of the nation-state.

The advent of market reforms, the One-Child Policy, and the Open Door Policy in the late 1970s led to a further elevation in children's status and to an intensification in the process of children's individualization. The last several decades have witnessed the introduction of a new, global discourse on children's individual needs and rights to official and public thinking in China. They have also seen an increase in caregivers' emotional and financial investment in the individual child, along with the emergence of children as independent consumers in a new market-driven capitalist economy.

In contrast to Maoist-era thinking, the discourse of "scientific childrearing" which has come to dominate government, media, and pedagogical discourse in contemporary China requires that parents give increased attention to their child's emotional and educational needs. The result has been a retreat of the extended family and of the postsocialist Party-state from childrearing in favor of the nuclear family and the private sphere. This trend has been facilitated by the promotion of a new, neoliberal relationship to the child, as a "self-cultivating," "self-regulating" subject who is expected to be creative, independent, and innovative in order to succeed in the new market economy. This discourse further supports the idea that children have unique psychological needs and require personal freedom to express their inner worlds.

The post-socialist Chinese state has not relinquished its interest in shaping children's subjectivities but rather has modified its governing logic and techniques while seeking to integrate neoliberal ideas and practices with national-collectivist agendas. Increasingly geared to "a regime of human capital accumulation and intense competition" (Kuan 2015: 210), state publications promote new individualizing paradigms of childcare and education as a means to improve the people's "quality" (*suzhi*) and to hasten the country's modernization and integration within the global market economy. Government plans such as the "education for quality" reform program launched in the late 1990s reflect the attempts of schools to insert market discipline in children through the fostering of the values of autonomy and self-governance, thereby indicating that the post-socialist Party-state in China is seeking to produce "neo-liberal subjects par-excellence" (Greenhalgh and Winckler 2005: 236).

On the other hand, state schools in contemporary China are also at pains to teach children the "traditional" precepts of Confucianism, which now enjoys a renewed importance in government discourse as a superior moral logic and as an embodiment of the "true essence" of Chinese national culture. Further, a more repressive logic of governing the child through corporal punishment or strict discipline is still in evidence in some state schools, particularly those in rural areas, as well as in popular titles purporting to teach contemporary parents how to raise successful, "quality" children.

Chinese parents find themselves in the rather difficult position of having to reconcile these contradictory themes of obedience and auton-omy in their everyday interactions with children. As the discussion in chapter 2 illustrated, some parents, especially those who belong to, or aspire to belong to, the country's newly constituted middle classes, accept that China's increasing links to the global economy mean that they must adopt new childrearing techniques in order to encourage children's individuality, creativity, and independent thinking. Others, however, resist these new strategies or attempt to adapt them to pre-existing models of childcare, which draw on a socialist-collectivist morality on which they themselves were raised. The filial ethos, with its emphasis on respect and obedience for elders and seniors, also continues to serve as an alternative source of guidance to many caregivers in both rural and urban settings.

The tension between autonomy and obedience is equally evident in public and official views of children's new, central roles in the market economy. As the discussion in chapter 4 has shown, the rise of consumer society in China, underpinned by a global media and a worldwide commodity distribution system, is being shaped by children's tastes and preferences. Though caregivers are eager to give their children the material benefits they themselves could not enjoy in previous eras, children's new status as independent consumers is also cause for much popular anxiety in China. It threatens to destabilize intergenerational relations within the family and is seen as upsetting the balance between the newly celebrated value of individualism and the still influential notion of collective responsibility.

Moreover, Chinese children's avid consumption of foreign popular media products, especially those which originate in countries such as Japan or the United States, is regarded as a threat to Chinese national identity and as a challenge to the powerful role that the Party-state seeks to play in shaping young people's attitudes and values. These concerns translate into an ambiguous consumer socialization at home and at school, and to widespread criticism of children's perceived materialism and excessive Internet and computer game use. These are seen as detrimental both to children's moral and psychological health as well as to the fostering of national loyalty.

As chapter 4 has shown, this criticism is largely unfounded, but it does illustrate the intensity of current public debates in China concerning the proper relation between society and the state; public and private interests; the use of repressive power versus the defense of individual rights; and the roles of "tradition" and "modernity," "locality" and "globality" in the construction of a twenty-first-century Chinese national and cultural identity. Children and childhood constitute a central site for these crucial debates.

CHILDREN UNDER THE ONE-CHILD POLICY: EMPOWERMENT AND DISCRIMINATION

The growing empowerment and individualization of children in contemporary China is a product not only of new ideational currents or of the consumer revolution the country has undergone in recent decades, but also of the Chinese government's One-Child Policy introduced in the late 1970s. One of the central arguments of the book is that the policy has resulted not only in the acceleration of modernization and economic growth in China but also – and no less importantly – in the restructuring of adult–child relations and the elevation of children's status within the family and society. However, the policy has also produced a series of social problems that influence the lives of boys and girls across the country in complex, non-uniform ways.

By limiting couples to one or two children, China's birth control regulations have contributed to a re-definition of normative family form and have brought greater involvement by parents in childcare. In urban areas, where the regulations are stricter, they have led to a focusing of the attention of many adults upon each child and to children's increasing ability to assert their will in areas such as family consumption. At the same time, however, the One-Child Policy has also produced unrealistic expectations for singletons' success and the fear that parents will not have enough support in old age. In response to the state's call "to reproduce less in order to nurture better" and to "raise the quality of the population," many Chinese singletons in the cities now suffer from acute academic pressure and, contrary to their common perception as "little emperors," are subject to intensified surveillance and regimentation by over-anxious parents and grandparents.

The contradictions of the One-Child Policy are particularly stark when we consider its effects on the status of girls in China. Due to the diminishing family size, urban singleton girls have experienced relative empowerment within the family and have come to enjoy better access to family investment. However, the modification of the original policy in the mid-1980s to allow rural couples to have two children if the first-born is a girl has resulted in deepening discrimination against girls, particularly in rural areas. In some parts of the country, unwanted girls have been given up for adoption while others have suffered neglect and maltreatment. The One-Child Policy, which had initially been gender-neutral, has therefore contributed to growing gender inequality in contemporary China. The modified "single-son" policy in rural areas has also given rise to the common use of sex-selective abortions, which in turn have contributed to the imbalanced gender structure of the country's population.

As the discussion in chapter 3 made clear, the various gendered effects of the Chinese government's population policy are a product not only of differing views regarding the value of girls but also of different economic conditions in the country's rural and urban areas, as well as between rural migrants and permanent residents in the city. Living standards of children in contemporary China are highly uneven, with children in metropolises such as Beijing and Shanghai experiencing a far more commoditized existence than their rural counterparts in the country's western regions. Among relatively affluent families in the cities, the avid consumption on behalf of singletons, particularly in education, resembles in many ways the practices of urban, middle-class families elsewhere in the world. However, in China, the consumption of educational products and skill-enhancement activities is motivated not only by parents' class aspirations but also by the effects of the One-Child Policy, which makes the single child the focus of urban household consumption.

The investment in children's schooling also receives impetus from the long-standing emphasis in China on education and striving for excellence from a young age. Like urban caregivers, parents with rural backgrounds regard children's education as key to social mobility and self-improvement. They are willing to spend well beyond their means on children's schooling in order to help them leave farming behind and secure better, more lucrative jobs in the cities. However, rural children continue to face substantial disadvantages in access to education, health, and welfare services. Unlike their city peers, many of these children must struggle for the attainment of a physically and emotionally sound environment in which to develop.

UNEQUAL CHILDHOODS UNDER CHINA'S MARKET REFORMS

As noted in chapters 5 and 6, the level of education in rural areas has seen a rapid increase, and the number of rural children excluded from primary and lower-secondary schools has dropped in recent decades. Yet exclusion from education before the age of seven continues to exist in China and is almost entirely a rural problem. Furthermore, most of the children who remain locked out of access to compulsory education at the middle school level are rural, and many are children of ethnic minorities residing in China's poorest western regions. The disavowal of minority cultural practices and languages by teachers and school curricula contributes to these children's estrangement from school. It also impinges upon the ability of many ethnic minority children to construct a coherent sense of social identity while gaining a rightful place in China's national collectivity.

Gender inequality is another issue affecting the childhood experiences of many children, particularly in poorer rural areas. While there is nearly no significant gender inequality in the education of urban girls or in rural compulsory education, many girls in the countryside continue to face inequality when they reach senior middle school or beyond. This gap is a product of persistent beliefs about the social roles and inherently limited capabilities of girls. However, it is exacerbated by increasing economic pressures that force many rural parents in China to sponsor the education of only one child, often a boy.

Rural to urban migration constitutes one of the main ways of alleviating poverty in developing countries. However, in China, the mass migration of peasants to the cities has had many negative consequences for the education, wellbeing, and familial relations of children. Due to financial constraints and the dual (rural or urban) household registration system (*hukou*), farmers have no recognized legal status in cities, limited access to public services, and are unable to afford decent housing, transportation, and educational costs. Many migrant parents therefore choose to leave their children behind, entrusting their care to grandparents or other persons in the village. As chapter 5 has shown, this new vulnerable group of "left-behind children" often do not receive the necessary guidance to prepare school tasks. They have less time for study or play, and the prolonged parental absence affects their sense of emotional security. Many have little opportunity for real contact with an absent parent and, although they understand the need for the parent to leave, they can become alienated from the migrating parent due to the long periods of separation.

Children who do live with their migrant parents in the city do not necessarily fare better than those who had been left behind in the countryside. On paper, rural to urban migration has opened up new opportunities to rural migrant children who have moved to the cities. These children have come to cherish new personal dreams and new career expectations. As chapter 6 argues, however, the *hukou* system still contributes to stratified citizenship in China, and, in general, children who come from the countryside have remained second-class citizens in the city. These children suffer from material and social marginalization and their adaptation to city life has been hampered both by institutional exclusion based on their lack of a local *hukou*, and by cultural prejudices and social discrimination built on the back of the urban–rural divide.

Despite many years of hard work in the cities, most migrant workers in China are still trapped in the segregated migrant labor market, earning only a fraction of their urban counterparts' average incomes. They live in poor neighborhoods and their children have until recently been barred from attending public schools, enrolling in sub-standard, self-run institutions that are poorly equipped and seriously under-staffed. These "migrant schools" cannot offer children sufficient educa-tion to gain higher-level schooling, higher education, and access to professional work that could help them win urban citizenship and become socially included. Although migrant children have recently gained permission to attend public schools in China's largest cities, they often suffer prejudice and discrimination at these schools based on their low social class and rural origin. Many are treated as inferiors, not only by their urban peers but also by their teachers, and are not accepted as full members of their school or the urban community.

In summary, the economic reforms launched by the Chinese govern-ment in 1978 have greatly improved the lot of children across the country, especially in comparison to Maoist-era conditions. However, they have also deepened both the perceived and objective gaps between children of various social backgrounds. The growing importance of a child-rights discourse, the increasing popularity of child psychology, and the One-Child Policy have all contributed to changed patterns of childcare and a reconceptualization of children as autonomous indi-viduals worthy of rights and respect, but these trends have been mostly evident among urban, middle-class families.

While affluent Chinese caregivers in the city struggle to negotiate between new, liberal notions of childhood and ingrained beliefs about the proper way of raising the young, urban families of lesser means or those residing in the countryside face challenges of a different type. Many rural and migrant children, and in particular girls, are still unable to enjoy a full course of basic education, let alone the right to express their individuality, as contemporary legal codes, school teachers, and parenting guide-books currently advise. Their childhoods are therefore starkly different from those of their more affluent peers in the city.

STUDYING CHILDREN IN TWENTY-FIRST-CENTURY CHINA: FUTURE DIRECTIONS

As urbanization continues and the ranks of the Chinese middle classes are predicted to grow over the next few decades, we may see a diffusion of new – and contested – models of childrearing and education to broader parts of Chinese society. We may also observe an improvement in the life conditions of rural and migrant children who have thus far been unable to enjoy the same education and development opportunities as local children in the cities. Conversely, however, distinctive patterns of children's care associated with an idealized global "middle-class modernity" may continue to serve as a key mechanism for the creation and maintenance of social difference in China. Social exclusion and discrimination of rural or non-Han children based on their perceived lack of quality (*suzhi*) may further deepen the country's current divides, by reproducing these children's lower status in decades to come.

A thorough exploration of these future trajectories will require additional studies on the childrearing patterns and the lives of Chinese boys and girls, not only in urban, affluent areas but also in the countryside and among families of migrant and urban lower-class backgrounds. There is also a need for additional studies that would document the life conditions and subject formation processes of ethnic minority children; and to studies about sexual minority (or LGBT) children; street children; child laborers, and children with illness and disability in China.

At present, these remain understudied topics within the nascent field of China's childhood studies. However, they are crucial to understanding what is currently at stake in public debates not only about children's care and education, but also about cultural and national identities, the dynamics of urbanization and emergent class formations, and the changing relationship between the individual and the state in contemporary China.

Finally, there is also need for a greater emphasis on the voices of children themselves and a recognition of their agency and active role as meaning makers. Only by documenting Chinese children's interactions with both adults and peers, and by allowing children of various backgrounds to report about their worlds and experiences in their own words, can we gain a more thorough understanding of the nature of Chinese childhood today.

References

Abelmann, Nancy (2003) *The Melodrama of Mobility: Women, Talk, and Class in Contemporary South Korea*. Honolulu, HI: University of Hawai'i Press.

Anagnost, Ann (1995) "A Surfeit of Bodies: Population and the Rationality of the State in Post-Mao China." In *Conceiving the New World Order: The Global Politics of Reproduction*. Faye D. Ginsburg and Rayna Rapp (eds.). Berkeley, CA: University of California Press, pp. 22–41.

Anagnost, Ann (1997) "Children and National Transcendence in China." In *Constructing China: The Interaction of Culture and Economics*. Kenneth G. Lieberthal, Shuen-fu Lin, and Ernest P. Young (eds.). Ann Arbor, MI: Center for Chinese Studies, University of Michigan, pp. 195–222.

Anagnost, Ann (2004) "The Corporeal Politics of Quality (*suzhi*)." *Public Culture* 16(2): 189–208.

Anagnost, Ann (2008) "Imagining Global Futures in China: The Child as a Sign of Value." In *Figuring the Future: Globalization and the Temporalities of Children and Youth*. Jennifer Cole and Deborah Durham (eds.). Santa Fe, NM: School for Advanced Research Press, pp. 49–73.

Appadurai, Arjun (1990) "Disjuncture and Difference in the Global Cultural Economy." In *Global Culture: Nationalism, Globalization and Modernity*. Mike Featherstone (ed.). London: Sage Publications, pp. 295–310.

Apter, Norman D. (2014) "All in the Family: New Approaches to Child Relief in Post-Mao China." *Modern China* 40(1): 3–39.

Archard, David (2004) *Children: Rights and Childhood* (2nd edn). London and New York: Routledge.

Ariès, Philippe (1962) *Centuries of Childhood: A Social History of Family Life*. Robert Baldick, trans. New York: Vintage Books.

Bai, Limin (2005a) "Children at Play: A Childhood beyond the Confucian Shadow." *Childhood* 12(1): 9–32.

Bai, Limin (2005b) *Shaping the Ideal Child: Children and Their Primers in Late Imperial China*. Hong Kong: The Chinese University Press.

Bakken, Børge (1993) "Prejudice and Danger: The Only-Child in China." *Childhood* 1: 46–61.

Bakken, Børge (1999) *The Exemplary Society: Human Improvement, Social Control, and the Dangers of Modernity in China.* Oxford: Oxford University Press.

Banister, Judith (1984) "Population Policy and Trends in China, 1978–83." *The China Quarterly* 100: 717–41.

Banister, Judith (1987) *China's Changing Population.* Stanford, CA: Stanford University Press.

Banister, Judith (2004) "Shortage of Girls in China Today." *Journal of Population Research* 21: 19–45.

Bastid, Marianne (1987) "Servitude or Liberation? The Introduction of Foreign Educational Practices and Systems to China from 1840 to the Present." In *China's Education and the Industrialized World.* Ruth Hayhoe and Marianne Bastid (eds.). Armonk, NY: M.E. Sharpe, pp. 3–20.

Bhabha, Homi K. (1994) *The Location of Culture.* London: Routledge.

Bin, Zhao (1996) "The Little Emperors' Small Screen: Parental Control and Children's Television Viewing in China." *Media, Culture & Society* 18(4): 639–58.

Binah-Pollak, Avital (2014) "Discourses and Practices of Child-Rearing in China: The Biopower of Parenting in Beijing." *China Information* 28(1): 27–45.

Bluebond-Langner, Myra, and Jill E. Korbin (2007) "Challenges and Opportunities in the Anthropology of Childhoods: An Introduction to 'Children, Childhoods, and Childhood Studies.'" *American Anthropologist* 109(2): 241–6.

Branigan, Tania (2013) "China's One-Child Policy's Human Cost Fuels Calls for Reform." *The Guardian*, August 16. Available at: http://www.theguardian.com/world/2013/aug/16/china-one-child-policy-calls-reform

Bray, Francesca (1997) *Technology and Gender: Fabrics of Power in Late Imperial China.* Berkeley, CA: University of California Press.

Bu, Wei (2006) "Internet Use among Chinese Youth." In *Chinese Youth in Transition.* Jieying Xi, Yunxiao Sun, and Jing Jian Xiao (eds.). Aldershot: Ashgate, pp. 215–32.

Buckley, Chris (2015) "Henan Delegates Protest Inequality in University Admissions." Sinosphere: Dispatches from China, *The New York Times*, March 10.

Caputo, Virginia (1995) "Anthropology's Silent 'Others': A Consideration of Some Conceptual and Methodological Issues for the Study of Youth and Children's Cultures." In *Youth Cultures: A Cross-Cultural Perspective.* Vered Amit-Talai and Helena Wulff, (eds.). New York: Routledge, pp. 19–42.

Chan, Anita (1985) *Children of Mao: Personality Development and Political Activism in the Red Guard Generation.* London: Macmillan.

Chan, Aris (2009) "Paying the Price for Economic Development: The Children of Migrant Workers in China." Geoffrey Crothall (ed.). *China Labour Bulletin*, Special Report, November 2009. Available at: http://clb.org.hk/en/files/share/File/research_reports/Children_of_Migrant_Workers.pdf

Chan, Kara (2006) "Consumer Socialization of Chinese Children in Schools: Analysis of Consumption Values in Textbooks." *Journal of Consumer Marketing* 23(3): 125–32.

Chan, Kara (2009) "Advertising and Children in China." In *Advertising and Chinese Society: Impacts and Issues*. Hong Cheng and Kara Chan (eds.). Køge: Copenhagen Business School Press, pp. 265–83.

Chan, Kara, and Xiao Cai (2009) "Influence of Television Advertising on Adolescents in China: An Urban-Rural Comparison." *Young Consumers* 10(2): 133–45.

Chan, Kara, and Fanny Chan (2008) "Children's Television Programs in China: A Discourse of Success and Modernity." In *Discourses of Cultural China in the Globalizing Age*. Doreen D. Wu (ed.). Hong Kong: Hong Kong University Press, pp. 113–28.

Chan, Kara, and Fan Hu (2008) "Attitudes toward Material Possessions among Chinese Children." *Young Consumers* 9(1): 49–59.

Chan, Kara, and James U. McNeal (2006a) "Children and Media in China: An Urban-Rural Comparison Study." *Journal of Consumer Marketing* 23(3): 79–88.

Chan, Kara, and James U. McNeal (2006b) "Rural Chinese Children as Consumers: Consumption Experience and Information Sourcing." *Journal of Consumer Behaviour* 5(3): 182–92.

Chang, Hongqin, Xiao-yuan Dong, and Fiona MacPhail (2011) "Labor Migration and Time Use Patterns of the Left-behind Children and Elderly in Rural China." *World Development* 39(12): 2199–210.

Chao, Ruth K. (1994) "Beyond Parental Control and Authoritarian Parenting Style: Understanding Chinese Parenting through the Cultural Notion of Training." *Child Development* 65(4): 1111–19.

Chee, Bernadine W.L. (2000) "Eating Snacks and Biting Pressure: Only Children in Beijing." In *Feeding China's Little Emperors: Food, Children, and Social Change*. Jun Jing (ed.). Stanford, CA: Stanford University Press, pp. 48–70.

Chen, Feinian, Guangya Liu, and Christine A. Mair (2011) "Intergenerational Ties in Context: Grandparents Caring for Grandchildren in China." *Social Forces* 90(2): 571–94.

Chen, Qijia, and Hui Song (2009) Riben Dongman Yingxiangli Diaocha Baogao [A Report on the Influence of Japanese Animation]. Beijing: Renminchubanshe.

Chen, Tina Mai (2003) "Female Icons, Feminist Iconography? Socialist Rhetoric and Women's Agency in 1950s China." *Gender & History* 15(2): 268–95.

Chen, Weidong (2006) "Chinese Children's Leisure." In *Chinese Youth in Transition*. Jieying Xi, Yunxiao Sun, and Jing Jian Xiao (eds.). Aldershot: Ashgate, pp. 41–51.

Chen, Xinxin, Qiu Qiong, Scott Rozelle, Yaojiang Shi, and Linxiu Zhang (2009) "Effect of Migration on Children's Educational Performance in Rural China." *Comparative Economic Studies* 51(3): 323–43.

Chen, Yiu Por, and Zai Liang (2007) "Educational Attainment of Migrant Children: The Forgotten Story of China's Urbanization." In *Education and Reform in China*. Emily Hannum and Albert Park (eds.). New York: Routledge, pp. 117–32.

Chen, Yuanyuan, and Shuaizhang Feng (2012) "Access to Public Schools and the Education of Migrant Children in China." Institute for the Study of Labor Report. Available at: http://ftp.iza.org/dp6853.pdf

Cheng, Fucai, and Debbie Lam (2010) "How Is Street Life? An Examination of the Subjective Wellbeing of Street Children in China." *International Social Work* 53(3): 353–65.

Chi, Jin, and Nirmala Rao (2003) "Parental Beliefs about School Learning and Children's Educational Attainment: Evidence from Rural China." *Ethos* 31(3): 330–56.

Chin, Ann-Ping (1988) *Children of China: Voices from Recent Years*. Ithaca, NY: Cornell University Press.

China Daily (2004) "'Care For Girls' Gaining Momentum." July 8. Available at: http://www.chinadaily.com.cn/english/doc/2004-07/08/content_346700.htm

China Daily (2005) "Parents Pay Too Much for Education." April 1. Available at: http://www.china.org.cn/english/Life/124528.htm

China Daily (2011) "12-Year-Old's Poetic Bid Ends Homework Toil." January 28. Available at: http://www.chinadaily.com.cn/china/2011-01/28/content_11934134.htm

China Daily (2014) "Soaring Number of Migrants to Attend China's Gaokao." June 6. Available at: http://usa.chinadaily.com.cn/china/2014-06/06/content_17569529.htm

China Internet Network Information Center (CNNIC) (2014) "Statistical Report on Internet Development in China." January. Available at: http://www1.cnnic.cn/IDR/ReportDownloads/201404/U020140417607531610855.pdf

China Labour Bulletin (2007) "Small Hands: A Survey Report on Child Labour in China." Research Report No. 3, September. Available at: http://www .clb.org.hk/en/files/share/File/general/Child_labour_report_1.pdf

China.org.cn (2009) "60 Years of Educational Reform and Development." State Council Information Office and the China International Publishing Group (CIPG), Beijing. September 14. Available from http://www.china.org.cn/ china/2009-09/14/content_18520870.htm

China.org.cn. (2015) "Law of the PRC on the Protection of Minors." Available at: http://www.china.org.cn/english/government/207410.htm

Chen, Lydia, Iris Li, and Chryssa Rask (2012) *Reflections on the Development of the Private Education Industry in China 2012.* Deloitte Report. Available at http://www2.deloitte.com/cn/en/pages/technology-media-and -telecommunications/articles/reflections-development-private-education -industry-china2012.html

Coale, Ansley J., and Judith Banister (1994) "Five Decades of Missing Females in China." *Demography* 31: 459–79.

Cockain, Alex (2011) "Students' Ambivalence toward their Experiences in Secondary Education: Views From a Group of Young Chinese Studying on an International Foundation Program in Beijing." *The China Journal* 65: 101–18.

Cockain, Alex (2012) *Young Chinese in Urban China.* London and New York: Routledge.

Communist Party of China (2000) "The Decision of the CPC Central Committee and the State Council on Deepening Education Reform and Promoting Quality Education in an All-around Way (13 June 1999)." In *China Facts and Figures Annual Handbook*, 25, Robert J. Perrins (ed.). Gulf Breeze, FL: Academic International Press, pp. 230–41.

Connelly, Rachel, Kenneth Roberts, and Zhenzhen Zheng (2012) "The Role of Children in the Migration Decisions of Rural Chinese Women." *Journal of Contemporary China* 21(73): 93–111.

Corsaro, William A. (1997) *The Sociology of Childhood.* Thousand Oaks, CA: Pine Forge Press.

Crabb, Mary W. (2010) "Governing the Middle-class Family in Urban China: Educational Reform and Questions of Choice." *Economy and Society* 39(3): 385–402.

Croll, Elisabeth J. (1980) *Feminism and Socialism in China.* London: Routledge and Kegan Paul.

Croll, Elisabeth J. (1985) "Introduction: Fertility Norms and Family Size in China." In *China's One-Child Family Policy.* Elisabeth Croll, Delia Davin, and Penny Kane (eds.). New York: St. Martin's Press, pp. 1–36.

Croll, Elisabeth J. (2006) *China's New Consumers: Social Development and Domestic Demand*. London and New York: Routledge.

Culp, Robert (2006) "Rethinking Governmentality: Training, Cultivation, and Cultural Citizenship in Nationalist China." *Journal of Asian Studies* 65(2): 529–44.

Cunningham, Maura E. (2014) "The Vulnerability of China's Left-Behind Children." March 21. Available at: http://blogs.wsj.com/chinarealtime/2014/03/21/the-vulnerability-of-chinas-left-behind-children/

Dardess, John (1991) "Childhood in Premodern China." In *Children in Historical and Comparative Perspectives: An International Handbook and Research Guide.* Joseph M. Hawes and N. Ray Hiner (eds.). New York: Greenwood Press, pp. 71–94.

Davey, Gareth (2008) "Children's Television, Radio, Internet, and Computer Usage in a City and a Village of China." *Visual Anthropology* 21(2): 160–5.

Davin, Delia (1998) *Internal Migration in Contemporary China*. New York: St. Martin's Press.

Davis, Deborah S. (1995) "Introduction: Urban China." In *Urban Spaces in Contemporary China: The Potential for Autonomy and Community in Post-Mao China*. Deborah S. Davis, Richard Kraus, Barry Naughton, and Elisabeth J. Perry (eds.). Cambridge: Cambridge University Press, pp. 1–22.

Davis, Deborah S. (2000) "Introduction: A Revolution in Consumption." In *The Consumer Revolution in Urban China*. Deborah S. Davis (ed.). Berkeley, CA: University of California Press.

Davis, Deborah, and Stevan Harrell (1993) "Introduction: The Impact of Post-Mao Reforms on Family Life." In *Chinese Families in the Post-Mao Era*. Deborah Davis and Stevan Harrell (eds.). Berkeley, CA: University of California Press, pp. 1–22.

Davis, Deborah S., and Julia S. Sensenbrenner (2000) "Commercializing Childhood: Parental Purchases for Shanghai's Only Child." In *The Consumer Revolution in Urban China*. Deborah S. Davis (ed.). Berkeley, CA: University of California Press, pp. 54–79.

Davis-Friedmann, Deborah (1991) *Long Lives: Chinese Elderly and the Communist Revolution* (expanded edn). Stanford, CA: Stanford University Press.

Démurger, Sylvie, and Hui Xu (2013) "Left-Behind Children and Return Decisions of Rural Migrants in China." Institute for the Study of Labor (IZA) Discussion Paper No. 7727. Available at: http://ftp.iza.org/dp7727.pdf

Deng, Meng, and Kim Fong Poon-McBrayer (2012) "Reforms and Challenges in the Era of Inclusive Education: The Case of China." *British Journal of Special Education* 39(3): 117–22.

Diamant, Neil (2000) *Revolutionizing the Family: Politics, Love, and Divorce in Urban and Rural China, 1949–1968*. Berkeley, CA: University of California Press.

Donald, Stephanie Hemelryk (1999) "Children as Political Messengers: Art, Childhood, and Continuity." In *Picturing Power in the People's Republic of China: Posters of the Cultural Revolution*. Harriet Evans and Stephanie Hemelryk Donald (eds.). Lanham, MD: Rowman & Littlefield, pp. 79–150.

Donald, Stephanie Hemelryk (2002) "Crazy Rabbits! Children's Media Culture." In *Media in China: Consumption, Content and Crisis*. Stephanie Hemelryk Donald, Michael Keane, and Hong Yin (eds.). London and New York: RoutledgeCurzon, pp. 128–38.

Donald, Stephanie Hemelryk (2004) "Little Friends: Children and Creative Consumption in the People's Republic of China." *International Journal of Cultural Studies* 7(1): 45–53.

Donald, Stephanie Hemelryk (2005) *Little Friends: Children's Film and Media Culture in China*. Lanham, MD: Rowman & Littlefield.

Donald, Stephanie Hemelryk, and Yi Zheng (2008) "Richer Than Before: The Cultivation of Middle-Class Taste: Education Choices in Urban China." In *The New Rich: Future Rulers, Present Lives*. David Goodman (ed.). London: Routledge, pp. 71–82.

Dong, Qiang, Xiaoyun Li, Hongping Yang, Keyun Zhang (2008) "Gender Inequality in Rural Education and Poverty." *Chinese Sociology and Anthropology* 40(4): 64–78.

Dong, Qingwen (2002) "Chinese Family Consumer Socialization: A Study of Chinese Urban Adolescents' Involvement in Family Purchasing Activities." In *Chinese Communication Studies: Contexts and Comparisons*. Xing Lu, Wenshan Jia, and Ray D. Heisey (eds.). Westport, CT: Ablex, pp. 135–46.

Drulhe, Christile (2002) "The Little Emperor in the City: The Child and the Family in Urban China." Michael Black, trans. *China Perspectives* 39: 17–27.

Ebenstein, Avraham (2011) "Estimating a Dynamic Model of Sex Selection in China." *Demography* 48: 783–811.

The Economist (2013) "Why Is China Relaxing Its One-Child Policy?" December 10. Available at: http://www.economist.com/blogs/economist-explains/2013/12/economist-explains-8?fsrc=scn/tw/te/bl/ee/chinarelaxingpolicy

The Economist (2014) "Rural Schools: Down and Out in Rural China." August 23. Available at: http://www.economist.com/news/china/21613293-many-teenagers-chinese-countryside-do-not-finish-secondary-school-bodes-ill

The Economist (2015) "Fertility: Tales of the Unexpected." July 11. Available at: http://www.economist.com/node/21657416/print

Ellsworth, Nancy J., and Chun Zhang (2007) "Progress and Challenges in China's Special Education Development: Observations, Reflections, and Recommendations." *Remedial and Special Education* 28(1): 58–64.

Erwin, Kathlyn (2000) "Heart-to-Heart, Phone-to-Phone: Family Values, Sexuality, and the Politics of Shanghai's Advice Hotlines." In *The Consumer Revolution in Urban China*. Deborah S. Davis (ed.). Berkeley, CA: University of California Press, pp. 145–70.

Evans, Harriet (1997) *Women and Sexuality in China: Female Sexuality and Gender since 1949*. New York: Continuum.

Evans, Harriet (1999) "Comrade Sister: Gendered Bodies and Spaces." In *Picturing Power in The People's Republic of China: Posters of the Cultural Revolution*. Harriet Evans, and Stephanie Hemelryk Donald (eds.). Lanham, MD: Rowman & Littlefield, pp. 63–78.

Evans, Harriet (2008) *The Subject of Gender: Daughters and Mothers in Urban China*. Lanham, MD: Rowman & Littlefield.

Falbo, Toni (2012) "Only Children: An Updated Review." *The Journal of Individual Psychology* 68(1): 38–49.

Falbo, Toni, and Dudley L. Poston (1993) "The Academic, Personality, and Physical Outcomes of Only Children in China." *Child Development* 64: 18–35.

Fan, C. Cindy (2008) "Migration, *Hukou* and the City." In *China Urbanizes: Consequences, Strategies, and Policies*. Yusuf Shahid, and Tony Saich (eds.). Washington, DC: World Bank, pp. 65–90.

Fan, Ying, and Yixuan Li (2010) "Children's Buying Behavior in China: A Study of their Information Sources." *Marketing Intelligence & Planning* 28(2): 170–87.

Fang, Lai, Chengfang Liu, Renfu Luo, Linxiu Zhang, and Xiaochen Ma (2012) "Private Migrant Schools or Rural/Urban Public Schools: Where Should China Educate Its Migrant Children?" Working Paper 224, REAP (Rural Education Action Project) Stanford University, April.

Farquhar, Judith (2001) "For Your Reading Pleasure: Self-Health [*Ziwo baojian*] Information in 1990s Beijing." *Positions* 9(1): 105–30.

Farquhar, Mary Ann (1999) *Children's Literature in China: From Lu Xun to Mao Zedong*. Armonk, NY: M.E. Sharpe.

Featherstone, Mike (1990) "Global Culture: An Introduction". In *Global Culture: Nationalism, Globalization, and Modernity*. Mike Featherstone (ed.). London: Sage, pp. 1–14.

Feng, Xiao-Tian, Dudley L. Poston, and Xiao-Tao Wang (2014) "China's One-child Policy and the Changing Family." *Journal of Comparative Family Studies* XLV(1): 17–29.

Field, Norma (1995) "The Child as Laborer and Consumer: The Disappearance of Childhood in Contemporary Japan." In *Children and the Politics of Culture.* Sharon Stephens (ed.). Princeton, NJ: Princeton University Press, pp. 51–78.

Fong, Vanessa L. (2002) "China's One-Child Policy and the Empowerment of Urban Daughters." *American Anthropologist* 104(4): 1098–109.

Fong, Vanessa L. (2004a) "Filial Nationalism among Chinese Teenagers with Global Identities." *American Ethnologist* 31(4): 631–48.

Fong, Vanessa L. (2004b) *Only Hope: Coming of Age under China's One-Child Policy.* Stanford, CA: Stanford University Press.

Fong, Vanessa L. (2007a) "Morality, Cosmopolitanism, or Academic Attainment? Discourses on 'Quality' and Urban Chinese-Only-Children's Claims to Ideal Personhood." *City & Society* 19(1): 86–113.

Fong, Vanessa L. (2007b) "Parent-Child Communication Problems and the Perceived Inadequacies of Chinese Only Children." *Ethos* 35(1): 85–127.

Froissart, Chloé (2003) "The Hazards of the Right to an Education: A Study of the Schooling of Migrant Worker Children in Chengdu." *China Perspectives* 48: 21–36.

Fu, Keung Ong, Chang Ying Li, and He Xue Song (2009) "Correlates of Psychological Wellbeing of Children of Migrant Workers in Shanghai, China." *Social Psychiatry & Psychiatric Epidemiology* 44(10): 815–24.

Fuligni, Andrew J., and Wenxin Zhang (2004) "Attitudes toward Family Obligation among Adolescents in Contemporary Urban and Rural China." *Child Development* 74: 180–92.

Fung, Heidi (1999) "Becoming a Moral Child: The Socialization of Shame among Young Chinese Children." *Ethos* 27(2): 180–209.

Furth, Charlotte (1987) "Concepts of Pregnancy, Childbirth, and Infancy in Ch'ing Dynasty China." *The Journal of Asian Studies* 46(1): 7–35.

Furth, Charlotte (1995) "From Birth to Birth: The Growing Body in Chinese Medicine." In *Chinese Views of Childhood.* Anne Behnke Kinney (ed.). Honolulu, HI: University of Hawai'i Press.

Gao, Wenshu, and Merritt Wilson (2010) "Providing an Education for Left-Behind and Migrant Children." In *The China Population and Labor Yearbook: The Sustainability of Economic Growth from the Perspective of Human Resources.* Fang Cai, Meiyan Wang, and Dewen Wang (eds.). Leiden: Brill, pp. 75–91.

Gates, Hill (1993) "Cultural Support for Birth Limitation among Urban Capital-Owning Women." In *Chinese Families in the Post-Mao Era.* Deborah Davis, and Stevan Harrell (eds.). Berkeley, CA: University of California Press, pp. 251–74.

Gaubatz, Piper R. (1995) "Urban Transformation in Post-Mao China: Impacts of the Reform Era on China's Urban Form." In *Urban Spaces in Contemporary China: The Potential for Autonomy and Community in Post-Mao China*. Deborah S. Davis, Richard Kraus, Barry Naughton, and Elisabeth J. Perry (eds.). Cambridge: Cambridge University Press, pp. 28–60.

Geng, Liuna, Wenjun Zhou, and Yiqing Hu (2012) "The Implicit and Explicit Sense of Belonging in Migrant Children in China." *Social Behavior & Personality: An International Journal* 40(7): 1175–82.

Gillette, Maris Boyd (2000) "Children's Food and Islamic Dietary Restrictions in Xi'an." In *Feeding China's Little Emperors: Food, Children, and Social Change*. Jun Jing (ed.). Stanford, CA: Stanford University Press, pp. 71–93.

Glosser, Susan L. (2003) *Chinese Visions of Family & State, 1915–1953*. Berkeley, CA: University of California Press.

Goh, Esther C.L. (2011) *China's One-Child Policy and Multiple Caregiving: Raising Little Suns in Xiamen*. New York: Routledge.

Goh, Esther C.L. (2013) "'You Must Finish Your Dinner': Meal Time Dynamics Between Grandparents, Parents and Grandchildren in Urban China." *British Food Journal* 115(3): 365–76.

Goh, Esther C.L., and Leon Kuczynski (2014) "'She Is too Young for These Chores' – Is Housework Taking a Back Seat in Urban Chinese Childhood?" *Children & Society* 28(4): 280–91.

Gold, Thomas (1991) "Youth and the State." *The China Quarterly* 127: 594–612.

Gong, Qian, and Peter Jackson (2013) "Mediating Science and Nature: Representing and Consuming Infant Formula Advertising in China." *European Journal of Cultural Studies* 16: 285–309.

Gong, Xiaodong, Arthur van Soest, and Ping Zhang (2005) "The Effects of the Gender of Children on Expenditure Patterns in Rural China: A Semiparametric Analysis." *Journal of Applied Econometrics* 20(4): 509–27.

Goodburn, Charlotte (2014) "The End of the *Hukou* System? Not Yet." China Policy Institute Policy Paper 2014: No 2. Available at: http://www.nottingham.ac.uk/cpi/documents/policy-papers/cpi-policy-paper-2014-no-2-goodburn.pdf

Goodkind, Daniel (2011) "Child Underreporting, Fertility, and Sex Ratio Imbalance in China." *Demography* 48: 291–316.

Gottschang, Susan (2000) "A Baby-Friendly Hospital and the Science of Infant Feeding." In *Feeding China's Little Emperors*. Jing Jun (ed.). Stanford, CA: Stanford University Press, pp. 160–84.

Greenhalgh, Susan (2003) "Planned Births, Unplanned Persons: 'Population' in the Making of Chinese Modernity." *American Ethnologist* 30(21): 196–215.

Greenhalgh, Susan (2011) "Governing Chinese Life: From Sovereignty to Bio-political Governance." In *Governance of Life in Chinese Moral Experience: The Quest for an Adequate Life*. Everett Zhang, Arthur Kleinman, and Tu Weiming (eds.). London: Routledge, pp. 146–62.

Greenhalgh, Susan, and Edwin A. Winckler (2005) *Governing China's Population: From Leninist to Neoliberal Biopolitics*. Stanford, CA: Stanford University Press.

Guan, Xiaomeng (2009) "Spoiled Generation Paves Way for New Age Parenting." *China Daily*, July 14. Available at: http://www.chinadaily.com.cn/china/2009-07/14/content_8427903.htm

Guan, Ying (2003a) "Consumption Patterns of Chinese Children." *Journal of Family and Economic Issues* 24(4): 373–9.

Guan, Ying (2003b) "Spare-Time Life of Chinese Children." *Journal of Family and Economic Issues* 24(4): 365–71.

Guo, Jing, Li Chen, Xiaohua Wang, Yan Liu, Cheryl Hiu Kwan Chui, Huan He, Zhiyong Qu, and Donghua Tian (2012) "The Relationship between Internet Addiction and Depression among Migrant Children and Left-Behind Children in China." *Cyberpsychology, Behavior & Social Networking* 15(11): 585–90.

Guo, Yuhua (2000) "Family Relations: The Generation Gap at the Table." In *Feeding China's Little Emperors: Food, Children, and Social Change*. Jun Jing (ed.). Stanford, CA: Stanford University Press, pp. 94–113.

Hannerz, Ulf (2002 [1989]) "Notes on the Global Ecumene." In *The Anthropology of Globalization: A Reader*. Jonathan Xavier Inda, and Rentao Rosaldo (eds.). Malden, MA: Blackwell, pp. 37–45.

Hannum, Emily C. (2002) "Educational Stratification by Ethnicity in China: Enrollment and Attainment in the Early Reform Years." *Demography* 39(1): 95–117.

Hannum, Emily C., and Jennifer Adams (2007) "Girls in Gansu, China: Expectations and Aspirations for Secondary Schooling." In *Exclusion, Gender and Education: Case Studies from the Developing World*. Maureen A. Lewis, and Marlaine E. Lockheed (eds.). Washington, DC: Center for Global Development, pp. 71–98.

Hannum, Emily C., Peggy A. Kong, and Yuping Zhang (2009a) "Family Sources of Educational Gender Inequality in Rural China: A Critical Assessment." *International Journal of Educational Development* 29(5): 474–86.

Hannum, Emily, Tanja Sargent, and Shengchao Yu (2009b) "Poverty, Parental Ill Health, and Children's Access to Schooling in Rural Gansu, China." *Provincial China* 1(2): 24–60.

Hannum, Emily, Meiyan Wang, and Jennifer Adams (2010) "Rural-Urban Disparities in Access to Primary and Secondary Education under Market Reforms." In *One Country, Two Societies: Rural-urban Inequality in Contemporary China*. Martin King Whyte (ed.). Cambridge, MA: Harvard University Press, pp. 125–46.

Hansen, Mette Halskov (1999) *Lessons in Being Chinese: Minority Education and Ethnic Identity in Southwest China*. Seattle, WA: University of Washington Press.

Hansen, Mette Halskov (2012) "Recent Trends in Chinese Rural Education: The Disturbing Rural-Urban Disparities and the Measures to Meet Them." In *Towards a New Development Paradigm in Twenty-First Century China: Economy, Society and Politics*. Erik Florence, and Pierre Defraigne (eds.). London and New York: Routledge.

Hansen, Mette Halskov (2015) *Educating the Chinese Individual: Life in a Rural Boarding School*. Seattle, WA: University of Washington Press.

Hansen, Mette Halskov, and T.E. Woronov (2013) "Demanding and Resisting Vocational Education: A Comparative Study of Schools in Rural and Urban China." *Comparative Education* 49(2): 242–59.

Hardman, Charlotte (1973) "Can There Be an Anthropology of Children?" *Journal of the Anthropological Society of Oxford* 4: 85–99.

Hardt, Michael, and Antonio Negri (2001) *Empire*. Cambridge, MA: Harvard University Press.

Hershatter, Gail (2004) "State of the Field: Women in China's Long Twentieth Century." *The Journal of Asian Studies* 63(4): 991–1065.

Heywood, Colin (2001) *A History of Childhood: Children and Childhood in the West from Medieval to Modern Times*. Cambridge: Polity.

Honig, Emily, and Gail Hershatter (1988) *Personal Voices: Chinese Women in the 1980s*. Stanford, CA: Stanford University Press.

Hou, Wenzhuo (2002) "Privately Run Migrant Schools in Beijing: Vital Community Resources Existing on Sufferance." *China Rights Forum* 2: 14–21.

Hsiung, Ping-chen (2005) *A Tender Voyage: Children and Childhood in Late Imperial China*. Stanford, CA: Stanford University Press.

Hsu, Francis L.K. (1967 [1949]) *Under the Ancestors' Shadow: Kinship, Personality, and Social Mobility in China*. Stanford, CA: Stanford University Press.

Hu, Anjun, Dongmei Li, and Mingming Liu (2011) "Research on Influencing Factors of Welfare Level about Left-Behind Children in China Rural Areas." *Journal of Agricultural Science* 3(2): 223–9.

Hu, Shen (2000) *Suzhi lun: Chensi zhuti zishen zhi mi* [*On quality: Contemplating the concept of self and the subject*]. Beijing: Huayi Chubanshe.

Huang, Shu-Min, Kimberley C. Falk, and Su-Min Chen (1996) "Nutritional Well-Being of Preschool Children in a North China Village." *Modern China* 22(4): 355–81.

Human Rights Watch (2013) "'As Long as They Let Us Stay in Class': Barriers to Education for Persons with Disabilities in China: Report." July 15. Available from: http://www.hrw.org/sites/default/files/reports/china0713_ForUpload.pdf

Ikels, Charlotte (1993) "Settling Accounts: The Intergenerational Contract in an Age of Reform." In *Chinese Families in the Post-Mao Era*. Deborah Davis and Stevan Harrell (eds.). Berkeley, CA: University of California Press, pp. 307–33.

Ikels, Charlotte (1996) *The Return of the God of Wealth: The Transition to a Market Economy in Urban China*. Stanford, CA: Stanford University Press.

Inda, Jonathan Xavier, and Renato Rosaldo (2002) "Introduction: A World in Motion." In *The Anthropology of Globalization: A Reader*. Jonathan Xavier Inda, and Rentao Rosaldo (eds.). Malden, MA: Blackwell, pp. 1–34.

Ishii, Kenichi (2013) "Nationalism and Preferences for Domestic and Foreign Animation Programmes in China." *The International Communication Gazette* 75(2): 225–45.

Jacka, Tamara (1992) "The Public/Private Dichotomy and the Gender Division of Rural Labour." In *Economic Reform and Social Change in China*. Andrew Watson (ed.). London and New York: Routledge, pp. 117–43.

James, Allison (2007) "Giving Voice to Children's Voices: Practices and Problems, Pitfalls and Potentials." *American Anthropologist* 109(2): 261–72.

James, Allison, and Alan Prout (1997 [1990]) "A New Paradigm for the Sociology of Childhood? Provenance, Promises and Problems." In *Constructing and Reconstructing Childhood: Contemporary Issues in the Sociological Study of Childhood*. Allison James, and Alan Prout (eds.). London: Falmer Press, pp. 7–33.

James, Allison, Chris Jenks, and Alan Prout (1998) *Theorizing Childhood*. Cambridge: Polity.

Jenks, Chris (1996) *Childhood*. London: Routledge.

Jia, Zhaobao, and Wenhua Tian (2010) "Loneliness of Left-Behind Children: A Cross-Sectional Survey in a Sample of Rural China." *Child: Care, Health & Development* 36(6): 812–87.

Jia, Zhaobao, Lizheng Shi, Yang Cao, James Delancey, and Wenhua Tian (2010) "Health-Related Quality of Life of 'Left-Behind Children': A Cross-Sectional Survey in Rural China." *Quality of Life Research* 19(6): 775–80.

Jiang, Quanbao, Shuzhuo Li, and Marcus W. Feldman (2011) "Demographic Consequences of Gender Discrimination in China: Simulation Analysis of Policy Options." *Population Research and Policy Review* 30: 619–38.

Jiao, Shulan, Guiping Ji, and Qicheng Jing (1986) "Comparative Study of Behavioral Qualities of Only Children and Sibling Children." *Child Development* 57: 357–61.

Jing, Jun (2000) "Food, Children, and Social Change in Contemporary China." In *Feeding China's Little Emperors: Food, Children and Social Change*. Jun Jing (ed.). Stanford, CA: Stanford University Press, pp. 1–26.

Jones, Andrew F. (2002) "The Child as History in Republican China: A Discourse on Development." *Positions* 10(3): 695–727.

Kane, Penny (1985) "The Single-Child Family Policy in the Cities." In *China's One-Child Family Policy*. Elisabeth Croll, Delia Davin, and Penny Kane (eds.). New York: St. Martin's Press, pp. 83–113.

Katz, Ilan, Xiaoyuan Shangs, and Yahua Zhang (2011) "Missing Elements of a Child Protection System in China: The Case of LX." *Social Policy and Society* 10(1): 93–102.

Keenan, Barry (1977) *The Dewey Experiment in China: Educational Reform and Political Power in the Early Republic*. Cambridge, MA: Harvard University Press.

Kessen, William, ed. 1975. *Childhood in China*. New Haven, CT: Yale University Press.

Kim, Sung Won, and Vanessa L. Fong (2014) "A Longitudinal Study of Son and Daughter Preference among Chinese Only-Children from Adolescence to Adulthood." *The China Journal* 71: 1–24.

Kinney, Anne Behnke (ed.) (1995a) *Chinese Views of Childhood*. Honolulu, HI: University of Hawai'i Press.

Kinney, Anne Behnke (1995b) "Introduction." In *Chinese Views of Childhood*. Anne Behnke Kinney (ed.). Honolulu, HI: University of Hawai'i Press, pp. 1–14.

Kinney, Anne Behnke (2004) *Representations of Childhood and Youth in Early China*. Stanford, CA: Stanford University Press.

Kipnis, Andrew B. (2001) "The Disturbing Education of 'Peasants.'" *The China Journal* 46: 1–24.

Kipnis, Andrew B. (2006) "*Suzhi*: A Keyword Approach." *The China Quarterly* 186: 295–313.

Kipnis, Andrew B. (2008) "Education and the Governing of Child-Centered Relatedness." In *Chinese Kinship: Contemporary Anthropological Perspectives*. Susan Brandtstädter, and Gonçalo D. Santos (eds.). London: Routledge, pp. 204–22.

Kipnis, Andrew B. (2011a) *Governing Educational Desire: Culture, Politics, and Schooling in China*. Chicago, IL: University of Chicago Press.

Kipnis, Andrew B. (2011b) "Subjectification and Education for Quality in China." *Economy and Society* 40(2): 289–306.

Kleinman, Arthur, Yunxiang Yan, Jing Jun, Sing Lee, Everett Zhang, Tianshu Pan, Fei Wu, and Jinhua Guo (2011) "Introduction: Remaking the Moral Person in a New China." In *Deep China: The Moral Life of the Person: What Anthropology and Psychiatry Tell Us about China Today*. Arthur Kleinman, Yunxiang Yan, Jing Jun, Sing Lee, Everett Zhang, Tianshu Pan, Fei Wu, and Jinhua Guo (eds.). Berkeley, CA: University of California Press, pp. 1–35.

Kong, Peggy A. (2010) "To Walk Out: Rural Parents' Views on Education." *China: An International Journal* 8(2): 360–73.

Koo, Anita (2012) "Is There Any Chance to Get Ahead? Education Aspirations and Expectations of Migrant Families in China." *British Journal of Sociology of Education* 33(4): 547–64.

Korbin, Jill (1991) "Cross-Cultural Perspectives and Research Directions for the 21st Century." *Child Abuse & Neglect* 15: 67–77.

Kuan, Teresa (2011) "'The Heart Says One Thing but the Hand Does Another': A Story about Emotion-Work, Ambivalence and Popular Advice for Parents." *The China Journal* 65: 77–100.

Kuan, Teresa (2012) "The Horrific and the Exemplary: Public Stories and Education Reform in Late Socialist China." *Positions* 20(4): 1095–125.

Kuan, Teresa (2015) *Love's Uncertainty: The Politics and Ethics of Child Rearing in Contemporary China*. Oakland, CA: University of California Press.

Kwong, Julia (2004) "Educating Migrant Children: Negotiations between the State and Civil Society." *The China Quarterly* 180: 1073–88.

Kwong, Julia (2006) "The Integration of Migrant Children in Beijing Schools." In *Education and Social Change in China: Inequality in a Market Economy*. Gerard A. Postiglione (ed.). Armonk, NY: M.E. Sharpe, pp. 163–78.

Kwong, Julia (2011) "Education and Identity: The Marginalisation of Migrant Youths in Beijing." *Journal of Youth Studies* 14(8): 871–83.

Lan, Pei-chia (2014) "Segmented Incorporation: The Second Generation of Rural Migrants in Shanghai." *The China Quarterly* 217: 243–65.

Lareau, Annette (2003) *Unequal Childhoods: Class, Race, and Family Life*. Berkeley, CA: University of California Press.

Lee, Ming-Hsuan (2011) "Migration and Children's Welfare in China: The Schooling and Health of Children Left Behind." *The Journal of Developing Areas* 44(2): 165–82.

Leng, Lee, and Albert Park (2010) "Parental Migration and Child Development in China." In *Gansu Survey of Children and Families*, University of Pennsylvania. Available at: http://repository.upenn.edu/gansu_papers/24

Li, Hongbin, Junjian Yi, and Junsen Zhang (2011) "Estimating the Effect of the One-Child Policy on the Sex Ratio Imbalance in China: Identification Based on the Difference-in-Differences." *Demography* 48: 1535–57.

Liang, Wenyan, Longlong Hou, and Wentao Chen (2008) "Left-Behind Children in Rural Primary Schools: The Case of Sichuan Province." Ted Wang, trans. *Chinese Education and Society* 41(5): 84–99.

Liang, Zai, and Yiu Por Chen (2007) "The Educational Consequences of Migration for Children in China." *Social Science Research* 36: 28–47.

Liang, Zai, Lin Guo, and Charles Chengrong Duan (2008) "Migration and the Well-Being of Children in China." *Yale China Health Journal* 5: 25–46.

Liao, Minli, and Jun Sung Hong (2011) "Child Labor in the People's Republic of China: An Ecological Systems Analysis." *International Social Work* 54(4): 565–79.

Lim, Louisa (2011) "And You Thought the Tiger Mother Was Tough." NPR, December 14. Available at: http://www.npr.org/2011/12/14/143659027/and-you-thought-the-tiger-mother-was-tough

Lin, Yi (2008) *Cultural Exclusion in China: State Education, Social Mobility and Cultural Difference.* New York: Routledge.

Lin, Yi (2011) "Turning Rurality into Modernity: *Suzhi* Education in a Suburban Public School of Migrant Children in Xiamen." *The China Quarterly* 206: 313–30.

Liu, Chenying, Tsunetsugu Munakata, and Francis N. Onuoha (2005) "Mental Health Condition of the Only-Child: A Study of Urban and Rural High School Students in China." *Adolescence* 40(160): 831–45.

Liu, Fengshu (2006) "Boys as Only-Children and Girls as Only-Children – Parental Gendered Expectations of the Only-Child in the Nuclear Chinese Family in Present-Day China." *Gender and Education* 18(5): 491–505.

Liu, Fengshu (2009) "It Is Not Merely About Life on the Screen: Urban Chinese Youth and the Internet Cafe." *Journal of Youth Studies* 12(2): 167–84.

Liu, Li-Juan, Xun Sun, Chun-Li Zhang, Yue Wang, and Qiang Guo (2010) "A Survey in Rural China of Parent-Absence through Migrant Working: The Impact on their Children's Self-Concept and Loneliness." *BMC Public Health* 10: 1–8.

Liu, Zhijun (2009) "*Liushou* Children in a Chinese Village: Childhood Apart from Parents [Dongpai, Nankang, Jiangxi]." *Chinese Sociology and Anthropology* 41(3): 71–89.

Lozada, Eriberto P., Jr. (2000) "Globalized Childhood? Kentucky Fried Chicken in Beijing." In *Feeding China's Little Emperors: Food, Children, and Social Change.* Jing Jun (ed.). Stanford, CA: Stanford University Press, pp. 114–34.

Lu, Yao (2012) "Education of Children Left Behind in Rural China." *Journal of Marriage & Family* 74(2): 328–41.

Luo, Renfu, Linxiu Zhang, Chengfang Liu, Scott Rozelle, Brian Sharbono, and Jennifer Adams (2012) "Behind before They Begin: The Challenge of Early Childhood Education in Rural China." *Australasian Journal of Early Childhood* 37(1): 55–64.

Luo, Wangshu (2013) "Migrant Children in Beijing to Take *Gaokao*." *China Daily*, January 21. Available at: http://www.chinadaily.com.cn/china/2013-01/21/content_16150176.htm

Luo, Zhongyun (2003) "New Consumption Trends for Children." *Beijing Review* 46(6): 26–8.

Lupher, Mark (1995) "Revolutionary Little Red Devils: The Social Psychology of Rebel Youth, 1966–1967." In *Chinese Views of Childhood*. Anne Behnke Kinney (ed.). Honolulu, HI: University of Hawai'i Press, pp. 321–43.

May, Shannon (2010) "Bridging Divides and Breaking Homes: Young Women's Lifecycle Labour Mobility as a Family Managerial Strategy." *The China Quarterly* 204: 899–920.

Maynes, Mary Jo, and Ann Beth Waltner (2001) "Women's Life-Cycle Transitions in World-Historical Perspective: Comparing Marriage in China and Europe." *Journal of Women's History* 12(4): 11–21.

McLoughlin, Caven S., Zheng Zhou, and Elaine Clark (2005) "Reflections on the Development and Status of Contemporary Special Education Services in China." *Psychology in the Schools* 42(3): 273–83.

McNeal, James U. and Mindy F. Ji (1998) "The Role of Mass Media in the Consumer Socialization of Chinese Children." In *AP – Asia Pacific Advances in Consumer Research* Volume 3. Kineta Hung, and Kent B. Monroe (eds.). Provo, UT: Association for Consumer Research, pp. 6–12.

McNeal, James U., and Chyon-Hwa Yeh (1996) "Consumer Behaviour Patterns among Chinese Children." *Asia Pacific Journal of Marketing and Logistics* 8: 31–47.

McNeal, James U., and Chyon-Hwa Yeh (2003) "Consumer Behavior of Chinese Children: 1995–2002." *Journal of Consumer Marketing* 20(6): 542–54.

Meyerhoefer, Chad D., and C.J. Chen (2011) "The Effect of Parental Labor Migration on Children's Educational Progress in Rural China." *Review of Economics of the Household* 9(3): 379–96.

Milwertz, Cecilia N. (1997) *Accepting Population Control: Urban Chinese Women and the One-Child Family Policy*. Richmond: Curzon Press.

Ming, Holly H. (2014) *The Education of Migrant Children and China's Future: The Urban Left Behind*. London and New York: Routledge.

Morgan, Stephen L. (2014) "Growing Fat on Reform: Obesity and Nutritional Disparities among China's Children, 1979–2005." *The China Quarterly* 220: 1033–68.

Murphy, Rachel (2004) "Turning Peasants into Modern Chinese Citizens: 'Population Quality' Discourse, Demographic Transition and Primary Education." *The China Quarterly* 177: 1–20.

Murphy, Rachel (2014a) "Sex Ratio Imbalances and China's Care for Girls Programme: A Case Study of a Social Problem." *The China Quarterly* 219: 781–807.

Murphy, Rachel (2014b) "Study and School in the Lives of Children in Migrant Families: A View from Rural Jiangxi, China." *Development & Change* 45(1): 29–51.

Naftali, Orna (2008) "Treating Students as Subjects: Globalization, Childhood, and Education in Contemporary China." In *The Production of Educational Knowledge in the Global Era*. Julia Resnik (ed.). Rotterdam: Sense Publishers, pp. 251–74.

Naftali, Orna (2009) "Empowering the Child: Children's Rights, Citizenship and the State in Contemporary China." *The China Journal* 61: 79–104.

Naftali, Orna (2010a) "Caged Golden Canaries: Childhood, Privacy, and Subjectivity in Contemporary Urban China." *Childhood: A Journal of Global Child Research* 17(3): 297–311.

Naftali, Orna (2010b) "Recovering Childhood: Play, Pedagogy, and the Rise of Psychological Knowledge in Contemporary Urban China." *Modern China* 36(6): 589–616.

Naftali, Orna (2014a) *Children, Rights, and Modernity in China: Raising Self-Governing Citizens*. Basingstoke: Palgrave Macmillan.

Naftali, Orna (2014b) "Chinese Childhood in Conflict: Children, Gender, and Violence in China of the 'Cultural Revolution' Period (1966–76)." *Oriens Extremus* 53: 85–110.

Naftali, Orna (2014c) "Marketing War and the Military to Children and Youth in China: Little Red Soldiers in the Digital Age." *China Information* 28(1): 3–25.

National Bureau of Statistics of China (2011) "Communiqué of the National Bureau of Statistics of People's Republic of China on Major Figures of the 2010 Population Census (No. 1)." April 28. Available at: http://www.stats.gov.cn/english/NewsEvents/201104/t20110428_26449.html

National Bureau of Statistics of China (2013) "What Census Data Can Tell Us about Children in China: Facts and Figures 2013." NBS/UNFPA/UNICEF China. December 16. Available at: www.unicef.cn/en/uploadfile/2013/1216/20131216111141945.pdf

National Bureau of Statistics of China (2014) "Statistical Communiqué of the People's Republic of China on the 2013 National Economic and Social Development." February 24. Available at: http://www.stats.gov.cn/english/PressRelease/201402/t20140224_515103.html

Nie, Yilin, and Robert J. Wyman (2005) "The One-Child Policy in Shanghai: Acceptance and Internalization." *Population and Development Review* 31(2): 313–36.

Pease, Catherine E. (1995) "Remembering the Taste of Melons: Modern Chinese Stories of Childhood." In *Chinese Views of Childhood*. Anne Behnke Kinney (ed.). Honolulu, HI: University of Hawai'i Press, pp. 279–320.

People's Daily (2007) "China's Children Too Busy for Playtime." May 13. Available at: http://english.people.com.cn/200705/13/eng20070513_374164.html

Pepper, Suzanne (1996) *Radicalism and Education Reform in 20th-Century China: The Search for an Ideal Development Model*. Cambridge: Cambridge University Press.

Philips, Tom (2015) "China May Bring in 'Two-Child Policy' to Tackle Demographic Timebomb." *The Guardian*, July 23. Available at: http://www.theguardian.com/world/2015/jul/23/china-may-adopt-two-child-policy-this-year-as-demographic-timebomb-looms

Plum, M. Colette (2012) "Lost Childhoods in a New China: Child-Citizen-Workers at War, 1937–1945." *European Journal of East Asian Studies* 11(2): 237–58.

Pong, Myra (2015) *Educating the Children of Migrant Workers in Beijing: Migration, Education, and Policy in Urban China*. London and New York: Routledge.

Postiglione, Gerard A. (2011) "Education." In *Understanding Chinese Society*. Xiaowei Zang (ed.). London and New York: Routledge, pp. 80–95.

Postiglione, Gerard A., Zhiyong Zhu and Ben Jiao (2004) "From Ethnic Segregation to Impact Integration: State Schooling and Identity Construction for Rural Tibetans." *Asian Ethnicity* 5(2): 195–217.

Potter, Sulamith Heins, and Jack M. Potter (1990) *China's Peasants: The Anthropology of a Revolution*. Cambridge: Cambridge University Press.

Pu, Wei, and Jue Huang (1998) "An Analysis of the Latest Developments in Children's Media in China." *Social Sciences in China* 19(4): 154–61.

Pun, Ngai (2005) "Understanding Child Labor Use in the Dormitory Labor Regime of China." *Harvard Asia Pacific Review* 8(2): 26–8.

Qiao, Dong Ping, and Yuk-chung Chan (2005) "Child Abuse in China: A Yet-to-be-Acknowledged 'Social Problem' in the Chinese Mainland." *Child & Family Social Work* 10(1): 21–7.

Qiao, Dong Ping, and Qian Wen Xie (2015) "Public Perceptions of Child Physical Abuse in Beijing." *Child & Family Social Work* 20(2): 1–13.

Riskin, Carl (2010) "Inequality: Overcoming the Great Divide." In *China Today, China Tomorrow: Domestic Politics, Economy, and Society.* Joseph Fewsmith (ed.). Lanham, MD: Rowman & Littlefield, pp. 91–108.

Rose, Nikolas (1989) *Governing the Soul: The Shaping of the Private Self.* London: Routledge.

Rosen, Stanley (1982) *Red Guard Factionalism and the Cultural Revolution in Guangzhou (Canton).* Boulder, CO: Westview Press.

Rosen, Stanley (2003) "Chinese Media and Youth: Attitudes toward Nationalism and Internationalism." In *Chinese Media, Global Contexts.* Chin-Chuan Lee (ed.). London New York: RoutledgeCurzon, pp. 97–118.

Rosen, Stanley (2004) "The Victory of Materialism: Aspirations to Join China's Urban Moneyed Classes and the Commercialization of Education." *The China Journal* 51(1): 27–51.

Rosen, Stanley (2008) "Film and China's Youth Culture." *Education About Asia* 13(3): 38–43.

Ross, Heidi (2005) "China Country Study." Paper commissioned for the UNESCO *Education for All (EFA) Global Monitoring Report 2006, Literacy for Life.* Available at: http://unesdoc.unesco.org/images/0014/001461/146108e.pdf

Ross, Heidi (2006) "Challenging the Gendered Dimensions of Schooling." In *Education and Social Change in China.* Gerard A. Postiglione (ed.). New York: M.E. Sharpe, pp. 25–50.

Saari, Jon L. (1990) *Legacies of Childhood: Growing up Chinese in a Time of Crisis, 1890–1920.* Cambridge, MA: Harvard University Press.

Scharping, Thomas (2003) *Birth Control in China: Population Policy and Demographic Development.* London and New York: RoutledgeCurzon.

Scheper-Hughes, Nancy (1992) *Death Without Weeping: The Violence of Everyday Life in Brazil.* Berkeley, CA: University of California Press.

Scheper-Hughes, Nancy, and Carolyn Sargent (1998) "Introduction: The Cultural Politics of Childhood." In *Small Wars: The Cultural Politics of Childhood.* Nancy Scheper-Hughes and Carolyn Sargent (eds.). Berkeley, CA: University of California Press, pp. 1–33.

Schoenhals, Martin (1993) *The Paradox of Power in a People's Republic of China Middle School.* Armonk, NY: M. E. Sharpe.

Schwarcz, Vera (1986) *The Chinese Enlightenment: Intellectuals and the Legacy of the May Fourth Movement of 1919.* Berkeley, CA: University of California Press.

Schwartzman, Helen B. (2001) "Introduction: Questions and Challenges for a 21st-Century Anthropology of Children." In *Children and Anthropology: Perspectives for the 21st Century*. Helen B. Schwartzman (ed.). Westport, CT: Bergin and Garvey, pp. 1–14.

ShanghaiDaily.com (2014) "Boy's Death Highlights Tragedy of China's Left-Behind Children." January 27. Available at: http://www.shanghaidaily.com/national/Boys-death-highlights-tragedy-of-Chinas-leftbehind-children/shdaily.shtml

Sharma, Yojana (2013) "Asia's Parents Suffering 'Education Fever.'" BBC News, October 22. Available at: http://www.bbc.com/news/business-24537487

Shen, Anqi, Georgios Antonopoulos, and Georgios Papanicolaou (2013) "China's Stolen Children: Internal Child Trafficking in the People's Republic of China." *Trends in Organized Crime* 16(1): 31–48.

Silverstein, Merril, and Zhen Cong (2013) "Grandparenting in Rural China." *Generations – Journal of the American Society on Aging* 37(1): 46–52.

Solinger, Dorothy J. (1999) *Contesting Citizenship in Urban China: Peasant Migrants, the State, and the Logic of the Market*. Berkeley, CA: University of California Press.

Stafford, Charles (1995) *The Roads of Chinese Childhood: Learning and Identification in Angang*. Cambridge: Cambridge University Press.

Stephens, Sharon (1995) "Introduction: Children and the Politics of Culture in 'Late Capitalism.'" In *Children and the Politics of Culture*. Sharon Stephens (ed.). Princeton, NJ: Princeton University Press, pp. 3–48.

Sun, Baicai, and Jingjian Xu (2010) "Why Ethnic Minority Children Are More Likely to Drop Out of School: A Cultural Capital Perspective: Evidence from Ethnic Minority Rural Communities in the Northwest." *Chinese Education and Society* 43(5): 31–46.

Sun, Tao (2009) "Parental Mediation of Children's TV Viewing in China: An Urban-Rural Comparison." *Young Consumers* 10(3): 188–98.

Sun, Yunxiao, and Xiao Zhao (2006) "Only Children in China." In *Chinese Youth in Transition*. Jieying Xi and Yunxiao Sun (eds.). Aldershot: Ashgate, pp. 199–207.

Szablewicz, Marcella (2010) "The Ill Effects of 'Opium for the Spirit': A Critical Cultural Analysis of China's Internet Addiction Moral Panic." *Chinese Journal of Communication* 3(4): 453–70.

Thøgersen, Stig (2002) *A County of Culture: Twentieth-Century China Seen from the Village Schools of Zouping, Shandong*. Ann Arbor, MI: University of Michigan Press.

Tilt, Bryan (2006) "Chinese Children's Consumption: A Commentary." In *Chinese Youth in Transition.* Jieying Xi, Yunxiao Sun, and Jing Jian Xiao (eds.). Aldershot: Ashgate, pp. 70–6.

Tobin, Joseph J., Yeh Hsueh, and Mayumi Karasawa (2009) *Preschool in Three Cultures Revisited: China, Japan, and the United States.* Chicago, IL: University of Chicago Press.

Tsui, Ming, and Lynne, Rich (2002) "The Only Child and Educational Opportunity for Girls in Urban China." *Gender & Society* 16(1): 74–92.

Tsung, Linda (2014) "Trilingual Education and School Practice in Xinjiang." In *Minority Education in China: Balancing Unity and Diversity in an Era of Cultural Pluralism.* James Leibold, and Chen Yangbin (eds.). Hong Kong: Hong Kong University Press, pp. 161–86.

Tu, Wei-ming (1976) "The Confucian Perception of Adulthood." *Daedalus* 105(2): 109–23.

UNDP China (2013) "China National Human Development Report 2013: Sustainable and Liveable Cities: Toward Ecological Civilization." Research Report, June. Beijing: China Publishing Group Corporation, China Translation & Publishing Corporation. Available at: http://www.cn.undp.org/content/dam/china/docs/Publications/UNDP-CH-HD-Publication-NHDR_2013_EN_final.pdf

Unger, Jonathan (1982) *Education under Mao: Class and Competition in Canton Schools, 1960–1980.* New York: Columbia University Press.

Vickers, Edward (2009) "The Opportunity of China? Education, Patriotic Values and the Chinese State." In *Education as a Political Tool in Asia.* Marie Lall, and Edward Vickers (eds.). London: Routledge, pp. 53–82.

Walkerdine, Valery (2005) "Developmental Psychology and the Study of Childhood." In *Childhood: Critical Concepts in Sociology.* Vol. 3. Chris Jenks (ed.). New York: Routledge, pp. 13–25.

Waltner, Ann (1995) "Infanticide and Dowry in Ming and Early Qing China." In *Chinese Views of Childhood.* Anne Behnke Kinney (ed.). Honolulu, HI: University of Hawai'i Press, pp. 193–217.

Wang, Chunguang (2007) "Education and Social Inequality in China Elite Groups Perpetuating Their Privileged Status." *China Perspectives* 3: 110–16.

Wang, Dan (2011a) "The Dilemma of Time: Student-Centered Teaching in the Rural Classroom in China." *Teaching and Teacher Education* 27: 157–64.

Wang, Dan (2011b) "The New Curriculum and the Urban–Rural Literacy Gap: The Case of One County in Western China." *Chinese Education and Society* 44(6): 87–101.

Wang, Jin, Jun Zhao, and Nan Li (2008) "The Upbringing and Education of Migrant Workers' Children in the Pearl River Delta." *Social Sciences in China* 29: 121–35.

Wang, Jing (2001) "The State Question in Chinese Cultural Studies." *Inter-Asia Cultural Studies* 2(1): 35–52.

Wang, Lihua, and Tracey Holland (2011) "In Search of Educational Equity for the Migrant Children of Shanghai." *Comparative Education* 47(4): 471–87.

Wang, Lin (2015) "Quanmian er hai fang kai zhengce zheng zhuajin tuijin" ["Stepping up efforts to promote a comprehensive two-child policy"]. *Di yi caijing ribao* [*China Business News*], July 22. Available at: http://www.yicai.com/news/2015/07/4648139.html

Wang, Lu (2008) "The Marginality of Migrant Children in the Urban Chinese Educational System." *British Journal of Sociology of Education* 29: 691–703.

Wang, Qingfeng, and Fang Lan (2012) "Beijing Closes Four Migrant Children Schools." *Caixin Online*. July 20. Available at: http://english.caixin.com/2012-07-20/100413467.html

Wang, Su (2014) "Closer Look: Unifying the Hukou System Is a Start, but It's Just That." *Caixin Online*. July 31. Available at: http://english.caixin.com/2014-07-31/100711516.html

Wang, Xiaobing, Chengfang Liu, Linxiu Zhang, Yaojiang Shi and Scott Rozelle (2013) "College is a Rich, Han, Urban, Male Club: Research Notes from a Census Survey of Four Tier One Colleges in China." *The China Quarterly* 214: 456–70.

Wang, Zheng (2001) "Call Me *Qingnian* but Not *Funü*: A Maoist Youth in Retrospect." *Feminist Studies* 27(1): 9–36.

Wang, Zheng (2011) *Never Forget National Humiliation: Historical Memory in Chinese Politics and Foreign Relations*. New York: Columbia University Press.

Watson, James L. (2000) "Food as a Lens: The Past, Present, and Future of Family Life in China." In *Feeding China's Little Emperors: Food, Children and Social Change*. Jun Jing (ed.). Stanford, CA: Stanford University Press, pp. 199–212.

Watson, James L. (2006) "McDonald's in Hong Kong: Consumerism, Dietary Change, and the Rise of a Children's Culture." In *Golden Arches East: McDonald's in East Asia*, 2nd edn. James L. Watson (ed.). Stanford, CA: Stanford University Press, pp. 77–109.

Wei, Jianwen, and Jiawei Hou (2010) "The Household Registration System, Education System, and Inequalities in Education for Migrant Children." *Chinese Education and Society* 43(5): 77–89.

Wen, Ming, and Danhua Lin (2012) "Child Development in Rural China: Children Left Behind by Their Migrant Parents and Children of Nonmigrant Families." *Child Development* 83(1): 120–36.

White, Tyrene (2005) "Domination, Resistance and Accommodation in China's One-Child Campaign." In *Chinese Society: Change, Conflict, and Resistance*, 2nd edn. Elizabeth J. Perry and Mark Selden (eds.). London and New York: Routledge, pp. 187–207.

White, Tyrene (2006) *China's Longest Campaign: Birth Planning in the People's Republic, 1949–2005*. Ithaca, NY: Cornell University Press.

Whyte, Martin King (2003) "Introduction." In *China's Revolutions and Intergenerational Relations*. Martin King Whyte (ed.). Ann Arbor, MI: University of Michigan Press, pp. 3–30.

Whyte, Martin King (2004) "Filial Obligations in Chinese Families: Paradoxes of Modernization." In *Filial Piety: Practice and Discourse in Contemporary East Asia*. Charlotte Ikels (ed.). Stanford, CA: Stanford University Press, pp. 106–27.

Wicks, Ann Barrott and Ellen B. Avril (2002) "Introduction: Children in Chinese Art." In *Children in Chinese Art*. Ann Barrott Wicks (ed.). Honolulu, HI: University of Hawai'i Press, pp. 1–30.

Woerdahl, Randi (2010) "The Dao of Consumer Socialization: Raising Children in the Chinese Consumer Revolution." In *Childhood and Consumer Culture*. David Buckingham and Vebjrg Tingstad (eds.). London: Palgrave Macmillan, pp. 178–93.

Wolf, Margery (1970) "Child Training and the Chinese Family." In *Family and Kinship in Chinese Society*. Maurice Freedman (ed.). Stanford, CA: Stanford University Press, pp. 37–62.

Wolf, Margery (1985) *Revolution Postponed: Women in Contemporary China*. Stanford, CA: Stanford University Press.

World Bank (1997) *China 2020: Development Challenges in the New Century*. Washington, DC: World Bank.

Woronov, T. E. (2004) "In the Eye of the Chicken: Hierarchy and Marginality among Beijing's Migrant Schoolchildren." *Ethnography* 5: 289–313.

Woronov, T. E. (2007a) "Chinese Children, American Education: Globalizing Child Rearing in Contemporary China." In *Generations and Globalization: Youth, Age, and Family in the New World Economy*. Jennifer Cole and Deborah Durham (eds.). Bloomington, IN: Indiana University Press, pp. 29–51.

Woronov, T. E. (2007b) "Performing the Nation: China's Children as Little Red Pioneers." *Anthropological Quarterly* 80(3): 647–72.

Woronov, T. E. (2008) "Raising Quality, Fostering 'Creativity': Ideologies and Practices of Education Reform in Beijing." *Anthropology & Education Quarterly* 39(4): 401–22.

Woronov, T. E. (2009a) "Governing China's Children: Governmentality and 'Education for Quality'." *Positions* 17(3): 567–89.

Woronov, T. E. (2009b) "Migrant Children and Migrant Schooling: Policies, Problems and Possibilities." In *Labour Migration and Social Development in Contemporary China*. Rachel Murphy (ed.). New York: Routledge, pp. 96–114.

Woronov, T. E. (2011) "Learning to Serve: Urban Youth, Vocational Schools and New Class Formations in China." *The China Journal* 66: 76–99.

Wu, David Y. H. (1996) "Parental Control: Psychocultural Interpretations of Chinese Patterns of Socialization." In *Growing Up the Chinese Way: Chinese Child and Adolescent Development*. Sing Lau (ed.). Hong Kong: The Chinese University Press, pp. 1–26.

Wu, Jinting (2012a) "Disenchantment and Participatory Limits of Compulsory Education: Lessons from Southwest China." *Compare: A Journal of Comparative and International Education* 42(4): 1–25.

Wu, Jinting (2012b) "Governing *Suzhi* and Curriculum Reform in Rural Ethnic China: Viewpoints from the Miao and Dong Communities in Qiandongnan." *Curriculum Inquiry* 42(5): 652–80.

Xiao, Hong (2001) *Childrearing Values in the United States and China: A Comparison of Belief Systems and Social Structure*. Westport, CT: Praeger.

Xiao, Yang (1955) "Haizi bu shi fumu de sichan [Children are not the private property of parents]." *Renmin ribao* [*People's Daily*], May 11, p. 3.

Xinhua News Agency (2011) "'Wolf Dad' Stirs Debate over 'Stick Parenting'." *China Daily*, November 19, 2011. Available at: http://www.chinadaily.com.cn/photo/2011-11/19/content_14125255.htm

Xinhua News Agency (2013) "China to Ease One-Child Policy." November 15. Available at: http://news.xinhuanet.com/english/china/2013-11/15/c_132891920.htm

Xinhua News Agency (2014a) "China to Boost Education for Disabled Children." January 20. Available at: http://news.xinhuanet.com/english/china/2014-01/20/c_133060494.htm

Xinhua News Agency (2014b) "China Spends Billions on Rural Education." February 13. Available at: http://news.xinhuanet.com/english/china/2014-02/13/c_133113169.htm

Xinhua News Agency (2014c) "China's Exam Reform: A Test of Fairness?" June 7. Available at: http://english.peopledaily.com.cn/n/2014/0607/c90882-8738281.html

Xinhua News Agency (2014d) "Xinhua Insight: China's Birth-Control Policy Enters New Era." January 23. Available at: http://news.xinhuanet.com/english/china/2014-01/23/c_133069039.htm

Xinran (2003) *The Good Women of China: Hidden Voices*. New York: Anchor Books.

Xiong, Yihan (2015) "The Broken Ladder: Why Education Provides No Upward Mobility for Migrant Children in China." *The China Quarterly* 221: 161–84.

Xu, Fenglian, Xiaoxian Liu, Colin W. Binns, Cuiqin Xiao, Jing Wu, and Andy H. Lee (2006) "A Decade of Change in Breastfeeding in China's Far North-West." *International Breastfeeding Journal* 1: 1–7.

Xu, Jie (2010) "Children's Materialism in Urban and Rural China: Media Exposure, Cognitive Development and Demographics." *The Journal of International Communication* 16(1): 58–74.

Xu, Jing (2014) "Becoming a Moral Child amidst China's Moral Crisis: Preschool Discourse and Practices of Sharing in Shanghai." *Ethos* 42: 222–42.

Xu, Tao, Z. Wu, K. Rou, S. Duan, and H. Wang (2010) "Quality of Life of Children Living in HIV/AIDS-Affected Families in Rural Areas in Yunnan, China." *AIDS Care* 22(3): 390–6.

Xu, Xu (2011) "'Chairman Mao's Child': *Sparkling Red Star* and the Construction of Children in the Chinese Cultural Revolution." *Children's Literature Association Quarterly* 36(4): 381–409.

Yan, Fei (2005) "Education Problems with Urban Migratory Children in China." *Journal of Sociology and Social Welfare* 32(3): 3–10.

Yan, Yunxiang (2000) "Of Hamburger and Social Space: Consuming McDonald's in Beijing." In *The Consumer Revolution in Urban China*. Deborah S. Davis (ed.). Berkeley, CA: University of California Press, pp. 201–25.

Yan, Yunxiang (2003) *Private Life under Socialism: Love, Intimacy, and Family Change in a Chinese Village, 1949–1999*. Stanford, CA: Stanford University Press.

Yan, Yunxiang (2006) "McDonald's in Beijing: The Localization of Americana." In *Golden Arches East: McDonald's in East Asia*, 2nd edn. James L. Watson (ed.). Stanford, CA: Stanford University Press, pp. 39–76.

Yan, Yunxiang (2009) *The Individualization of Chinese Society*. Oxford: Berg.

Yan, Yunxiang (2010) "Introduction: Conflicting Images of the Individual and Contested Process of Individualization." In *iChina: The Rise of the Individual in Modern Chinese Society*. Mette Halskov Hansen and Rune Svarverud (eds.). Copenhagen: NIAS Press, pp. 1–38.

Yan, Yunxiang (2011) "The Changing Moral Landscape." In *Deep China: The Moral Life of the Person: What Anthropology and Psychiatry Tell Us about China*

Today. Arthur Kleinman, Yunxiang Yan, Jing Jun, Sing Lee, Everett Zhang, Tianshu Pan, Fei Wu, and Jinhua Guo (eds.). Berkeley, CA: University of California Press, pp. 36–77.

Yang, Changzheng (2006) "Popular Culture among Chinese Youth." In *Chinese Youth in Transition.* Jieying Xi, Yunxiao Sun, and Jing Jian Xiao (eds.). Aldershot: Ashgate, pp. 171–92.

Yang, C. K. (1959) *The Chinese Family in the Communist Revolution.* Cambridge, MA: MIT Press.

Yang, Juhua (2007) "The One-Child Policy and School Attendance in China." *Comparative Education Review* 51(4): 471–95.

Yang, Mayfair Mei-hui (1994) *Gifts, Favors, and Banquets: The Art of Social Relationships in China.* Ithaca, NY: Cornell University Press.

Yang, Yunfan, Huan Wang, Linxiu Zhang, Sean Sylvia, Renfu Luo, Yaojiang Shi, Wei Wang, and Scott Rozelle (2013) "The Han-Minority Achievement Gap, Language and Returns to Schools in Rural China." Working paper 258, April. REAP (Rural Education Action Project), Stanford University. Available from reapchina.org/reap.stanford.edu

Yao, Lu, and Zhou Hao (2013) "Academic Achievement and Loneliness of Migrant Children in China: School Segregation and Segmented Assimilation." *Comparative Education Review* 57(1): 85–116.

Ye, Jingzhong, Yihuan Wang, and Keyun Zhang (2010) "Rural-Urban Migration and the Plight of 'Left-Behind Children' in Mid-West China." In *Rural Transformations and Development – China in Context: The Everyday Lives of Policies and People.* Norman Long, Jingzhong Ye, and Yihuan Wang (eds.). Cheltenham: Edward Elgar, pp. 253–75.

Ye, Jingzhong, James Murray, and Yihuan Wang (2011) *Left-Behind Children in Rural China: Impact Study of Rural Labor Migration on Left-Behind Children in Mid-West China.* Beijing: Social Sciences Academic Press and Paths International Ltd.

Ye, Jingzhong, Chunyu Wang, Huifang Wu, Congzhi He, and Juan Liu (2013) "Internal Migration and Left-Behind Populations in China." *The Journal of Peasant Studies* 40(6): 1119–46.

Ye, Weili, and Xiaodong Ma (2005) *Growing up in the People's Republic: Conversations between Two Daughters of China's Revolution.* New York: Palgrave Macmillan.

Yeo, Kenneth (2011) "Private Education a Sunrise Industry in China." *ChinaDaily.com.cn* (*HK Edition*). January 12. Available at: http://www.chinadaily.com.cn/hkedition/2011-01/12/content_11830900.htm

Yi, Hongmei, Linxiu Zhang, Renfu Luo, Yaojiang Shi, Di Mo, Xinxin Chen, Carl Brinton, and Scott Rozelle (2012) "Dropping Out: Why Are Students Leaving

Junior High in China's Poor Rural Areas?" *International Journal of Educational Development* 32: 555–63.

Yoxall, James W. (2007) "Disparities among the Orphans of China." *Southeast Review of Asian Studies* 29: 248–54.

Yu, D., B. Zhang, L. Zhao, and H. Wang (2008) "Snacks Consumption in Chinese Children and Adolescents at the Ages of 3–17 Years." *Wei Sheng Yan Jiu* 37(6): 710–13.

Yu, Haibo (2009) *Identity and Schooling among the Naxi: Becoming Chinese with Naxi Identity.* Lanham, MD: Lexington Books.

Yu, LiAnne (2014) *Consumption in China: How China's New Consumer Ideology Is Shaping the Nation.* Cambridge: Polity.

Zang, Xiaowei (2000) *Children of the Cultural Revolution: Family Life and Political Behavior in Mao's China.* Boulder, CO: Westview Press.

Zelizer, Viviana A. (1985) *Pricing the Priceless Child: The Changing Social Value of Children.* New York: Basic Books.

Zeng, Junxia, Xiaopeng Pang, Linxiu Zhang, Alexis Medina, and Scott Rozelle (2014) "Gender Inequality in Education in China: A Meta-Regression Analysis." *Contemporary Economic Policy* 32(2): 474–91.

Zhang, Hong (2007) "From Resisting to 'Embracing'? The One-Child Rule: Understanding New Fertility Trends in a Central China Village." *The China Quarterly* 192: 855–75.

Zhang, Li (2008) "Private Homes, Distinct Life Styles: Performing a New Middle Class." In *Privatizing China: Socialism from Afar.* Li Zhang and Aihwa Ong (eds.). Ithaca, NY: Cornell University Press, pp. 23–40.

Zhang, L., X. Li, L. Kaljee, X. Fang, X. Lin, G. Zhao, J. Zhao, and Y. Hong (2009) "'I Felt I Have Grown up as an Adult': Caregiving Experience of Children Affected by HIV/AIDS in China." *Child: Care, Health & Development* 35(4): 542–50.

Zhang, Min, Weiping Wu, Lei Yao, Ye Bai, and Guo Xiong (2014) "Transnational Practices in Urban China: Spatiality and Localization of Western Fast Food Chains." *Habitat International* 43: 22–31.

Zhang, Yue-Zhou, Hongbo Liu, and Lijuan Cao (2014) *Food Consumption in China: The Revolution Continues.* Cheltenham: Edward Elgar.

Zhao, Bin, and Graham Murdock (1996) "Young Pioneers: Children and the Making of Chinese Consumerism." *Cultural Studies* 10(2): 201–17.

Zhao, Suisheng (2004) *A Nation-State by Construction: Dynamics of Modern Chinese Nationalism.* Stanford, CA: Stanford University Press.

Zhao, Xia (2006) "Chinese Children's Consumption." In *Chinese Youth in Transition.* Jieying Xi, Yunxiao Sun, and Jing Jian Xiao (eds.). Aldershot: Ashgate, pp. 59–69.

Zhong, Shiqing, and Jinyang Zhang (1996) "Child Farmers, Child Laborers, and Child Merchants Increase Daily: Schools, Teachers, and Society Should Put a Stop to This." *Chinese Education and Society* 29(1): 58–61.

Zhu, Wei Xing, Li Lu, and Therese Hesketh (2009) "China's Excess Males, Sex Selective Abortion, and One Child Policy: Analysis of Data from 2005 National Intercensus Survey." *British Medical Journal* 338: 1–6.

Index

eating disorders 108
fast food 109–10
obesity 107, 108
safety concerns 106
snacks 107
weight differentials 107–8
foreign study 105

gang members 177
gender bias, parental 26, 71, 77,
 78–9
gender equality
 education (singletons) 83–4
 Maoist era 33–5
gender imbalance 15, 71, 76–82,
 93, 186
girls
 abandonment 79–80
 autonomy 62–3
 Care for Girls program 81–2
 education 103, 133–5, 136,
  153–4, 187
 empowerment 15, 71, 83–6,
  185–6
 ethnic minority girls 135, 136
 gender-specific expectations of
  62–3, 85, 134, 187
 infanticide 25–6
 late imperial society 23, 25–6
 left-behind girls 148
 Maoist era 34
 migrant girls 157, 158, 170
 neglect and maltreatment 15, 71,
  78–9, 186
 rural girls 71, 82, 84, 103, 133–5,
  153–4, 186, 187
 singletons 15, 71, 83–4, 185–6
 trafficking 93
 in two-child families 84
 unfavorable social status 78

unreported births 71, 77, 79, 80,
 93
globalization processes 6–7, 8
Goh, Esther C.L. 65, 92
grandparents
 caretaking role 38, 43, 47–8, 145,
  148, 149–50, 159
 child autonomy, views on 62
 "unscientific" childrearing
  knowledge 48
Great Leap Forward 77, 99

Han Chinese 3, 78, 135, 137, 138,
 139, 140
Han-centered scholarship 11
harmonious society (hexie shehui) 8,
 102
hierarchy of age and status 23–4
 reversal of 33, 35, 89–90, 95
HIV/AIDS, consequences for
 children's education 143–4
homework 49, 50, 51, 112
Hong Kong 11, 55
household chores
 girls 134
 migrant children 88, 170, 171
 rural children 88, 148
 singletons 88
household registration (hukou) 18,
 156, 157, 159, 161, 177, 178, 188
 change proposals 178–9
Hu Jintao 81, 102, 127
Hu Shi 29

idealized notion of childhood 10,
 14, 42
illiteracy rates 34
 disabilities, people with 141
 ethnic minorities 135
 rural areas 129